READING ACTIVITIES
FOR MIDDLE AND
SECONDARY SCHOOLS

A HANDBOOK FOR TEACHERS

Second Edition

READING ACTIVITIES FOR MIDDLE AND SECONDARY SCHOOLS

A HANDBOOK FOR TEACHERS

Second Edition

Carl B. Smith
Peggy Gordon Elliott

TEACHERS COLLEGE, COLUMBIA UNIVERSITY
NEW YORK AND LONDON

Published by Teachers College Press, 1234 Amsterdam Avenue,
New York, N.Y. 10027

Library of Congress Cataloging-in-Publication Data

Smith, Carl Bernard
  Reading activities for middle and secondary schools.
  Includes index.
  1. Reading (Secondary education)—Handbooks,
  Manuals, etc.—I. Elliott, Peggy G.   II. Title.
LB1632.S555   1986   428 .4'07'12   86-23015
ISBN 0-8077-2826-8 (pbk.)

Manufactured in the United States of America

91 90   2 3 4 5 6

CONTENTS

Preface   vii

1. A SOLUTION FOR CONTENT TEACHERS   1

    1.1   The Teacher Makes Decisions   2
    1.2   Critical Features of Each Textbook   4
    1.3   A Solution for Content Teachers: Bookthinking   6
    1.4   The Importance of a Content Book   8
    1.5   Attitude of Utility   10
    1.6   Reading Is an Interaction   11
    1.7   Readability Level   14
    1.8   General Reading Skills   18

2. MOTIVATING STUDENTS TO READ   21

    2.1   Motivate with Reality   22
    2.2   Motivate with Success   33

3. FLEXIBILITY AND PERSONAL CHOICES   45

    3.1   Choosing Topics for Reading   46
    3.2   Deciding by Interest   49
    3.3   Reacting Personally to Reading   52
    3.4   Selecting a Purpose for Reading   55
    3.5   Developing Flexibility   58

4. BUILDING VOCABULARY   63

    4.1   Using Vocabulary Assessment Techniques   64
    4.2   Building Vocabulary for Reading and Thinking   68
    4.3   Building Subject-Specific Vocabulary   77

5. SHARPENING RECALL   88

    5.1   Literal Comprehension   89
    5.2   Categorizing   97
    5.3   Association   102
    5.4   Organizing   110

6. TEACHING HOW TO ANALYZE   **117**

   6.1 Determining the Author's Purpose 117
   6.2 Getting the Main Idea 122
   6.3 Checking the Line of Reasoning 129

7. PRODDING CRITICAL THINKING   **144**

   7.1 Establishing Criteria 145
   7.2 Using Personal Standards 153
   7.3 Using External Standards 156
   7.4 A Questioning Attitude 161

8. USING AND EXTENDING READING   **166**

   8.1 Predicting 167
   8.2 Concluding 174
   8.3 Emotional and Creative Responses 180
   8.4 Reading and Problem Solving 187

9. STUDY TECHNIQUES FOR SPECIAL TEXTS   **193**

   9.1 Study Critically 194
   9.2 Technical Directions and Illustrations 208
   9.3 Reading Symbols and Charts 213

10. TEACHING WRITING WITH READING   **223**

   10.1 A Process Approach 224
   10.2 Establishing a Purpose 229
   10.3 Responding to Reading 234
   10.4 Revising for Clarification 239

APPENDIX A: Activities for Slow Learners Chart   **245**

APPENDIX B: Check Your Teaching Against These Questions   **248**

INDEX   **249**

PREFACE

This is an activity book, not a theory book. The expanded second edition is designed to provide even more samples and models to follow in developing activities that will help students to read more effectively. It helps answer specific questions about reading for meaning, rather than present theory or argumentation for a methodology of teaching reading. The book suggests activities, most of which apply to all content reading, and it encourages teachers to adapt the activity to the specific text and specific concerns of the subject being learned.

While this book contains many subject-specific activities, teachers from other areas may replace the passages shown with ones from their own textbooks and use the techniques and questions provided to promote reading and writing in their subjects.

As much as possible, jargon and technical language which might be foreign to the majority of content teachers have been eliminated, with the intent of making the ideas useful and instructive for both preservice and inservice teachers.

A middle or secondary school content teacher has an academic specialty which he or she knows and enjoys. It is reasonable to assume that the content teacher wants to communicate enjoyment and knowledge of his or her subject to the students who come to class. However, the teacher's personal knowledge and enjoyment of a subject, such as science or home economics — regardless of how complete it may be — does not guarantee transmittal. The teacher's internalized knowledge must be translated into teachable segments; only then can books, students, and teachers come together to share that knowledge. To that end, the teacher determines what the critical information is and what the best techniques are for communicating and for learning the information.

To accomplish these goals the teacher first needs to analyze the discipline (social studies, mathematics, or whatever) to determine its features and their order within the discipline.

The second step in the process of communicating the knowledge and joy of a subject is to help the students use the tools of learning in that subject; books, exploratory activities, writing, and discussions are the tools of thinking. So the content teacher has a major responsibility to teach students to think with particular books as much as he or she does to teach them to use a calculator, a map, or the diagram of a machine. If in fact the subject is unique enough to deserve its own time slot in the school program, then the subject textbook will merit the teacher's explanation and demonstration.

USING THIS BOOK

For preservice teachers.

A. In a college class, the activities in this text could be used as parts of assignments to develop lessons for the particular subject the student is interested in teaching. For each chapter in the text, the student would have to create at least one lesson, projecting ideas and showing how to apply them to concepts in a basic text for middle and secondary schools. The approval texts on the state adoption list or those that are most frequently used in the area would be appropriate bases for these lessons.

B. For those classes that have practicum activities, this text could serve either as a general reference of things to do or as a planned lab experience (that is, do tutorial work with students and try out at least one of the activities in each of the chapters).

For inservice teachers:

A. In all subject areas teachers find that, from time to time, reading or reading-related problems are preventing them from attaining the curricular goals they and their students hope to achieve. Some of the reading problems are infrequent, but some are persistent. For the classroom teacher faced with either of these situations, this book is a tool that provides sample lessons which can either be used in their entirety or as guides to developing such lessons in order to address the problem faced.

B. In a secondary reading class or laboratory, there is an unending need for plans, approaches, and ideas for assisting students who have been assigned to such classes. This handbook can serve well as a resource book for these classes by providing a large supply of instructional approaches for the teacher or director to use with the secondary readers.

ORGANIZATION OF THIS BOOK

Its organization as a handbook makes this book ideal for daily reference. As the students or teachers identify specific issues, they can concentrate on those skills, or they can use one section of the book devoted to vocabulary or critical reading for a period of time. The major thrust of each section is summarized at its beginning so a teacher can determine quickly which student needs will be addressed by the material that follows.

This book is divided into ten different sections describing various teaching goals, each of which contains subcategories with classroom activities. Each of the sections speaks to a major question that a conscientious teacher might raise about instruction using a book.

The activities in this book are the result of the experience of the authors and their teacher friends. Users are encouraged to write the authors to indicate their own experience with these activities or ones they have used for similar purposes. We especially thank Jane Leitzman and Kathryn Schnier, two creative teachers who provided numerous ideas for activities in this book.

LABELS AND LEVELS

Within each section, discussions and activities are identified with the following numbering system:
1, 2, 3, and so on = section number and introductory discussion;
1.1, 1.2, and so on = major subheads for the section;
1.1A, 1.1B, 1.2A, 1.2B, and so on = specific activities for the subheads.

ACTIVITY LEVEL

We have attempted to provide suggestions for all levels of student achievement. They are labeled as follows:
 *middle school and above
 junior high only
 secondary only
Each of the activities is mature enough in concept to be adapted to any level, but many are simple enough in plan to be used with students whose reading level is low (grade four or five, for example). In addition, at the end of the book there is a chart of activities for slow learners, which indicates the sections to be used in teaching them.

CARL B. SMITH
PEGGY GORDON ELLIOTT

---

*Activities marked with an asterisk are appropriate for students whose reading level is that of grade 4, 5, or 6.

1

A SOLUTION FOR CONTENT TEACHERS

Almost every content teacher, especially one who teaches a required subject, has wrestled with the problem of making that subject interesting and valuable to students. Simply presenting information and asking students to read books, hoping that something magical will happen along the way, is not sufficient. What the serious teacher does, then, is find a way of showing students that the ideas presented in books and in lectures are alive and useful. And that's no easy task. It is a task that demands both insight into the content of the subject matter and insight into the way youngsters learn. One of the teacher's key decisions, then, is to bring the books of the subject matter to life, to show students how to think with a book.

This chapter, different from the others in this book, has some initial activities designed for the teacher alone, and then some for student work. By design, this book presents ideas or model activities which content teachers can use to help their students understand or practice various aspects of the reading process. But the first few activities are for teachers who want to analyze the decisions they make about books and their students. The remainder of activities are aimed at helping students appreciate the value and importance of the books and articles they read in a subject area.

It must be reiterated that this is not a theory text, but rather an activity handbook. The activities are described in such a way that they may serve as samples or models that the teacher can use to build follow-up activities to accomplish the listed objective. Therefore, it is not a "busy-work" book. It is a resource book for teachers interested in helping students learn how to use subject books effectively and intelligently.

1.1 THE TEACHER MAKES DECISIONS

Books are an important means for making individuals independent learners. Almost every instructor strives to develop independent learners. In order to help students achieve that independence, a teacher makes decisions about how the course will be organized, how students will conduct themselves in that course, and especially how they will interact with and use textbooks and related materials.

1.1A CONTENT TEACHER DECISIONS

Level   Teacher Education activity.

Objective   To guide teachers in identifying instructional decisions and a means for making them.

Description   Use the following exercise as a means for working out the kinds of decisions a teacher makes about books.

In planning a course, a teacher makes the following significant decisions about the class text and supplementary materials. Decide which alternative you would choose.

BOOK DECISIONS

Question	Alternatives	Choice
1. How demonstrate the importance of a text?	1.1 Discuss it.	_____
	1.2 Problem solving.	_____
	1.3 Base tests on it.	_____
	1.4 Other.	_____
2. How promote reader–author interaction?	2.1 Invite author in.	_____
	2.2 Use context activities.	_____
	2.3 Students write to author.	_____
	2.4 Other.	_____
3. How choose (or cope with) reading difficulty of text?	3.1 Rewrite to students' level.	_____
	3.2 Selective assignments.	_____
	3.3 Study guides.	_____
	3.4 Other.	_____
4. How apply general reading skills to text?	4.1 Use pattern of questions.	_____
	4.2 Demonstrate with comparisons.	_____
	4.3 Other.	_____
5. How develop particular skills for this content?	5.1 Solving Problem.	_____
	5.2 Students search.	_____
	5.3 Other.	_____

6. How relate text to student interest?	6.1 Students explore text.	_____
	6.2 Match common interests to text topics.	_____
	6.3 Other.	_____
7. How use books in class?	7.1 For tests.	_____
	7.2 For solving problems.	_____
	7.3 Other.	_____

Thus each teacher has to review what important decisions are related to reading books in his or her class. Each teacher has to decide whether to pay attention to books or to limit his or her students' resources by saying, in effect, that they must "get it all" by listening to lectures or by watching movies. Once the decision is made that books are important for independent learning, then thinking with books becomes important. And so a major decision that a teacher has to deal with is, "How do I get students to engage in bookthinking?"

Some of the decisions related to "How do I get students involved in bookthinking?" deal with the difficulty of the book and the capabilities of the students. Any book written at an intense conceptual level or written with an elaborate style containing difficult vocabulary is going to baffle many students, especially in those classes that every student is required to take. A teacher also has to decide how to identify and define the critical features of the subject matter and the particular skills that a person needs in order to read a textbook in his subject matter. After all, if this subject matter is unique enough to have its own place in the curriculum, then that means that its presentation in a textbook is different from those of other subjects. If the presentation is different, then the students' bookthinking has to be different. So one of the decisions that the teacher has to make is, "How am I going to help students deal with the unique thinking that goes on in the text?"

Related to that is the transfer of general bookthinking skills—that is, general reading skills—into the particular text that the teacher has chosen. To make that decision, the teacher has to ask, "What are the applicable general reading skills that I want to think about and apply in helping students, through practice activities, to gain an understanding of my text?" An elaboration of these decisions and the concept of bookthinking can be found in the first two chapters of *Teaching Reading in Secondary School Content Subjects* by C. Smith, S. Smith and L. Mikulecky (Holt, Rinehart and Winston, 1978).

1.2 CRITICAL FEATURES OF EACH TEXTBOOK

True though it be that students have many of the thinking skills necessary to read every textbook in their curriculum, there are some special or unique features of each subject matter that demand particular teaching on the part of each content teacher. For example, the story problem in math and its abbreviated information; map and chart reading in social studies; graph and chart reading in science, math and vocational subjects; diagrams and illustrations in all subjects with a technical bent; and pronunciation guides in foreign languages and in music, and in other kinds of speech and language courses. The teacher must decide which of these features is unique to his subject, and develop explanatory and practice activities to help the students use them effectively.

It may seem presumptuous to call graphs and maps part of reading activities, but insofar as the content teacher's responsibility is to teach students to use content books as tools to independent learning, then bookthinking or reading–thinking with a book includes all aspects of the printed matter in those books. The teacher not only has to identify the thinking processes and techniques, but also has to find ways of teaching and practicing them—the reason for this book.

1.2A IDENTIFYING SPECIAL CONTENT FEATURES, TEACHING

Level　　　　　Teacher. Teacher–trainee.

Objective　　　To help teachers identify the content-specific features of the books and other printed matter in their subjects.

Description　　1. Teachers should page through sample books, journals, and other printed matter in subjects they teach and check off those aspects that are not likely to be found in books on other subjects.

2. With their checklists in hand, teachers should decide how they could explain to students or demonstrate or provide practice in using those features to understand and appreciate the subject to be learned. The activities in this book should help with learning and practice activities. Parts of this book then could serve as lesson plans or as sample lessons for teachers as they help their students become independent learners through intelligent use of the text—that is, through bookthinking.

3. Below is the beginning of a checklist teachers can use to guide their review of texts and the subsequent activities they want to teach. Each teacher should list those features that seem special to understanding his or her text.

SPECIAL FEATURE CHECKLIST

Area	*Special Features*	*Sample Activity Number in This Book*
Vocational	explanatory diagram	_____
	vocabulary	
	_____	_____
	_____	_____
	_____	_____
	_____	_____
Science	vocabulary	
	charts	_____
	_____	_____
	_____	_____
	_____	_____
Health	match text with illustrations	
	_____	_____
	_____	_____
	_____	_____
	_____	_____
Physical Education	rules	
	_____	_____
	_____	_____
	_____	_____
English/Literature	symbolism	
	_____	_____
	_____	_____
	_____	_____

Social Studies	time lines	_____
	maps	_____
	_____	_____
	_____	_____
	_____	_____
	_____	
Mathematics	graphs	
	_____	_____
	_____	_____
	_____	_____
	_____	_____
Others	_____	_____
	_____	_____
	_____	_____
	_____	_____

1.3 A SOLUTION FOR CONTENT TEACHERS: BOOKTHINKING

As with any educational problem, there is no single technique for a solution. For the content teacher interested in helping students use books intelligently, there is needed a thoughtful review of the students' abilities and the decisions needed to improve them. For general motivation teachers must show the value and utility of information in a content text. After that there should be a gradual movement toward independent use of the book. Initially, however, *bookthinking* has to be directed and not simply assigned. In directing reading–thinking there should be a concern for purpose, vocabulary, order of ideas, and making judgments.

None of this discussion should be misconstrued as detracting from learning the subject of the course. It is in fact an attempt to improve learning and teaching—to make them more effective. Instead of letting a book be an adversary in the learning process, as is often the case, teachers need to find ways of turning the book into an ally. One way to do that is to give it more time. The assignment of time constitutes one means for emphasis or for showing a priority. But having students spend more time does not in itself help them use books more effectively. Students need insights into the vocabulary, purposes, and organization of the writing in a content area. So the answer for the content teacher is not to become a reading teacher, but to decide what it takes to have students think effectively using the book as an essential tool for learning in the subject area. What does it require?

1.3A NEEDS ASSESSMENT: BOOKTHINKING

Level   Teacher activity.

Objective   To outline a means for noting class needs in bookthinking: art, science, math, social studies, English, vocational, health and physical education.

Description   1. First decide which areas of reading–thinking you want to inspect and emphasize in your course.

    _____ discussing values ⎤

    _____ using information ⎬ motivation

    _____ student interest ⎦

    _____ promoting an attitude of interaction with author

        _____ vocabulary difficulty

        _____ concept difficulty

    _____ unique features of content

        _____ vocabulary

        _____ organization

        _____ others

    _____ transfer general reading skills to subject matter reading

        _____ making inferences

        _____ others

    _____ study reading–learning to study with a book

        _____ purpose setting

        _____ asking questions

        _____ others

2. With a chart like the one below, a teacher can note the strengths and weaknesses of students in the class. A simple notation system would include (+) for strength, (−) for weakness, (0) for total lack of skill. Then a tally across the sheet would indicate who needs help, which skills to work on with certain groups, and which skills to let sit. Construct a chart like the sample and list those skills that you want to emphasize for your subject.

CLASS INSPECTION: BOOKTHINKING
+ = shows strength   − = shows weakness   0 = no skill

Students	Value of Work	Utility of Information	Interaction with Author	Readability Level	Study-Reading	Other
1.						
2.						
3.						
4.						
5.						
6.						
7.						
n_k						

1.4 THE IMPORTANCE OF A CONTENT BOOK

One of the ways that a teacher can demonstrate to students the importance of a book from the start is to give them a practice exercise to find information in the book that cannot be found anywhere else. In that way, the book becomes important because it is the only source of information to answer a particular question or solve a problem.

In almost every subject matter, that kind of practice exercise can be set up. It would be best if the problem requires the students to examine the textbook or the supplementary book that is to be used for the solution so that the students have to look at the table of contents or use the index or make use of the glossary, thus getting a chance to explore the book and its components as part of the exercise of answering the question or series of questions. For example, in social studies, ask students to use the index or table of contents to see why the Israeli raid on Entebbe was an important international event. (It was also the subject of a movie.)

*1.4A FINDING UNIQUE INFORMATION

Level   Middle school and above.

* Activities marked with an asterisk are appropriate for students whose reading level is that of grade four, five, or six.

Objective   To show that books contain unique (and perhaps interesting) information.

Description   1. Ask a question whose technical answer must be searched out in the text. It would be helpful if the answer that the students are searching for is also seen as valuable information for the students as individuals. For example, U.S. concern over our returning the Panama Canal to the Republic of Panama gave rise to a proposal to create a new canal. A science teacher might ask, "Is it possible to use atomic explosives in order to dig a canal like the Panama Canal? How could it be done, and how should the explosives be placed? What kinds of experiments have been done in the United States and elsewhere that would indicate that atomic explosives might be used safely for such a project?"

2. Discuss that series of questions, with answers available in the textbook or in a journal, and conclude that it both creates an interesting problem, one of importance to students, and makes the textbook a valuable resource for problem solving and answering important questions.

3. Other subject teachers, using the Canal or any appropriate issue, could require searches of their texts for information that is technical or unique to the subject. For example, regarding the Canal:

   social studies "What other area has a landform that would lend itself to a canal linking the Atlantic and the Pacific Oceans?"

   mathematics "Assuming a depth of 60 feet and level land for a 200-mile canal, how many cubic yards of earth would have to be displaced?"

   English "Based on stories arising from other huge construction feats, what types of literature would you expect to come from the construction of a new canal?"

*1.4B USING DIAGRAMS AND TECHNICAL DETAILS; IMPORTANCE OF BOOK

Level   Middle school and above.

Objective   To show that the text is the repository of exact technical information.

Description   1. Using a topic with potential interest and the text, ask questions that require technical illustrations as part of the answers. For example, "Show the angles of the tunnels in the pyramid of Cheops and illustrate their protective devices."

2. Then ask, "How could you reach the burial chamber safely?

Where did that information come from? Who was it who wrote this text? What are his credentials?"

3. Diagrams and technical illustrations appear in early subject area, including plot diagrams and linguistic diagrams in English. Some of these, by right of their topics, will be of interest to students and show them that subject-specific diagrams or illustrations hold information different from other books. For example:

vocational subjects "In construction, what common geometric form is strongest?" (For example, diagram showing load capacity of triangular form.)

health "What is the most beneficial way for a human to lift a weight from the floor?" (For example, diagram of where strain occurs depending on lifting angle of body.)

1.5 ATTITUDE OF UTILITY

The example given above, of using atomic energy to dig a canal comparable to the Panama Canal, promotes the notion that information in this textbook can also be useful. Promote an attitude of utility by having students solve a problem that is reasonably close to their daily lives. Creating a sense of immediacy and reality through the textbook has a considerable benefit in establishing a relationship between the students and the books to be used.

---

*1.5A PROMOTING UTILITY OF TEXT

Level   Middle school and above.

Objective   To demonstrate that books are valuable because they contain personally useful information.

Description   1. For example, in a geography class, ask the students to find information about the mineral resources in the state where they live and what those minerals mean to the economy of their city or location. If the subject of mineral resources does not suit a particular state, then other economic factors such as manufacturing, farming, or recreation could be made part of the question.

2. By asking questions like the ones above, the students are asked to examine, through their own textbooks, what the specific features of their state are as they relate to friends and neighbors making a living. Perhaps their own futures are involved in the kind of analysis that they are doing.

3. Some follow-up questions could be: "What are the

opportunities for expanding the various industries of the state? Is there land for development (especially land for recreation, if the state is involved in a considerable amount of recreation and tourism)? Does it appear that some of the sources of income in the state that rely on the geographic features of the state are starting to dwindle? What does this mean for your future and for the future of your neighbors?"

4. As the details to answer those questions are found in the textbook, no matter what the subject, ask the students to explain how the textbook can be used to help them solve problems that are significant in the lives of their families and friends.

1.6 READING IS AN INTERACTION

One of the valuable findings of recent research on reading comprehension is that the better readers engage in an aggressive interaction with the text or with the author of the text. It is important, therefore, that all subject-matter teachers try to develop among their students a sense of interaction with the authors of the books that are used in the class.

In one of Ray Bradbury's famous novels of the future, *Fahrenheit 451*, there is a man named Upburner, a fireman whose sole occupation is to burn books. Gradually Upburner begins to see that his occupation does not promote the values that he feels are important. A focal incident is his conversion in his realization that a live person stands behind each of the books that he has been burning. He begins to think about all the effort and the life's blood that some human being put into the development of a book, and that image gnaws his consciousness into seeing not only the human value of a book but also the horror of his igniting his flamethrower and spreading destruction across "living" books.

In one sense, a similar kind of image must be communicated to students in content courses. Students must realize that there are live minds and ideas in those books. Given a considerable amount of practice in trying to work through a relationship with the author of a book or with the ideas in a book, students have a chance of developing a sense of the importance of a subject and the books associated with it.

An interactive attitude does not occur automatically and a considerable amount of time and practice is required to accomplish it. One of the incidental ways that a teacher can promote that attitude is to refer to the book in terms of its author. Talk about what the author of the book is saying or thinking or implying in his or her statements. Ask the students to investigate the author's credentials. Ask the students to write to the authors and to engage in discussion about ideas presented in textbooks. But most importantly, the teacher must do things that will force the students to engage their minds actively with the ideas and with the organization of the textbook. Deciding to promote that interaction constitutes one of the important decisions a teacher makes in trying to solve reading interest problems in any subject matter.

1.6A THINK AS YOU READ: CONTEXT CLUES; RULES FOR GOOD READING

Level   Junior high and above.

Objective   To help students follow an author's thought and organization.

Description   1. As a practice exercise for getting students used to following an author's thoughts, a teacher may use the exercise that follows, which cajoles students into thinking about the way their minds work as they read.
2. Distribute copies and have students fill in the blanks with the words they think the author used.
3. When everyone is finished, compare answers and discuss what makes some words more appropriate than others.

Think as you read

The first step toward better reading is improving your vocabulary. The second step is better thinking.

If you want to _____ well, you have to know why you are reading, what
                  1
_____ are looking for, and how fast you must get the _____. That means
        2   3
that a good _____ keeps alert for these things as he reads.
            4

Here are six _____ that can guide you in thinking while you read. Study
                5
each one carefully.

RULE I: *Set a purpose.* Before you read anything, make sure that you give
            yourself a _____ for reading it.
                       6
RULE II: *Pay attention.* Keep your _____ on what you are doing. You can't do
                                        7
            _____ things at once.
               8
RULE III: *Get the point.* What is the main _____ of the article? Make sure you
                                               9
            know the _____ of the words and of the sentences that you read.
                     10
RULE IV: *Find important details.* Don't try to remember _____, but make sure
                                                            11
            you remember the _____ facts.
                             12
RULE V: *Think as you read.* Your mind has to stay _____ or you won't
                                                       13
            _____ what you see on the paper.
               14
RULE VI: *Vary your speed.* Some things you can read _____; some things,
                                                        15
            slowly. Change your reading speed to _____ what you are reading.
                                                 16

WHY DO YOU READ?

Be honest with yourself. Do you know _____ you are reading? Right now,
for instance? Are you reading only because someone _____ these pages to
you? How much do you think you will _____ if your only purpose is to
_____ the pages?

   Now look at the _____ statements and reread the first _____ for good
reading.

   If you want to get the _____ out of your reading, you must set _____
for yourself for everything that you read. That's the reason the _____ rule
is *set a purpose*.

   How do you set a purpose for _____? In school work the _____ will
often set a purpose for you, but that _____ keep you from setting your own
_____. Here are some _____ that you should ask yourself before begin-
ning to read:

1. Am I looking for anything in _____?
2. What _____ will my teacher ask about this article?
3. Will I have to _____ a report about it? What _____ must I look for
   to write a good report?
4. What is there about the _____ or the topic of the article that _____
   me particularly?
5. Will I want to explain the _____ to someone else? What will I have to
   _____ if I want to retell what I have read?

   [Answers for blanks above: 1. read, 2. you, 3. answers, 4. reader, 5. rules,
6. purpose, 7. mind, 8. several, 9. idea, 10. meaning, 11. everything, 12.
important, 13. active, 14. understand, 15. quickly, 16. match, 17. why, 18.
assigned, 19. remember, 20. cover, 21. boxed, 22. rule, 23. most, 24. goals,
25. first, 26. reading, 27. teacher, 28. shouldn't, 29. purpose, 30. questions,
31. particular, 32. questions, 33. write, 34. information, 35. subject, 36.
interests, 37. passage, 38. remember.]

   This type of exercise requires the students to outguess the author or to
think ahead as they read and can be used in any subject matter. All you need
is a passage that you want students to think about. Type it, leaving blanks
that will promote thinking, and distribute it. Discuss the answers provided
by the class before giving the words originally used by the author. Promote
the concept that the students can learn to supply many of the original words
by getting a sense of how the author was thinking.

*1.6B USING CONTEXT CLUES

Level   Middle grades and above by using a selection that the students could ordinarily read.

Objective   To encourage thinking with an author by estimating the words he would use.

Description   One technique to use in making students conscious of how they can think with and interact with an author is to present them with *cloze procedure passages.* The cloze procedure consists of working with passages from which some words have been systematically deleted. From those passages where words have been omitted the students have to supply words that they think are appropriate for the empty slots.

1. There are several options available in the cloze technique. One is to delete every fifth or every eighth word in the text, no matter what the word is. The students will be able to fill in many of the blanks from their natural sense of language. There will be other blanks which do not lend themselves easily to a simple, automatic response, and the students will have to engage in textual analysis to determine what appropriate word keeps the ideas flowing and the sentence meaningful.

2. In other types of deletions, the teacher can omit words by categories to force students to examine carefully the surrounding text to determine what words would be appropriate. For example, important nouns could be deleted, or words that are defined in the text.

3. A cloze technique could even be used as a glossary or a dictionary exercise. The teacher could delete from the passage the key vocabulary from a chapter and thus force the students to examine the context of the passage and to use the glossary in order to try to figure out the definition of a term which would fill the blank.

1.7 READABILITY LEVEL

A book so difficult as to be frustrating will deal its own deathblow to students' interest and willingness to read a textbook. No one puts up with continuing frustration, and so gives up or avoids those things that are continually frustrating. For that reason the teacher's decision about the textbook and related materials weighs the relationship between the readability of the text and the ability of the students.

It is simplistic and unrealistic to say that once a student is in the ninth or tenth grade he ought to be able to read any text prepared for high school students. It would be very easy to demonstrate that many teachers, once outside their own subject area, would not be able to read independently some of the texts prepared for high school students. Methods of conducting studies to determine the reading difficulty of textbooks can be found in other places, such as Smith, Smith and Mikulecky,[1] and Fry,[2] and Spache and Spache.[3]

Even with the best intentions and even after making the decision to choose a text that is readable for the average students in the class or grade that a teacher teaches, there will still be difficulties. For those students having difficulties with the readability of the text, the teacher ought to provide practice activities and guidance to help them extract as much information from the text as possible under the circumstances.

*1.7A DIFFICULT VOCABULARY; STUDENT VOCABULARY LIST

Level   Middle grades and above.

Objective   To help students select the words which are difficult for them.

Description
1. As part of preliminary work on a selection, have students make lists of words that they consider difficult, that is, words for which they do not know the meaning or the pronunciation.
2. Divide the class into groups of six (two high, two average, two low students in each group).
3. Have the students place each difficult word on a three-by-five slip of paper or card. These should be shuffled and dealt out equally to each member of the group.
4. Have each member privately write a definition or synonym and use each word in a sentence. Then have each member place the words in a pile or in a small box.
5. Have each student check the definitions he or she needs, discussing with members of his or her group any words that remain unclear.
6. During the above activities, the teacher can work with poorer students, showing them how to skim over a chapter or a selection, identifying words that are unfamiliar or whose meaning they do not know. Have the students write those words on a sheet of paper, and then have them turn to the glossary for definitions or pronunciations of those words. A text that has included in the glossary the key technical and content words for the subject has given the students an initial start or an understanding of what is going on in the chapter.

[1] Smith, C., S. Smith, and L. Mikulecky, *Teaching Reading in Secondary Content Subjects: a Bookthinking Process.* New York: Holt Rinehart and Winston, 1978.
[2] Fry, Edward, *Reading Instruction for Classroom and Clinic.* New York: McGraw Hill, 1972.
[3] Spache, G. and E. Spache, *Reading in the Elementary School,* 3d ed. Boston: Allyn and Bacon, 1973.

*1.7B STUDY QUESTIONS

Level   Junior high and above.

Objective   To help slow readers participate in discussion of an article.

Description
1. One technique to help slow readers is to have the students look at the questions at the end of the chapter prior to reading it. Those questions or others provided by the teacher can act as an organizer which helps slower students to read the selection in an attempt to answer those questions.
2. Reading selectively and perhaps being tutored by teammates or peers enable the slower students to extract sufficient information to survive.
3. To help slow readers, the teacher often makes differentiated assignments. Those who find the text too difficult to read can be handed separate assignment instructions, or the teacher can meet with them to discuss the questions they are to read to answer. By design, for example, the answers to their questions may be contained in the subheads or picture captions or in key diagrams.
4. During the discussion in the next class meeting, the teacher may want to give the slow readers a chance to contribute before all the answers have been provided by the better readers.

1.7C USING STUDY GUIDES

Level   Junior high and above.

Objective   To provide a sample guide for study reading as a model.

Description
1. Gradually all students must learn to do their own bookthinking. Though the teacher will often provide directed study guidelines, he or she prods students to build study guides "on their own." In one sense, until they can construct their own, they do not know how to work intelligently with a book. With the teacher providing a model, it would be helpful for students to learn to construct their own study guides. An expanded description of the development of study guides can be found in Smith, Smith and Mikulecky (1978).
2. The teacher tries to take advantage of the students' increased sense of personal responsibility during the teenage years by having them work on a study guide that suits their own personal needs and capabilities. That means that they have to identify what their purposes are—for example, to answer the questions at the end of the text, or to get some major ideas, to work on a project, or to identify the essential vocabulary that they must

have; another goal might be to relate some of the key features of the chapter, such as charts, tables, maps, or diagrams, to the topic or to the purposes that the students had in looking for information in the text. In other words, it is possible for students to develop a study guide that enables them to extract enough information to pass the course and to participate at least minimally in the discussions that surround a topic, even though they could not have read the chapter independently. All students at the college and graduate level learn to make these accommodations, but most middle-school and secondary-school students have not achieved the kind of sophistication they need to make them on their own.

3. Slower students will need a considerable amount of guidance and practice with the classroom teacher before they can develop their own study guides. In this regard a simple duplicated set of instructions is often helpful, and perhaps peer tutoring or help from parents at home will help the slower students to use the directions of the study guide and to overcome readability problems in that way.

4. *Study Guide Outline.* Directions: Fill in this outline as a practice for building a study guide. Then discuss your outline with a classmate or a teacher.

SAMPLE STUDY GUIDE WORKSHEET

A. Topic: _____

B. Pages: _____

C. Major questions to answer:
1. What were the three causes of _____?
2. Who discovered X, Y, Z?

D. Words to know (key concepts):
1.
2.
3.   (Vocabulary can be teacher selected or can be selected by the students as
4.   they find words they want to define and use.)
5.

E. Diagrams or charts (special features):
(Here direct the students to be ready to explain certain aspects of important charts or graphic features.)

F. Summary ideas:
1. Pt. A   (For certain groups, the teacher or tutor may provide these summary
2. Pt. B   statements. Otherwise, students could develop their own summary
3. Pt. C   statements, guided by a directional statement on the study guide.)

G. Questions to ask the teacher or to discuss in class:
1.
2.   (Student must list at least one.)
3.

1.8 GENERAL READING SKILLS

There are some reading skills common to all kinds of reading. A reader of any text is expected to be able to recall important information, make inferences, extract themes and main ideas, and make judgments and application decisions about the information that he or she has interacted with. The problem is not students' lack of some of those skills; the problem is that many students do not realize they have them to apply to specific content texts. Teachers can explain how to transfer those general reading skills to a specific content area.

Even though a student feels comfortable in making inferences, drawing conclusions, and getting main ideas while reading a short story, he often does not realize that he can make his mind work in the same way when he is reading a math problem or a health book or a home economics text. The teachers of those subjects, then, have to make conscious decisions to alert students to use the kinds of thinking skills they have developed in other areas on the text of this particular subject. But a casual reminder in itself may not be enough. Oftentimes it takes practice, discussion, or a demonstration before many of the students understand what is involved in making inferences and in identifying themes in science books, grammar books, writing handbooks, or foreign language books.

The teacher tries to make students comfortable in dealing with the types of information and the organization of ideas as they occur in the textbook. Because of the students' constant exposure to stories on television and to the huge quantity of story reading in the elementary grades, they have no difficulty in responding to a question of information, sequence, or theme as long as it deals with life experiences. But, to many students, there does not seem to be any organization or procedure in a social studies text or a chemistry book, either because it is not a familiar chronological narrative or because it presents data and then arrives at a conclusion. The social studies material seems to be unmanageable to many students, and so they try to power their way through it. That is, they try to memorize everything. From their point of view, the science book and the health book are merely collections of facts which have to be memorized for a test or for some classroom application. That is where the teacher's knowledge of *how* the physical scientist or the social scientist or the health expert *thinks* can be very helpful. Once again, the students are brought back to the notion that reading is bookthinking, and that they are not asked merely to memorize details, but to think with or against an author presenting information, opinions, and judgments. It is also true that there are certain processes that the author may use in sorting information that can be helpful to the students in understanding the peculiarities of the content.

1.8A REASONING FROM INFORMATION; ANSWERING QUESTIONS

Level   Secondary grades in all content subjects.

Objective   To show students that story reading and content reading generate similar questions and similar thinking.

Description   1. Students need to know that they can build on what they know, and it is helpful to give them an image to guide their thinking. Tell them that this activity will show them that some of the work of the mind builds on the pyramid principle.
2. Draw two pyramids side-by-side on the chalkboard or on a transparency. Make them large enough to write information inside. Label one "fiction" and the other "information."

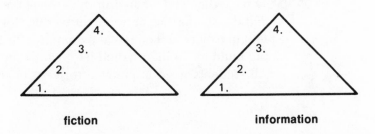

fiction   information

3. Explain that just as the actual pyramids needed a broad base, so the mind works from a base. Ask the students if they can identify similarities between the way a short story is built and the way an information article is built.
4. As needed, fill in the two pyramids with the following terms and explanations in step-by-step fashion:

First, in a story there are characters and events to carry forward the ideas and the action. They are the base on which the rest is built. So, too, in an information article there are facts and details that form the base. That is why discussions often start with questions like: "Who is involved?" (fiction) and "What are the important facts?" (information).

Second, in a story we want to know about the theme or main idea, just as we want to know the purpose or theme of an information article. That tells us we can categorize or understand the information base.

Third, beyond the theme we try to figure out how the story or information article was organized to solve the problem or reach the conclusion.

Fourth, we want to decide what the value of the story is, and the use of the conclusions in the information piece.

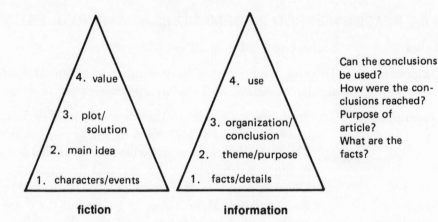

Is there a life value?
How is story problem solved?
What's the main idea?
Who's involved?

4. value
3. plot/ solution
2. main idea
1. characters/events

fiction

4. use
3. organization/ conclusion
2. theme/purpose
1. facts/details

information

Can the conclusions be used?
How were the conclusions reached?
Purpose of article?
What are the facts?

5. Discuss the need for an orderly sense of reading your class books and the similarities between answering story questions and content questions. Like mental pyramids, questions and their thinking build on an information base which supports other answers. All students need is practice to learn to reason well.

2 MOTIVATING STUDENTS TO READ

Students who do not like to read and students who cannot read well are *not* going to begin to either like to read or read better without some strong motivation to do so. Relating the need for reading to the realities of students' lives and the world in which they live is a forceful motivator for improving and increasing reading. Making the act of reading a comfortable, nonfrightening, nonthreatening experience is also a powerful motivator.

These four guidelines are offered as ground rules for each motivational technique you may want to attempt.

GUIDELINES FOR MOTIVATION

A motivational technique ought to be grounded in a realistic ongoing reason for reading. For example, if the students are taught a reading skill which they can regularly employ in working with their school assignments, they will generally respond quite positively because they will have a continuing use for it.

A motivational technique should require some form of commitment or action on the part of the students. For example, a razzle-dazzle presentation or performance about reading may be pleasant and interesting, but if the students have simply been *observers*, they are far less likely to become involved in the follow-up, no matter how entertaining the event.

A motivational technique should have built into it an ongoing follow-up of some sort. For example, students whose reading behaviors need to be adjusted or changed cannot be expected to alter significantly from one shot techniques, no matter how dramatic or appealing they may be.

A motivational technique should provide for some assurance of student success with the undertaking. For example, students who require special motivation do so most often because their past experiences have been frustrations or failures. Unless they see a very good opportunity for something different, they will not be persuaded to participate. (See Section 2.2)

2.1 MOTIVATE WITH REALITY

Relating the need for reading to the realities of students' lives and the world in which they live is a powerful motivator for improving and increasing reading.

The average teenager believes that practically everything he or she does is more interesting and consequential than school reading. One of the reasons for this is that the reading provided has so little to do with anything else in his or her life and world.

The teacher who assigns the reading usually believes the reading is necessary to clarify the content to the students or extend the students' understanding of it. The reading assigned is important to the teacher because the content area is important to the teacher. The teacher's life is involved in the particular content area for a minimum of forty hours a week. The teacher values the knowledge about the subject area, has spent years of study of the discipline, and it is an extension into his or her life. It even has direct reward in the form of a paycheck nine or ten months a year.

On the other hand, the students may not have even chosen to take the course; they actually may have tried very hard to get out of taking it. Very often they are there with no personal motivation to do more than sit out the semester and, maybe, to keep out of trouble. If they dislike to read or are poor readers, their strongest motivation is very likely to be to avoid the frustrations they experience with this reading that they believe has no relevance to them.

The "busyness" and the intensity of the adolescent experience does not leave students with much time. They will not spend time on things they cannot fit into this experience, unless they are convinced it is useful to them or potentially so.

Students are also accustomed to a society that has been willing to entice and seduce them into new behaviors and choices. All their lives, today's teenagers have been given demonstrations and compelling arguments for doing things that promised to make life better for them. From the *Sesame Street* alphabet on, everything from peanut butter to sneakers has been hard sold to them, usually on the basis of making them successful or improving their lives right now, or at the latest, by the time of their next dental checkup. Conditioned as they are to such sophisticated manipulations, it is not likely that they are going to do voluntarily something they dislike which has little identified instant real-life payoff or other inducement. Kotter's "sweathogs" in the popular television series, *Welcome Back, Kotter*, do not demand payoffs from the teacher because they are different from most students; they want them because they are just like the rest.

In addressing the reading problem, some teachers have recognized this characteristic of the students. They have attempted classroom hard sell or toy-in-the-cereal-box techniques. Cola and potato chips have rewarded the adolescents' completion of the reading assignment. The gimmicks worked for about as long as they dealt with the students' real lives, which was about as long as it took to drink the cola.

TEACHER ACTION

What then is the teacher to do? First, recognize that reading has not been singled out by the students as the skill in which they are refusing to be interested. They are refusing it on exactly the same basis that they would refuse to be interested in denture cream, retirement plans, or support hosiery. They are not willing to spend their time and energies on things from which they see no real-life transfer or payoff.

Second, accept the disinterested or poor readers for what in many cases they are: products of an instant gratification era who have been suckled on seduction.

Third, have faith in the teenagers' intelligence. With conviction borne of your own knowledge that they must read to survive, jump in and make use of what you know about the means of changing their behavior and the nature of their needs. The payoff will be slower than that of the peanut butter companies, but it will come if you are willing to go after it as aggressively as they have done so.

*2.1A   MOTIVATING THROUGH PURPOSE

Level   Middle grades and above.

Objective   To help the students identify the purpose for reading required materials in terms of what can be their own present life benefits.

Description
1. Ask the students to list how they think they may be able to benefit from the unit or activity they are beginning by quickly glancing at the topics and headings.
2. Depending on the length and importance of the work underway and the age of the students, indicate the minimum number of answers the students must provide. General vague reasons such as "will make me a better person" should be discouraged or disqualified. All answers which are reasonable attempts should be accepted. For example, a student in music might say, "I need to know the amount of training time needed to become a professional clarinet player."
3. Require the students to support a given number of their reasons (probably two). The most easily located documentation to

support their reasons will generally be found in newspaper and magazine stories about others engaging in the activity, lists of job requirements, lists of entry requirements, and so on. These sources should be suggested to the students as avenues to pursue for information and documentation. For example, a newspaper article about a popular sports figure who attributes his academic success to his ability to read well should be accepted as documentation. Even a testimonial from a dropout who equates some of his or her failure with not having accomplished what was required should be acceptable.

4. Attach an accountability factor to the activity so that the students understand that the task is an important and serious one. Accountability can be obtained by simply announcing the project is a course requirement.

5. Make an initial screening of the lists and supports after the students hand them in. In this way you can find out if any student has written only nonsense answers and deal with them. You can also make certain there are no answers that are so personal they might embarrass the student if he or she were asked to discuss them.

6. After the screening is done, return the lists to the students to use as a basis for class discussion and debate. In the discussion take time to point out:

   a. the sources for documentation of the ideas generally required an ability to read and react critically to information that was found primarily in print;
   b. one of the most important skills needed for experiencing *success* in the class or unit being undertaken is reading.

✓ *2.1B JOB-RELATED READING; REAL-WORLD READING

Level   Middle grades and above.

Objective   To acquaint the students with the academic skills they must demonstrate to obtain part- or full-time employment even as students.

Description   The skills customarily required of the students will be reading and math. For many students the reality of the value of these skills in the larger world will be dramatically demonstrated to them for the first time.

   1. Ask the students to identify three or four kinds of employment they would like to have and might possibly obtain given the time limits imposed on them by school attendance and their present level of skill.

2. Direct them to look for job listings in newspapers, grocery store bulletin boards, the school counselor's office, no-fee employment agencies like those operated by the state and county, and so on.
3. Ask the students to compare the lists of jobs they would like with the jobs available.
4. If there are match-ups, they should be told to get more detailed information about the jobs available.
5. Suggest to the students that they can get this detailed information by calling the telephone number indicated in the notices they found, going to see the contact person listed, or writing a request for information if their contacts provided a post office address.
6. Ask the students to get answers to the following questions:

   a. "What academic skills would you prefer an applicant to have for this job? Why?"
   b. "What skill do you consider the most important of these? Why?"

   Any other questions could be added to direct the students to other objectives the teacher might want to incorporate into the project.
7. Require a report of the students' findings. The information could be given in a variety of ways. Some suggested ways are:

   a. a copy of the requirements listed in the ad;
   b. a paragraph of written description of the requirements about which they were told in discussion with the employer;
   c. a teacher-made worksheet on which they could record such information as the answer to the key questions, where they obtained the information, and so on.

8. Share the work among class members with either a general class discussion or short individual presentations of findings by each student.
9. Follow up the discussion or presentations with the posting of the job listings and requirements for all the class to see and possibly use for actual employment opportunities.
10. On this posting identify in some vivid way each time there was a request or requirement for the applicant to have a basic academic skill (for instance, reading!). Underlining or circling in red or another bright color is an easy and effective way to do this. This last step is very important to the activity. The project will have provided the students with verification of the necessity to have some academic skills, particularly reading. They probably will have found that even for consideration for a job, many employers will require them to be able to read well.

While this information is not news to parents or to teachers, it will come as a shock to many students. For the ones who thought reading could somehow end with graduation, the external proof that it will *not* will become a strong motivation to become more able or interested in the area.

It should be noted in rural areas or small communities which have limited employment opportunities for high school students, students could be asked to describe the kinds of jobs that might exist. They would then go to the appropriate people, such as a gas station operator or store clerk, and obtain information from them on the basis of what the requirements would be if a job *were* available. Approaching the activity in this way will avoid eliminating the element of reality that makes it so appealing—especially if the teacher is careful to point out to the students all that they have accomplished in *a.* locating or identifying sources of employment information and *b.* having identified themselves to those who might eventually require employment assistance. Under these circumstances, though, it is crucial that the teacher approach the assignment as a serious one. Otherwise, the students will see the project as a typical school chore, and the information they gather will be regarded by them as suspect.

2.1C CAREER INFORMATION; ENTRY REQUIREMENTS

Level   Secondary only.

Objective   To inform the students of the general entry level requirements, activities, and rewards involved in various careers in which they might be interested.

Description There is a classic story about the student who always thought he wanted to be a physician until he realized he would have to work with sick people. He had not taken that into consideration, so he changed his mind! This situation describes many of the uninformed notions students harbor relative to career information. Yet, much of teen conversation, interest, and speculation revolves around career choices and aspirations.

1. Ask the students to identify two or three areas of career interest. Some students will not be able to narrow their list to that number, and others will have determined that only one appeals to them. If these variations are unacceptable because of class size or time constraints, a specified number probably should be two for everyone. Some students would be forced thereby to expand their choice list and engage in some exploration; those with large lists would be forced to engage in selection.
2. Make an oral check around the room to determine what areas

are under consideration and suggest that trade-offs be arranged so that a wide variety of fields can be investigated.

3. Direct the students to sources of career information. You could bring samples of such materials to class and show students how to locate information in them through the use of the tables of contents, indexes, and so on. Recent Career Education funding from the U.S. Department of Health, Education, and Welfare has provided most schools with ample books and materials. Indicate to the students where these are housed or take them to that section of the library and show them how to use the books. The school library and reference centers would be obvious suggestions. Governmental agencies use different titles in different states, but those related to or labeled economic security also provide rich sources of career information materials that can be suggested to the students.

4. Indicate the minimum number of sources students are expected to use.

5. Supply the students with a checklist or a worksheet such as the one in Figure 2–A to assist them in recording their findings. An advantage of the worksheet over narrative reports is that similar coverage will be completed for the different fields, thereby making comparative study of the various areas easily accomplished.

6. Have the students present their findings to the class.

7. Encourage discussion of the academic skills identified and how one develops them if they are weak or lacking.

8. Post the worksheets so that students have a continued opportunity to use the information gathered.

9. As a follow-up on the information gathering, provide the students with a second worksheet that would request them to examine themselves in light of the information they now have about the fields of their choice. A sample of such a worksheet is found in Figure 2–B.

10. Since students are often sensitive about sharing personal ideas, do not discuss any part of the second sheet in class except for the area dealing with academic skills. This area can easily lead students to a discussion of the merits of their present school work and how it relates to the totality of their present and future lives.

Reading is realistically motivated in this activity in a number of ways. It is used to find information about the students' real concerns and will undoubtedly be clearly identified by the requirements for the various fields as essential to career success.

Figure 2–A

OCCUPATIONAL INFORMATION WORKSHEET

Name of Occupation: _____
Usual requirements for entry:

    1.
    2.
    3.
    4.
    5.

Usual time needed to meet these requirements: _____
Availability of jobs in the field:

Generally very few openings   Always great many openings
  I _____ I
                           (mark along line)
Usual geographic location of the jobs in this field: _____
Salary ranges in this field:

    Beginners:
    Middle-level employees:
    Upper-level employees:

Advantages associated with this field (if any):

    1.
    2.
    3.
    4.

Disadvantages associated with this field (if any):

    1.
    2.
    3.
    4.

Description of tasks done by persons in this field:

Academic skills needed for success in this field (be as specific as possible):

Figure 2–B

PERSONAL OCCUPATIONAL INFORMATION WORKSHEET

Name of occupation: _____

What I have done or am doing to meet the requirements for entry?

How do I feel about the amount of time needed to meet the entry requirements?

How willing would I or could I be to wait for a position in the field?

Would the geographic limitations of the field be a problem to me?

Would I receive satisfaction or enjoyment from the tasks usually performed by people in this field? (explain)

Would the salary usually earned by people in this field provide me with a standard of living that would be satisfactory to me? (explain)

Which of the advantages claimed for this field do I find the most appealing? (explain)

Which of the disadvantages claimed for this field would be the most difficult for me to accept? (explain)

Do I presently possess all the academic skills required?

If not, which ones require improvement?

How can I improve them?

2.1D COMPARATIVE READING; ADVERTISING

Level   Junior high and above.

Objective   To demonstrate to the students the money that can be saved or made by careful reading of advertising.

Description
1. Ask the students to bring a newspaper to class. Each student should have the same paper for the same day, preferably the issue which has the weekly grocery store advertisements.
2. If it is unlikely that the students will all be able to obtain the same newspaper, call the education department of the local newspaper and request a complimentary class set of one issue. Most newspapers are happy to supply such sets, and many will even deliver them to the school for you. If you are unable to obtain the newspapers from a local source, contact a large well-known newspaper for copies. These papers are generally willing to supply throughout the entire geographical regions they serve.
3. As an introduction to the activity, go to the chalkboard and make a list of five widely advertised items which the students tell you they regularly purchase.
4. Set a time limit of ten or fifteen minutes and direct the students to find those items at the lowest price they can according to the newspapers they have. Some items will, of course, not be advertised; some will be listed at more than one price.
5. At the end of the time set, determine who has "made" the most money by his or her careful reading. Allow some time for disagreement and verification since the students are likely to become very involved and competitive.
6. Use any of the following variations of this activity.

   a. "Give" each student a certain amount of money and determine who is able to obtain the most goods and services with it.
   b. Assign one particular item (for instance, cosmetics or a six-pack of soda pop) and have the class compete to determine who can purchase it for the lowest price.
   c. Give a specific list of ten to fifteen items to a reading team of two players. Match a slower and faster reader where possible. Again, set a time limit and determine who made the most money with their careful reading.
   d. Most coupons carry a cash redemption value as well as a discount offer. Assign players or teams to determine how much cash can be obtained from the edition of the paper they are using.
   e. Make this a semester- or grading-period-long project. Keep a running total on the chalkboard or bulletin board of the amount of money they find they could save via coupons or mail redemption offers.

f. Begin a classroom coupon cooperative. Any student who contributes a coupon or special offer may take one from the co-op. If this project becomes popular some coupons that are highly prized may require the contribution of two that are less valued by the students for one of those highly valued, and so on.

g. If several classes become interested, collect the cash offered with proof of purchase and use it to buy books and magazines for the room. This then offers an opportunity to establish a class library selection committee and positions of responsibility related to print materials. (Since careful reading is the key to their financial success, the teacher can get a double reading participation payoff here by using that success to purchase *reading* materials. If, however, the classes really want to buy a goldfish tank or posters with any funds they accumulate collectively, the reading activity has still been successful because it was the source of their purchasing power.)

2.1E APPLICATIONS; DIRECTIONS; LICENSES

Level   Secondary.

Objective   To direct students to and assist them with the reading required for obtaining licenses for which they are old enough to apply. These licenses will primarily be driver's, hunting, and ham radio operator's. Many students may indicate that they would like CB radio licenses, but for most students the age requirement of eighteen is too high for them to qualify.

Description   1. Decide which license you wish to work with. It may be possible to work with more than one if the interests in the class suggest that. A show of hands as to who holds and who would like to hold each of the licenses would probably be sufficient to indicate the interest level in the different licenses. Since the ham radio operator's license requires a somewhat different approach from the other two, suggestions about it will be made at the end of this activity description.

2. Order the license manuals for the driver's or hunting licenses. A telephone call to the appropriate city or county department will yield you the addresses to which to write for a class supply of the manuals—or the local address at which they can be picked up. Students will likely already know where to get the manuals and will probably be delighted either to bring their own or get a supply for you. These manuals almost always are cost-free.

3. Go over the organization of the manual with the class. Discuss what topics are listed and how the information is referenced to help them to locate it.

4. Ask the students to take a class period or as a homework

assignment to do a quick reading of the manual. If the reading level is low enough to warrant it, assign only half of the manual or a chapter or two.

5. Have the students make a list of any words which they do not understand in their reading.

6. At the next class meeting put the list of words students find difficult on the blackboard. Work with the entire class for clear, brief meanings for each word.

7. If possible, leave the list on the board for reference.

8. If leaving the list on the board is not possible, either have the students copy the list or, as soon as you can, transfer it to a ditto so that they have a ready reference as they work with the reading.

9. Once there is a good understanding of the vocabulary, divide the class into as many groups as there are chapters or major sections of the manual. Try to balance the groups with strong and weak readers.

10. Charge each group with preparing the rest of the class for *the* test on the section of the manual they are assigned.

11. Remind each group that as their task they must:

    a. make certain all of the other readers will understand what the rule means;
    b. make certain all of the other readers will understand the reasons for the rule; and
    c. suggest ways all of the other readers will be able to remember the rule.

12. Suggest to the groups the two following comprehension aids they might want to use:

    a. an outline of the major and minor points in their section; and
    b. a study guide of questions or points to remember in their section.

13. After these basic suggestions, encourage the groups to create other ways to help all the readers understand and remember what they must read and know. Often the creative students, who have great imaginations, or the poorer readers, who know what they need in the way of assistance, will make very important suggestions for approaching this technical and generally dull reading matter in ways that all the readers will also find pleasant and helpful.

14. Allow some class time for planning so that if there are questions you can respond.

15. The work after the initial planning can be done outside of class unless there is no other opportunity for the students to work together. This is often the situation in schools where all the students are bused from long distances.

16. Have each group present its section of the material.
17. Prepare and give a test as similar to the official one that will be administered as you can devise.
18. Post the names of all the students who pass on a "License Ready" list and display the list conspicuously in the classroom.
19. If some students do not pass, discuss the probable causes of their failure and have them follow the suggestions given by the groups to improve their understanding.

Note: For ham radio operators, obtain these two basic books:

1. *The Radio Amateur's Handbook.* Annual editions written and published by the American Radio Relay League, Newington, Conn. 06111 Cost: about $7.50.
2. *The Radio Amateur's License Manual.* Annual editions written and published by the American Radio Relay League, Newington, Conn. 06111 (Cost: about $1.50.

These books may already be in the school library. If they are not, copies should be purchased and circulated from there, as the cost would generally prohibit class sets of the materials. A student seriously interested in obtaining his or her license will need a personal copy of each, so those who wish to work in this area will likely already have these necessary materials.

2.1F FILLING OUT APPLICATIONS

Other topics well suited for motivating the students with realistic reading activities are:

1. Work permits
2. Legal rights of minors, particularly those related to:

   a. driving a car
   b. driving a boat
   c. flying a plane
   d. liability for causing accidents and damage
   e. credit cards and accounts

2.2 MOTIVATE WITH SUCCESS

Making the act of reading a comfortable nonfrightening, nonthreatening experience is a powerful motivator.

The two most obvious characteristics that are shared by almost all weak or disinterested readers are: 1. they do not like to read, and 2. they do not do very well in reading related activities.

Since all of us have had to experience the frustrations and embarrassments of failure in some area of our lives, we should be able to relate to the feelings of the students who fail. We can understand why the students almost automatically back away from experiences that more often than not are going to put them through, at the worst, frightening and threatening kinds of feelings and, at the best, a general negative response of inadequacy and unhappiness.

If we examine our feelings closely, most of us will acknowledge that we tend to avoid situations that put us through frustration and unhappiness. And, if we pushed ourselves to the point of ruthless honesty, most of us would admit that we might not even be willing to show up at a sight that for several hours a day put us through such pain. What we do not do often enough is recognize that we are asking the weak readers to do precisely what we would be quite resistant to do ourselves—that is, to suffer repeatedly the embarrassment of displaying our weaknesses.

REASONS FOR READERS' DISTRESS

Five days a week the weak readers must present themselves at the "bookthinking place" to do what they already know they don't do well, which is "bookthink" or read. It is little wonder that, at the end of several hours of emotional discomfort, they are not willing to take those books home—and so the miserable cycle continues.

The whole process is not unlike the medieval rack if one considers the pressure and importance put on the quality of their bookthinking by all those who stand in judgment of the weak readers. History tells us that very few survived the rack; they either gave up or died in its awful process. To our knowledge there are no stories recorded of how people changed for the better as a result of increasing its pressure; indeed, the continued pressure was the cause of the giving up or dying.

To our knowledge there are also no stories recorded of how wonderfully reading improves by simply pouring on more pressure. There is, however, a myth abroad in the land that speaks to the topic of applying pressure to poor readers. It is the myth that demanding reading competency will automatically bring it forth. Certainly, demanding that more people be more accountable for students' reading progress is a desirable trend. But it is not accountability that is the problem with the myth or the trend. What is a problem and is doomed to failure is the myth that "racking" weak readers with more and more accountability *measures* (tests) or, if you please, *documentation*, of their shortcomings will in any way encourage them to improve.

What, then, can one do to stop the awful cycle? Since most of the weak readers' "racks" are emotional, that is an appropriate place to begin.

Despite the claims of antidepressant drugs and "do it yourself" psychotherapy, still far the best antidote for failure is some success. The teacher must work with the content reading so that the weak readers have some opportunity to experience a measure of success with it.

ADDRESSING THE READERS' PROBLEMS

Designing content instruction that promises some hope of bookthinking success for weak readers may not be as easy as it sounds. Four issues must be addressed in the teacher's usual thinking before it can get underway.

First, the teacher must be willing to admit that typical content area textbook instruction is probably contributing to the "no-win" cycle in which the weak readers find themselves.

Second, the teacher must also be committed to finding a way out of the cycle. This must be a serious determination to save the energies formerly spent on laments to colleagues and exhortations to students and to use those energies in *addressing* rather than *describing* the problem.

Third, the teacher must be willing in the short run to entertain alternatives to the grade level textbook as the primary source of student information and self-instruction. For many weak readers, allowing someone to read to them and help them until they have a good sense of the technical vocabulary and basic concepts in the area may make future comprehensible reading on their own possible. For other weak readers, having a tape recording of someone reading each chapter available in the school library may be an indispensable aid to their comprehension. For still other weak readers, a book entirely different from the one used by the other class members may be necessary. Any realistic alternative that allows the students an opportunity for a successful experience with their content reading should be considered by the teacher as an appropriate measure.

Fourth, the teacher should be willing to take some time from content specific instruction and devote it to instruction in how to read the content. The teacher of the subject is the most qualified to provide this kind of instruction. If he or she is experienced, those years of experience will have taught him or her the words and ideas that are most difficult for students to learn. The teacher probably will have developed ways to assist them with these difficulties. The beginning teacher can still remember how he or she personally dealt successfully with the details of the content area and can pass this direction and information along to the students. No teacher should feel guilty or uncomfortable about time spent in such bookthinking instruction. It is time that enhances the successful understanding of some students and makes successful understanding possible at all for others.

The teacher can expect to be quite effective with measures that allow students to experience success. However, some students may display an initial suspicion of the teacher's attempts. These students are familiar with one kind of failure associated with reading, and it has not made them willing to set themselves up for another kind. This resistance, if it does occur, will not last long if the teacher persists. The students are reluctant only because of their uncertainty that the reading approach has *really* changed, not because they do not want that change. After all, nobody ever willingly got on the rack when there was an alternative!

*2.2A READING TEST DIRECTIONS; IMPROVING TEST SCORES

Level   Middle grades and above.

Objective   To help students improve their test scores by more effective reading of test directions.

Description

1. Supply each student with a copy of the same test. You could use a set of standardized tests that are no longer used or you could construct a sample test for the demonstration teaching. There are books commercially available that can provide you with hundreds of test items of several different types to use as patterns or examples. Most of these books are entitled *How to Prepare for . . .* and then the name of a particular kind of test. There are probably already copies of many of these books in the school library.

2. Ask the students to designate with a circle or marker every place in the test that a direction is given.

3. Ask the students then to mark all of the examples that are provided.

4. Take each different set of directions and work with it individually.

5. Have the students read the directions to themselves.

6. Invite a volunteer to put the example given with the directions or an example she has made up herself on the board. Have her explain how it should be worked or answered according to the directions given.

7. When it is clear that all the students understand the directions and how they are used with the example, ask them to locate what they think are the most important words in the directions.

8. List these words on the board and discuss *a.* their meaning, and *b.* how misunderstanding of them could change a test answer so that it was incorrect.

9. Select test items to demonstrate how points would be lost if the students did not read the directions carefully.

10. If the word list did not include these key words related to test questions, add them to the list and discuss.

essay test words
clarify
compare
contrast
describe
discuss
explain
outline

objective test words
alike
antonym
eliminate
opposite
related
synonym

11. Ask the students to keep a personal list of the points they believe they "make" by careful rather than hasty reading of the directions on the next three tests they take.

12. Keep a chart of the total points the class believes have been "made" by this special reading and provide some kind of reward such as an extra trip to the library or a special reading day. Since one of the hopes for the instruction was to enhance everyone's opportunity for success, the reward *must* be for the group rather than for individuals.

*2.2B SUMMARIZING; LOCATING SUMMARY STATEMENTS

Level   Middle grades and above.

Objective   To demonstrate to students how to find summaries which they can use for clarification of what they are reading and as a check to their comprehension of it.

Description   1. Divide the class into pairs. Where possible, pair a strong reader with a weak reader.

2. Select a typical reading assignment, but be certain that it is one with a good overview introduction, a clearly stated conclusion, or a summary at the end of the passage. Select one that is as easy reading as possible and not more than three or four pages long. In math this may require using introductory material.

3. Ask the teams to read the passage, discuss it with each other, and agree as to what it is saying.

4. Have the students write the meaning that they have agreed upon in two or three sentences.

5. Ask the teams then to find the section in their assignment (the passage they have just finished) that most nearly states what they have just written themselves.

6. The students who have understood the passage will, of course, find that the summary, introduction, or conclusion is the section that most nearly tells what the passage is about. Pairing the strong readers with the weaker ones will have insured that everyone was successful in finding this.

7. Spend some time having the groups report their findings.

8. Spend some time discussing the advantages the students have in knowing this is how the print is presented. Emphasize how knowing this can contribute to their success with the reading by *a.* giving them a general understanding of the material in a short form, and *b.* giving them a means of checking their own understanding of the print by a synthesis already prepared for them.

9. Suggest that the students investigate the rest of the text to

determine if they can count on this format of summarizing for the rest of the textbook.

10. Assign each team a chapter or section of the textbook. The work can be done in class if time permits, but will probably need to be assigned as homework.

11. Again, ask the teams to read, discuss, and agree with each other as to the meaning of the chapter or section.

12. Direct each team to write a summary as they did before.

13. Have each team compare that summary with what is most like it in the section they have just finished.

14. Have each team report its findings.

15. Provide a textbook from another content area for each team. (With approximately thirty students per class, there would be fifteen books needed. Borrowing that many from other teachers could create a problem and would not be as effective as having each student bring one of his or her own from another class he or she is taking.) Work with the students in making their selections so that every text at their grade level is used.

16. Have the teams investigate these books in the same way they have done the other material.

17. Let each team report its findings.

18. The findings will generally indicate: *a.* a specific summary pattern for each textbook, and *b.* that the location of that summary is generally to be found in *i.* the beginning paragraph, *ii.* the ending paragraph, or *iii.* a separately labeled section such as "Overview," "Conclusion," "Looking Backward," and so on.

19. Make a chart listing each of the texts the students are using and where the summary material is found in each. Either post this information where all the students have continued access to it or transfer it to a ditto copy that each could keep for reference. If there is a school newspaper, some of the students would probably like to write up the project and the results to share with the rest of the school.

The sense of success that the students will derive from this activity is two-fold. One, they will feel more confidence in their ability to deal successfully with texts or other reading material, and two, they will be more successful because they have an additional means of using the reading material for their own understanding.

*2.2C CLASSIFYING; ORGANIZING INFORMATION

Level   Middle grades and above.

Objective To teach students a technique for classifying the material they have read so that they are less confused by large amounts of information and detail.

Description   1. Provide students with a particularly fact-laden piece of writing, such as that they would find in an encyclopedia or a reference book. You could even copy an entry from one of those kinds of books and duplicate it for the class. (Check with your librarian concerning the duplication of copyrighted material.)
2. If there are weak readers in the class, you should do the activity in teams of two. This way the weak readers can be paired with the strong readers, and everyone can be successful from the outset.
3. Ask the students to read the entry very carefully to themselves.
4. When everyone has finished reading, ask the students to go back and count each item of information they have read and place a number on the page beside the item.
5. When this has been done, see how closely the agreement is as to the number of items. Wide variations should be discussed and reconciled, but the totals need only be close, not exactly the same.
6. Ask each team then to organize the facts they have into some classification system. Make these rules:

   a. The system cannot be a nonsense system. (For example, the students should not divide the facts into "ones I like" and "ones I don't like.")
   b. The system cannot have more than six parts. (Otherwise the students will try to simply divide the information by paragraphs.)
   c. The system must include every one of the numbered items. (This may require the students to divide some of the items they had put together.)

7. Allow time for the students to work in class, or assign the task as homework.
8. To have fewer groups, you may want to increase the size of teams to four or six. Keep the balance between weak and strong readers, though.
9. Have the groups report their systems to the class.
10. Discuss the advantages and limitations of each of their systems.
11. If the journalistic system of using "Who, What, Where, When, How, and Why" does not emerge in the discussion, suggest that students try to fit their pieces of information into these categories.
12. When it is clear to them that the information they have read can all be put into these categories, ask them to use the format in Figures 2–C and 2–D when they read their next assignment. You could, of course, make up these worksheets and provide them to the students.
13. Continue using a format until the students become successful at organizing the information they read in a way that classifies and

Figure 2–C

ORGANIZER TO BE USED WHILE READING

Student Name _____ *Date* _____

Name of Chapter _____ *Pages* _____

WHO	WHAT
WHERE	WHEN
HOW	WHY

clarifies it to them. Remind them that this organization will improve their reading.

This activity gives the weak readers another opportunity for success with their reading by giving them another means of getting the information in the reading material. It also enhances the weak readers' chances for success in the classroom where reading is required.

*2.2D MAIN IDEAS; PARAGRAPH

Level   Middle grades and above.

Objective   To teach students how to identify main ideas in paragraphs so they can more successfully deal with the reading material.

Description   1. Select eight paragraphs on different but related subjects. For example, the first paragraph in the chapters of your textbook would be fine. Be certain to select material that has an explicitly stated main idea.

Figure 2–D

ORGANIZER TO BE USED AFTER READING

Student Name _____ *Date* _____

Name of Chapter _____ *Pages* _____

Directions: Place the labels in the spaces according to the amount of room you will need to record the information you have just read. The labels are: *Who, What, Where, When, How* and *Why.*

_____	_____
_____	_____
_____	_____

2. Type the material so that it is in the form of a list of sentences rather than paragraph style. See the example below:

   Paragraph Style
   The weather was terrible. The wind blew loudly. The snow fell for hours, and the temperature dropped below zero.

   List Style
   The weather was terrible.
   The wind blew loudly.
   The snow fell for hours, and the temperature dropped below zero.

3. Duplicate enough copies of the list to supply one to each member of the class. At least four lists should fit on a sheet of paper.

4. Cut the sentences in each list apart from one sheet of your lists.

Put the sentences from each list in a separate envelope. If you have prepared four lists on one sheet of paper, then you would have four envelopes for each sheet. Cut the second page of lists apart, but place *all* the sentences in *one* envelope. If money is available for supplies, you can simply request the number of envelopes you will need. If there is a shortage of funds, ask students to bring old envelopes from home. Within a week you will have an ample number. Or, if you prefer not to rely on students, you could purchase small plastic sandwich bags to use as an inexpensive substitute for the envelopes. The ones with the fold-over tops are the best for your purposes. The cutting and sorting required for this activity could be done by a student assistant or volunteer. To complete the activity you will need two sheets of "paragraph lists," and five envelopes per student. The same set of materials can be used for different classes. If you have a class of thirty, two boxes of envelopes or two large packages of sandwich bags will be sufficient.

5. Give each student an envelope from the first page.
6. Ask the student to find the most encompassing sentence in the envelope.
7. Remind the students that this sentence, which summarizes the paragraph and tries to draw together its meaning, is called the topic sentence.
8. When the students think they have found the topic sentence in the first envelope, have the class discuss it and agree on which sentence it is and why.
9. Repeat the process with the other three envelopes.
10. At this point in the activity, if there are very weak readers in the class, use the buddy system and pair weak and strong readers as teams. This is important so that the weak readers have a better opportunity for success with the activity. They will have more success with their reading after they are able to identify the main idea in the paragraph, but they also need a successful start with the undertaking.
11. Give the students the envelope with all the sentences from the four lists enclosed.
12. Ask the students to find the four main ideas in the jumbled sentences. Suggest that they *a.* try first to get together the statements that seem closely related, and then *b.* try to find the topic sentence for each group of related sentences.
13. This task will take time, so you should either assign it as homework or plan to spend an entire period on it.
14. Have the students share their results, discuss them, and agree upon the topic sentences.
15. Follow-up for this activity is needed to insure that attention to

the topic sentence becomes part of the students' regular reading process. Two follow-up activities you might use are:

Popular music lyrics   Have each student prepare an envelope as you did but have her use the lyric to some piece of popular music. You might consider having the students do this every other week or once a month. The lyric must, of course, have a topic sentence to qualify for use.

Student writing   When students turn in writing of their own, exchange the papers and have another student locate and mark each topic sentence. If no topic sentence can be found in a paragraph, the checker can return the paper to the writer for change before it is given to you for grading. This practice could become routine procedure with classroom writing and would assist all the students in having more success with both reading and writing.

*2.2E INTEREST READING; BOOKS FOR ENJOYMENT

Level   Middle grades and above.

Objective   To give every student an opportunity to do some reading in the classroom that is pleasurable and nonthreatening.

Description   1. Establish an area to house special student reading material. Make provision for the students to have some privacy about their materials if they wish. For example, a book shelf in the back of the room could be used. Large manila envelopes could be placed on the shelf for the students to drop their books into if they preferred not to leave them out on the shelf. This provision for privacy is *very important* because it will make it more possible for the student to bring what he really wants to read without the fear that he will be teased or laughed at about his choice or reading level when others are looking at the shelf.
2. Find a name for the area that appeals to the students. Perhaps a contest could be held to find a name, or it could be decided in a class discussion. Obvious names for the area would be Book Nook, Self-Shelf, and the like. Encourage the students to think up something new and fun.
3. Ask every student to identify some reading that he or she enjoys.
4. Ask the students to bring the reading matter to class, but stress that material can be put in the area only if he *likes* to read it.
5. Put any limits on the choices that you feel are necessary to prevent problems in the school. For example, one magazine might be used for a class in one school and forbidden even in

the library in another building. You will know the restrictions that are appropriate in your own situation.

6. Deal with the students who insist that they have never found *anything* that they liked to read by, first of all, believing they are sincere. Then, suggest materials you believe would be appropriate to their interests and/or reading levels depending on the amount of information you have about their needs.

7. If you are uncertain about the students' interests, ask them to fill out an interest inventory for you. A sample inventory that could be used if found on page 53.

8. If you are uncertain about the students' reading level, you could check their standardized test scores or select the level at which you think they are reading and use an assessment technique such as the *cloze* or *fistful of words* that are found in Sections 4.1D and 4.1B.

9. If the problem is a combination of interest and weak reading skill, there are a number of materials that you could suggest to the students that they may not have known about. If there is a reading resource teacher in your building, you should go to that person for suggestions about what is available in your building. You could also get this kind of information from the school librarian.

10. After selections have been made by the students and placed in the special area, set aside a regular time, daily or weekly, for reading.

11. Be alert to the kinds of materials the students enjoy and attempt to build those materials into your regular instruction whenever this is possible.

12. Allow the students to *enjoy* the reading they are doing and *resist* all urges to test or otherwise threaten them. Remind yourself that this is very likely the only pleasant experience some of the students have with reading materials. Remember that if you can change the way those students feel about printed matter, the payoff in increased learning will be important indeed.

*2.2F MOTIVATION THROUGH SUCCESS

Other means of motivating the students by providing them with a greater opportunity for success with their reading are:

1. Rewriting materials to a level they can better comprehend.
2. Taping the printed material so that they can hear it as they try to obtain some meaning from it.
3. Teaming the class so that weak and strong readers work together on projects that require the use of a great deal of printed material.

3

FLEXIBILITY AND PERSONAL CHOICES

Adolescent readers are maturing and therefore can be expected to grasp concepts that their elementary school counterparts cannot. Part of that maturing process is seen in a rejection of some of the topics that they enjoyed reading about a year or two earlier. Maturing readers are conscious of their growing independence and tend to be more selective in what they read. This is natural, and the teacher helps them understand that they are still "OK" despite their changing sense of values in interests and styles. The teacher encourages them to expand their interests and to increase their flexibility in the ways they use books.

With the growing maturity of adolescence, youths are better able to reflect on their past and its difference from present interests. Teachers will want to make sure that the habit of reading does not suffer because the youths associate it mistakenly with childhood—not to be confused with the seemingly more important events that are occurring right now. Teachers will want to take advantage of adolescence as the best possible time to demonstrate to students the control they have over their learning and ideas. Through the decisions they make about reading and learning they express their maturity and they become more and more independent. Related to reading, their major decisions are: 1. choice of topic, 2. choice of purpose for reading, and 3. determining how much energy they will apply to any particular reading activity.

Other characteristics of maturing readers include flexibility and inventiveness. With appropriate instruction and practice, readers become more flexible; that is, they learn how to increase or decrease their rate of reading to match their purposes and topics. Flexibility also includes using various reading strategies to accomplish different purposes and work on different writing styles. For example, readers will skim quickly over an article to get its flavor, or read very closely and take notes to make sure that they can construct a science apparatus or follow a detailed, step-by-step argument the writer is trying to make about a welfare system in a social studies text.

If the adolescents are avid readers, one of the things they must learn to do is to be selective. Their cognitive development now enables them to categorize topics, magazines, and books according to criteria that identify their importance. They realize that no one can or should read everything on a topic, and they must now learn how to sort the flowers from the weeds. As they do so, they must begin to invent their own sorting systems and their own techniques for achieving with books what is important for them.

Adolescents begin to understand that they have to take their places in the real world. For that reason they can be challenged to make decisions about reading based upon future life requirements.

3.1 CHOOSING TOPICS FOR READING

One of the clearest ways that maturing readers show that they are becoming their own decision-makers is that they want to choose the topics that they will read. As children they may have thought that most choices were made for them, especially when it came to the content subjects in school. Though they may have chosen a short story or a novel from the library for recreational purposes, they probably did not believe that they had the same kinds of choices operating for them in science or in art. They should now learn about the alternatives that exist in all fields and see that, whether related to class or to general reading, the number of topics available and the number of books and magazines available can satisfy them intellectually and emotionally.

Students have to learn to make choices. As children, they may have known that they were interested in science. They may even have gone to the library on occasions and asked for "books on science." But most of the time, as librarians attest, younger children tend to make their reading choices on the basis of categories such as "stories about animals," or "stories about sports," or books about the Hardy Boys or Nancy Drew or similar mysteries. Adolescents learn that beyond "biology books" they can read about the feeding habits of frogs, or the life cycles of turtles, or the reproductive mechanisms of deciduous trees. Gradually it becomes clear that the topic alternatives are almost endless. The choices are up to them.

CHOOSING PERSONAL READING TOPICS

The newspaper is an excellent example of how personal reading demands choices. The newspaper contains something for almost everyone, but almost no one reads it in its entirety. Even those who start at the front and work their way through the paper check the headlines or use some other cueing system to determine what they will stop to read and what they will pass over. Most readers want to be more selective than that. But the point needs to be developed for students that they can be better decision-makers in their personal reading where they already think that they are making frequent choices. People do not have to read every article in the movie fan magazine, unless they all make them feel so good that that is what they really want to do—nor do they have to read every article in every popular magazine about the latest sports hero, unless their hero worship dictates endless repetitions. As with all use of time, individuals have to learn to assign priorities. Which topics will they seek out and to what extent will they pursue them?

Maybe one of the reasons adolescents do not read newspapers and news magazines extensively is that they have not learned how to be selective in those publications. Social studies teachers and English teachers have special affinities for reading the popular press, and so need ways to help their students choose their topics, their magazines, and the time they will spend on them. In the broader realm of books and special interest publications, such as *Scientific American*, almost every teacher should be concerned with making his or her students wise decision-makers—if only for the selfish purpose of perpetuating interest in his or her own subject.

*3.1A CHOOSING A BOOK: TEACHER GUIDANCE

Level   Middle grades and above.

Objective   To provide a sense of direction in choosing books for content reading.

Description   The teacher's role is to help students make intelligent choices in their reading. The students want to become more independent, and the teacher wants them to make decisions that will promote that independence. So instead of making choices for the students as to topics that they will read, the subject teacher shows the students what the alternatives are, how they can use their interests to guide their choices, and how they can choose to satisfy class needs.

1. Discuss with the class the fact that most secondary school students have stood in a large library and thus have seen the thousands of books which are available. But that overpowering sense of mountains of books does not actually help make choices. For some, in fact, it may make the task of choosing a book or topic seem overwhelming. Who, after all, can roam through that maze of aisles and pick out a book or two that he or she wants to read? Besides, some of those books are too difficult. That is an additional frustration.

2. Next, discuss ways of viewing alternatives. Discuss the vantage points from which a topic can be viewed. Students who know next to nothing about insects may, for instance, select insects as a broad topic to read about, choosing books and articles that

have the general heading: *insects*, or *insects: general*. Such a choice attempts to open up the field to see what other ways there are to gain generalized knowledge about the topic. But as the students' knowledge increases, so do their options for other topics under the heading of insects. Ask students to list as many topics as they can under the general heading of insects. Each item on the class list represents a topic for reading. All the students have to do is circle the topics which hold greatest interest for them and find books or articles.

3. Then place the following outline on the board. (Other topics in other subject areas could use this as a model to be adopted.)

Categories of insects related to the way man lives:
    Household insects
    Farm insects
    Camping and hiking insects

Topics related to the life and production of insects:
    Life cycle of typical insects
    Multiplication of insects
    Predators and victims

Point out that the topics in this outline require no prior scientific knowledge of insects, only a real-life awareness of them. Those topics also become available, requiring only personal interest.

4. Now the students can choose to read either from the random class or from the categories outlined by the teacher. They could go to the library and report their findings at a future date announced by the teacher.

3.1B STUDENT-DETERMINED READABILITY

Level   Junior high and above.

Objective   To guide students in selecting books they can read independently.

Description   1. Tell students you will show them a way to judge the difficulty of a book for themselves. When they are choosing a selection to read for pleasure or for information, they will want to know if they can read it independently. On topics related to the course, have each student bring three books or journal articles to class. (Or provide sample pages which have a range of difficulty.)

    2. As much as possible, the students should make their own

determinations of whether or not they can read the books. One way for the students to decide this is to read one or two pages at random from a book. If they feel they comprehend without difficulty, then they should feel free to try the rest of the book or article. Have students use the sample page test and discuss the results.

3. Then try a faster test. On different sample pages, have students skim down the page and close a finger into their fists each time they encounter a word they don't know. If a single page produces two closed fists (ten unknown words), the page and probably the book will be quite difficult.

4. Discuss the results of the "fistful of words" technique. It is only a rough estimate, but it gives students a reasonable guide to follow. It is most applicable on pages that have 200 to 250 words. In other words, about 5 unknown words out of 100 running words. In conjunction with the students' own sense of textual difficulty, the fistsful of words technique gives them a sense of assurance in selecting materials for independent reading. Naturally, any such guideline should be used in conjunction with common sense. (For further discussion of this technique, see Smith, Smith and Mikulecky, 1978.)

3.2 DECIDING BY INTEREST

Students should use their interests as a legitimate reason for choosing a reading topic. Students should also seek to expand their interests and to realize that the older they get, the more personal their reading becomes. With additional experience and increased participation in choosing their own topics, their reading–thinking patterns become more and more personal.

The teacher guides the readers in identifying their interests and assures them that they will lead them to topics in which they are likely to succeed. The very fact that they have some interest in the topic means that they probably have enough background in it to proceed with further reading or study and should take advantage of that kind of head start.

The teacher can take the table of contents of the class text and ask the students to rate each topic on a one-to-four scale according to their perceived interests in pursuing the topic. The results of such an exercise would permit members of the class to stimulate each other's interest in topics by acknowledging their own interests. More than that, the teacher can use any avowed interest to form study groups, which will develop bibliographies and displays of related reading as the topics come up for discussion. Thus the students' own interests are fostered with a search for additional material, and they use that interest to promote the class's cumulative knowledge.

By having the students examine their interests through an interest inventory, the teacher creates an opportunity to discuss the value of personal interest in achieving success. If students seem to have no interest in a topic or a subject on which the school or society places high value as recorded in its prominent place in the curriculum, the students should ask themselves why it generates so much interest in the minds of other people. Perhaps such a discussion will broaden their knowledge and help expand their own interests. Then, too, students need to recognize that their interest in succeeding in school prompts them to read and to be selective in what they read.

*3.2A DECIDING ON CLASS READING; TEST PREPARATION

Level   Middle grades and above.

Objective   To guide the students in deciding what to read for study purposes.

Description   1. Often in school the students must choose to read a topic because they know that it will help them achieve a positive grade in a specific class. The students' interest in success guides their choice of what they read. But they have to become conscious of the purposes that guide them. Topics highlighted by the teacher, predicted as possible test questions, or offered as discussion issues for the group are topics to which the students will want to devote special attention in their reading. Without any special introduction, ask each student to take a sheet of paper and write as follows:

_____ Read it all till it is memorized..
_____ Read those sections which will answer what I think the test questions will be.
_____ Read those sections which are personally interesting to me.

Then ask the students to place a check mark in front of the statement above that indicates the way they read the last assigned chapter (or topic) in preparation for a test or a discussion. Ask them to explain why they read the way they did.

2. Discuss with the class the fact that students have to learn how to identify and keep track of those topics that seem to lead to achievement in a class:

a. What does the teacher talk about often or with considerable enthusiasm?
b. Which topics are related specifically to the objectives of the course?
c. Has the teacher given a list of concepts or key terms which were identified as important?

By making a note—at least a mental note—of those questions, the students know which topics to pick for special reading or study as they go ahead. In the same vein, related reading can be selected from the library and from daily reading to support the key ideas that are being stressed in the class.

3. Ask the students to review the current chapter or topic they are working on and to decide what sections they would read in preparation for a test. Let them join in groups of five or six to discuss their individual decisions. Have each group devise a checklist based on questions *a, b,* and *c* above to help them collect the information they need to decide on what they will read in preparation for a test.

3.2B IDENTIFYING RANGE OF INTERESTS

Current events, science, and home economics

Level   Junior high and above.

Objective   To demonstrate that a range of interests is expected in any class group.

Description 1. Have each student bring a newspaper to class, or have the local newspaper send multiple copies of the same issue to you. Each student selects five articles that interest him or her.
2. Collect the selected titles and list the alternatives on the chalkboard.
3. Discuss the range of interests that are revealed by the class and ask them how well they think they will each comprehend the first two or three choices that they have listed for themselves. Lead them to comment on the considerable range of interests reflected in a relatively limited search. What is conveyed by the potential range of interests that the class would demonstrate if they were given free rein in a small library and with newspapers and magazines? The alternatives expand enormously with the addition of each new resource.
4. Have them test the difficulty of the articles that they have chosen by using the fistful of words technique. (See 3.1B.) Some of their choices can be changed if they estimate that an article is too difficult and may lead to frustration instead of success. Have them read their top two or three selections in order to share them with their peers.
5. Have the students, in groups of six to eight, discuss the articles and their interests that prompted them to choose the articles.

3.3 REACTING PERSONALLY TO READING

As the students mature, their reading becomes more and more related to their personal interests. Not only do they want to read entertainment fiction that suits their needs, but they also want to use their growing experiential background to react personally to the study–reading that they do for classes. To help them make those personal reactions more productive, the teacher encourages the students to broaden their personal interests and reading while they are in school.

The fact that adolescents want to make decisions about reading from quite personal points of view reflects their expanding views of the world and their sense that they have to take charge of their personal destinies. And that is good. To capitalize on that sense of personal awareness, the teacher allows personal reactions and personal selections of books and projects, while at the same time requiring the students to match their ideas and interests against the requirements of the course and the authority of the authors. One role for the teacher to play is that of questioner and rhetorical doubter. "What makes you think that your reaction is correct? When you thought that you could skip the entire section on atomic energy, what were you eliminating from your knowledge base or, more pertinently, which questions on the test could you then not answer?" "When you say that the Republicans are full of bunk, do you mean that? Lincoln was a Republican. What should I then conclude on your view of Lincoln?" And so on.

We want to encourage personal reactions and personal decisions. Such decisions lead to mature thinking if the students are challenged occasionally. For these reasons students should learn to identify their interests and to try to identify what they personally want to get from a book or a class.

*3.3A PERSONAL INTEREST INVENTORY

Level   Middle grades and above.

Objective   To help individuals identify their personal interests and match readings to them.

Description   1. Have each student complete the interest inventory record given below. (It can be easily modified to suit the needs of most subject areas. Substitute the table of contents from the textbook for the topics given.)
2. On the bottom of the form, ask each student to list the three interests that he or she holds most strongly.
3. For each of the three identified interests, have the student choose a book or magazine from the library that he or she will read.
4. After the students have explored the library, discuss ways that they think they can use their interests to benefit their work in

class. Not everyone needs to offer a clear response. The discussion should reveal many opportunities, however.

INTEREST INVENTORY RECORD

---

1. What sports do you like to play? (Circle your answers.) What sports do you like to watch? (Underline your answers.)
   - a. Roller skating
   - b. Skiing
   - c. Football
   - d. Baseball
   - e. Basketball
   - f. Swimming
   - g. Bowling
   - h. Horseback riding
   - i. Boating
   - j. _____

2. Do you have pets? What kinds? _____

3. Do you collect things? (Circle your answers.)
   - a. Foreign money
   - b. Stamps
   - c. Rocks
   - d. Butterflies
   - e. Antique dolls
   - f. _____

4. Do you have hobbies and pastimes? (Circle your answers.)
   - a. Writing letters
   - b. Sewing or knitting
   - c. Dancing
   - d. Singing or playing a musical instrument
   - e. Playing cards
   - f. Working on cars
   - g. Repairing things
   - h. Drawing or painting
   - i. Driving a car
   - j. Cooking
   - k. Making things with tools
   - l. Experimenting in science
   - m. Going for walks
   - n. Fishing
   - o. Hunting
   - p. _____

5. What school subject do you like best? _____

6. What is the best book you have ever read? _____

7. Do you enjoy reading? _____

8. Do you like to have someone read to you? Who? _____

9. Apart from lessons, about how much time each day do you spend reading? __

10. Do your parents encourage you to read at home? _____

11. What are the names of some books you have been reading during the last two months? _____

12. Underline the kinds of reading you enjoy most: history, travel, plays, essays, adventure stories, science, poetry, novels, detective stories, fairy tales, mystery stories, biography, music, others.

13. What kind of work do you want to do when you finish school? _____

14. What newspapers do you read? _____

15. What sections of the newspaper do you like best? Check below.
    - a. Sports _____
    - b. Funnies _____
    - c. Stories _____
    - d. News _____
    - e. Editorials _____
    - f. Other _____

16. What magazines are received regularly at your home? (Underline those which you read.) _____

_____

17. Name your favorite magazines: _____

_____

18. Name the comic books you read and underline your favorites: _____

_____

19. All of the above are sources of interests for you. List three interests which you want to work on and three books or articles that you will read to foster those interests.

Interests	*Books/Articles*
a.	a.
b.	b.
c.	c.

*3.3B Choosing Subject Matter Books; Personal Interest

Level   Middle grades and above.

Objective   To use students' choices to expand their personal interest in the course.

Description   Identify five or six major areas of emphasis where students should read to expand their awareness of the subject and to better prepare themselves for the objectives of the class. Encourage students to use their present knowledge and interests in the area to select their readings, and distribute to each a pie design like the one below.

1. Draw a circle and divide it into pie-shaped chunks.
2. In each pie-shaped piece, write a category in which you want the students to read.
3. During the term, the students are to read some article or book that fits the category and also gives them better preparation to succeed in the course. (Brief oral reports on each item listed in the circle could form part of the students' grade.)
4. The circle below is designed for use in a vocational education course, but the idea could be adapted to any subject by changing the titles to those that fit the course. A brief bibliography could accompany this reading design.

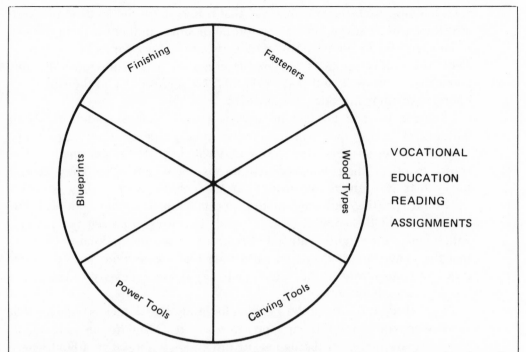

DIRECTIONS: Read a book or an article for each section. Write in title and author of book or article that you have read in each category. Be prepared to give your reaction to each one, especially on how you think it can be used.

3.4 SELECTING A PURPOSE FOR READING

Mature readers not only decide what they will read, but for which purpose. It is important that purpose is a choice. To make a choice implies the existence of alternatives.
Once the students see that they can take charge of their reading and be success-ful in that way, they have achieved an attitude that will give them the psychologi-cal energy to overcome many of the problems that other student readers face.

Though it seems clear that everyone has a choice in reading for personal pleasure, it is not obvious that readers also have choices to make concern-ing assigned readings. Like adults who think they have to clean their plates of every scrap of food because that was a childhood rule, nonselective readers pick up a magazine and devour it from start to finish—because that seems to be the thing to do with a "plateful" of reading. In school, after all, you always try to cover the entire book—even to rush through its last 167 pages as time runs short in the semester—and apologize profusely for every page that was not read and discussed.

In order for purpose setting to be effective, the readers must know how to get beyond the obvious distinctions between reading for enjoyment and reading for information and study. When people read for enjoyment, they relax and approach the text in a way that brings them the kinds of pleasure that they seek. Escape, adventure, erotic dreams, finding thrills in the use of language (as in poetry), laughter, or whatever, are forms of enjoyment that readers may seek. As readers mature, they make conscious decisions about their purposes, and that alerts their consciousness and their physical energies to their intended responses.

Choosing to read for general information also helps readers establish patterns of action that will accomplish that purpose. They can choose magazines, newspapers, and books that will keep them informed in the broad scope of their lives—which means, of course, that they choose topics that give them information in the categories that they consider important: politics and government, sports, entertainment, physical and mental health, the comics, science. And then they approach the reading with a "once-over-lightly" attitude because that serves the kind of purpose that they have set. If they find something that affects their lives directly, they can concentrate to the extent that they deem necessary to assimilate the necessary information.

Every student has to study. Reading for study also demands a choice that is more specific. Students can study to pass a test, to write an assignment, to participate in a class discussion, or just to keep abreast in a field where they have some competence. By recognizing and choosing specifically what kind of study purpose they have, students enable themselves to use the techniques most appropriate for their purposes. In reading to prepare for a test, for example, students should try to formulate the questions that they think will be asked and then read to formulate an acceptable answer. In contrast, reading to participate in a discussion suggests getting the theme and some salient details and then trying to make judgments that can be expressed in the discussion.

*3.4A PURPOSE SETTING

Level Middle grades and above.

Objective To demonstrate the effects of purpose setting on reading.

Description
1. Divide the class into five equal groups.
2. Give each group the same article to read: for example, a short story in an English class, a science report on a new development in plastics, an analysis of a recent governmental election for social studies, a description of Base 2 mathematics, and so on.
3. Either in writing or privately aloud, give each group a different purpose for reading the same article.

   Group 1: Read and tell the story.
   Group 2: Read and be prepared to take a ten-question quiz.

Group 3: Write the theme and give some supporting details.
Group 4: Answer these four questions:
Who . . . ?   What . . . ?
When . . . ?   Where . . . ?
Group 5: Tell why you do or do not agree with it.

4. Have each group share its ideas within the group and decide what response they will give.
5. Ask each group to explain to the whole class how they read the story in order to prepare for the purpose given. Discuss how the five different purposes should prompt different kinds of reading behavior.

3.4B PURPOSES FOR READING; ALTERNATIVE CHOICES

Level   Junior high and above.

Objective   To acquaint students with various purposes for reading in a given content area.

Description   1. Distribute the same article appropriate to your content area to all students. In each subject area it should offer opportunities for various purposes: for example, a·description of changing fashions for home economics, a humorous essay on the political scene for social studies, an argument over the value for science of cloning, a book review for English, and so on.
2. After the students have read the selection, ask them to think of various purposes that they and other students might have for reading the selection. Write each suggestion on the board.
3. If they have not come up with all of the following, list these additional items:
Possible purposes are:

to develop an image of an event or a process
to solve problems
to support ideas and requests
to argue against ideas and requests
to clarify a complex or a vague issue
to answer specific questions
to participate in discussions or conversations.

4. Discuss with the students the values arising from thinking about purpose before beginning reading. If the teacher did not give a preordained purpose for reading, students still would choose a wide variety of purposes for, and therefore approaches to, reading this article just by using their own interests.
5. For additional practice, have the students take a selection from

their text or from a journal on a current study topic, write a purpose for reading, discuss their various purposes, read the selection, and discuss their perceptions of the selection based on their preassigned purpose.

3.5 DEVELOPING FLEXIBILITY

Competent, mature readers learn to vary their purposes, their speed, and their techniques—in a word, they are flexible. One intention of every teacher is to make the students flexible reader–thinkers in his or her subject area. Part of working on that task is to remind students to use all the skills they have acquired through the years.

In a previous section there was a discussion of adjusting reading according to a purpose for reading. That is one example of flexibility. Depending on the purpose, readers skim for a few ideas, read with great care, take notes, or relax and let the music of the language and the images take over their imaginations. Just as purpose is one conscious, directing force in reading which brings about differing responses, so there are other conscious, directing activities that lead to a more flexible reader–thinker. Take the notion of speed as an example. By telling themselves to read faster (for a purpose), students can in fact process the information more quickly. In order to increase reading speed by a considerable margin, however, a considerable amount of practice is necessary. Readers also show flexibility by adjusting their approach or technique to the content being read. For example, a newspaper account of daily traffic accidents can be read quite casually (or not at all), whereas the directions for filling out an income tax report must be read formally and intently.

*3.5A INCREASING READING SPEED. FLEXIBILITY.

Level   Middle grades and above.

Objective   To increase through concentration the number of words per minute students are capable of reading.

Description 1. In the military, service personnel are often asked to "double time"—that is, to move twice as fast as they would ordinarily march. With a little practice, they learn to move as a group in double time. Students can also learn to read in double time. Use the double-time analogy with students and tell them that all they have to do is concentrate and practice. In other words, they have to tell themselves to read faster, and they will—with practice.

2. Using pages from the course text or another source where

similar types of material will be available over a period of four to six weeks, have all the students start reading when you say "go" and continue reading for three minutes. They should place a mark exactly where they were when you called time, count the number of words read, and divide by three. Tell them that that is their base figure—the number of words per minute that they read at present. They should place that number in the chart. Distribute one like the sample below.

3. Conduct a brief speed-reading exercise at least two, and preferably three, times a week. At the beginning of the class period give them an initial three-minute practice period and

READING RATE CHART

_____   _____
          (Name)   (Subject and time)

Date	Page Numbers	Number of Words	Time	Words Per Minute (Base Figure)

then a three-minute trial with their scores being recorded in the "Reading Rate Chart." The only direction that you need to give the students is that they are to read faster today than they did yesterday. The combination of your direction, which focuses attention on what they are to do, and the chart, with its scorecard features, will lead to a considerable improvement in speed over a four- to six-week period. The students *will* increase their rates. Many will double them.

4. Once a week, the students should check their own comprehension by writing a brief summary of what they have read and then reread to see that they have picked up the salient features of the passage. As a caution, you can remind them that their comprehension should not lag just because they are trying to increase their speed. The energy and concentration that they apply during those speed exercises usually will reduce problems with comprehension. If anything, their comprehension ought to improve a little with their speed. (This technique does not apply, of course, to students who have serious reading problems and cannot read the text in the first place.)

5. Every two weeks, check the "Reading Rate Charts" and circle the date when students double their base rates. Challenge them to triple their base rates by the end of the six-week practice period. Give the entire class a biweekly summary of the number who have doubled or tripled their base reading rates.

6. Reading speed without comprehension is meaningless, of course. Every legitimate test of speed should include a brief test of comprehension as well—either a summary of the passage or answers to a set of specific questions.

7. Remind students that a reader adjusts his rate to fit the purpose for reading—study, enjoyment, casual interest, general information, and so on.

3.5B SKIMMING THE TEXT; INCREASING SPEED; OVERVIEW

Level   Junior high and above.

Objective   To develop a systematic technique for skimming a reading selection.

Description 1. Distribute an article from a newspaper or magazine to the students. Its topic should be related to a current class topic so the transfer will remain strong. Tell them that you will give them thirty seconds to find the "Who, What and Where" of the article. "Go—thirty seconds—stop!" They will complain because you did not give them enough time. But that is part of the exercise.

2. Tell them that you will show them how to skim the article so they can respond quickly to questions like those you just asked. But it will take a little practice. It is called the *zigzag skim technique*. The readers move their fingers back and forth across the column of print in a zigzag fashion in order to skim the article for the kind of information that they want. Diagram the technique on the chalkboard. (See diagram below).

Earthquake Kills 800

3. Explain that the steady movement of the finger across the page forces the eye to follow at a smooth pace and to look only for the information that you set out to find: "Who, What, When, Where, How, Why?" Try it and see how it works.

4. The students need numerous practice attempts. Use newspaper and magazine columns because they are relatively narrow and permit easy early practice with the zigzag skim. As the students progress, shift them to wider columns and finally to the full width of the page that is typical of most textbooks.

5. As the students become more and more proficient, the angle of the zigzag can become wider until the finger motion is nearly (or actually) a straight line down the center of the column of print.

6. This kind of skimming is useful for getting the main idea and the basic information from an article. If that is all that is needed, the technique fits the situation. Like other techniques for increasing flexibility, this one must be practiced for it to serve its purpose. Practice at least two or three times a week

for a four- to six-week span. The practice time requires only three to five minutes at the beginning of each period. Have the students evaluate their progress in terms of the width of a column they can work on and the angle of the zigzags they use. In a month to six weeks, they will become proficient at the technique if it is practiced regularly.

7. Skimming often serves the students in previewing a chapter to see what it is about and in what direction the information is moving. The technique prepares the readers for finding more specific information or for engaging in a search of a more complex nature for later work in the class.

4

BUILDING VOCABULARY

A word that a person can both under-
stand and use is a valuable possession, something that
cannot be worn out, taken away, or lost except through dramatic circumstances. The more kinds of words people have at their disposal, the better equipped
they are to adapt to different situations that call for language. From the earliest stages
of language acquisition, children understand this. The teacher's task, then, is not so
much to promote a natural human interest in words as to exploit it fully in the
classroom.

Because of the organizational plan of most secondary schools, the junior and senior high school teacher is usually teaching in a specific subject area. If not, he or she is team teaching in a combination of content areas. The teacher's charge is to transmit certain parts of the content of the specific subject area to the students in such a way as to insure that the students have "learned" it.

The means the secondary teacher has at his or her disposal for helping students "learn" are usually books and other printed material, class discussion time, and sometimes audiovisual and appropriate laboratory equipment. Printed materials constitute by far the largest amount of the resources, and attention to printed materials occupies the greatest amount of the teacher's class time. It is fair to say that print carries the bulk of the instructional load even in areas such as science and mathematics.

Obviously, these printed materials, which are so central to the instructional program of secondary schools, are only an instructional aid so long as students can obtain meaning from them. And, that meaning rides on the students' understanding of the words in the print. The words and their arrangement are the carriers of the concepts the students are expected to understand and master.

GUIDELINES

Two things become clear when one realizes how consequential it is for students to develop adequate vocabularies. One is that every content teacher will have to work with vocabulary. No matter how well the students read when they leave elementary school, they cannot be expected to have vocabulary sufficient to carry the subject area concepts taught in the secondary school. Nor, should the secondary teacher expect the elementary teacher to have taught this vocabulary. The very nature of the secondary teacher's training has qualified him or her to have a depth of knowledge and understanding in a specific area that cannot be expected from one with less specialized content preparation. As the concepts of a particular subject grow more specialized and complex, the words that carry those concepts do also, and the teacher specifically trained for the area becomes the one most qualified, if not the only one, who can provide this specialized vocabulary instruction.

The second point is that vocabulary instruction must be continuous. There is no time at which someone can be declared "finished" with vocabulary teaching or learning. As long as the students and the teacher continue to learn new concepts, there is a need for new words. They are necessary to clarify meaning and to give the students a means for identifying, ordering, and using that meaning to relate to what they already know and what they seek to know.

4.1 USING VOCABULARY ASSESSMENT TECHNIQUES

Time is one of the teacher's instructional resources. It should be carefully planned to guard against waste or loss. It is as inexcusable to force students to spend time on what is already well known as it is to fail to spend time on what must be known and is not. It is critical for the teacher to determine what is known and what is not known before instruction begins.

Since each new concept the teacher introduces will bring with it new words or new uses for words already known, virtually every topic covered will require attention to vocabulary instruction.

Historically, secondary teachers have either ignored the problem of new words and new uses or relied heavily on a vocabulary list of some sort.

The problems inherent in ignoring the new words are obvious. The academically able and independent students will discover the meanings either through their ability to work with context clues, their previous knowledge of similar terms, or their willingness to look up meanings without being directed to do so. The less independent learners and the academically weak students will simply struggle through and avoid as many of the new terms as they can, thus further weakening their position.

In classes where only a formal vocabulary list is employed, there are problems also. The typical vocabulary list comes from a word book and consists of words someone speculated the students would not know. The instruction for the use of the list will generally be to look up the words and write the definitions and/or to use the words in a sentence. Ordinarily, the sentences will be handed to the teacher for grading, often even without a class discussion of them. Since there are usually a great many words on such lists, and there are usually a number of these lists in such books, the students and the teacher will spend a great deal of time producing and grading the activities they require. If no efforts are made to relate them to the work underway, the lists are not likely to help the students very much and the time the students might have spent learning a word they really needed to know will have been used up in the list activity.

There is certainly nothing wrong with organizing vocabulary instruction around the use of vocabulary lists. It is not the idea of a list that is a problem. It is the irrelevance of the words to the topic the students are studying and the lack of some systematic application of the new words to their needs that create student indifference to the words and constitute the problem.

When the students show a negative response to any vocabulary study approach, it is almost always the result of their inability to see a need for the study. If the students can be shown a clear need for such study, they can be expected to be far more diligent and enthusiastic about it. They are getting something for the time invested. This accounts for the great industry of students preparing for competitive scholarship exams. They know the words they are learning will be valuable to them in obtaining scores worth scholarship money to them.

Taking time to assess what the student vocabulary needs are addresses the problem of motivation for learning the new words and their uses. It also saves valuable instructional time that would be wasted providing instruction about words already known or not necessary for the enterprise underway.

The following vocabulary assessment techniques give the teacher quick and easy methods of finding out which words require special instruction for the class. By using these techniques the teacher can plan relevant vocabulary study or build his or her own lists that will provide students with new words actually needed. Using the techniques will insure that the time used for vocabulary study is directed to clearly identified needs.

*4.1A VOCABULARY SELECTION; STUDENT CHOICE

Level   Middle grades and above.

Objective   To determine what words in a selection must be taught.

Description   1. Divide the class into teams. The teams should represent a variety of reading abilities, low to high, and probably be no more than three or four members each. Otherwise, there will not be opportunity for each team member to be totally involved.

2. Explain that these teams will function as "preparation teams" or "information squads." The teams will operate on a rotation basis so that everyone in the class will participate. The team responsibilities will be:

   a. read a selection two or three days before it is assigned to the class as a whole;
   b. decide what words are going to be "troublemakers" and list them;
   c. supply the list to the teacher before he or she assigns the reading to the rest of the class.

3. Take the list which the students provide and make a decision as to how much time will probably be required for word study in order for the students to be successful with the material.

4. Determine what will be the most effective approach for this particular list of words. (See 4.2 and 4.3 for suggestions.)

5. To simplify the management of the system, number or name the teams and keep a list of them inside the cover of the text being used. Then at the beginning of each grading period, simply take five minutes, and both you and the class can jot down the team number in the table of contents by each selection for which it will be responsible. If you know the dates you will need their lists, these can be penciled in also.

*4.1B VOCABULARY DEVELOPMENT; STUDENT CHOICE

Level Middle grades and above.

Objective To determine the approximate number of words in a section that must be taught.

Description
1. Ask the students to ready silently a 100-word passage of a selection which you will be assigning in the next book.

2. As the students read, ask them to close a finger into their fists when they come to a word they do not know.

3. Have the students write the number of unknown words (number of fingers) they find in the 100-word section.

4. Repeat the process a couple of times if the selection is quite long. Even if the selection is short, the process should be gone through more than once.

5. Determine the number of words with which most students had difficulty.

6. Use as a rule of thumb:

   a. Ten difficult words or more (two fists) per passage indicates that the students will require direct vocabulary instruction since they are trying to read at a frustration level.

b. Less than five difficult words (one fist) per passage indicates that the students can probably work with the material with minimal assistance in vocabulary.

7. Consider using this "instant" method with most material so that you will be able to better predict the appropriate amount of vocabulary instruction for particular sections of the text and other printed materials. The method certainly does not pretend to be scientific, but it is an effective gross screener.

4.1C READABILITY LEVEL

Level   Can be adapted to any grade level and subject area.

Objective   To determine the reading difficulty of a passage.

Description
1. Select three 100-word passages in the printed material which you will be using. One passage should be taken from the beginning, one from the middle, and one from the end.
2. For each passage, count the number of words that have three or more syllables. You do *not* count proper names, compound words, or verb forms that become three syllables by adding *ed* or *es*.
3. Determine what the average sentence length of each passage is.
4. Add the number of three or more syllable words *and* the average sentence length.
5. Multiply the sum by 0.4.
6. Your result is the "Fog Index" of the passage.[1]
7. The "Fog Index" score represents the approximate grade level needed to read the passage.
.8. When the "Fog Index" grade level is much higher than the grade level of the class, you will obviously have to spend a great deal of time on directed vocabulary study. While the "Fog Index" does not identify specific words which will create difficulty, it is an efficient way to make comparisons among materials and to get a general indication of the students' probable difficulties with a given selection.

*4.1D DIFFICULTY LEVEL; CLOZE TECHNIQUE

Level   Middle grades and up.

Objective   To determine the reading difficulty of specific printed material.

Description
1. Select a reading passage of approximately 275 words from material that you will be using with your students.
2. Leave the first sentence intact. Starting with the second

---

[1] The Fog Formula was developed by Dr. Robert Gunning.

sentence, select at random one of the first five words. As you type the passage leave an underlined blank fifteen spaces long for the word you leave out.

3. Omit every fifth word until you have a total of fifty underlined blanks. Finish the sentence.

4. Type one more sentence intact.

5. Before passing out the tests, explain to the students that they will be taking a test that will try to measure the difficulty of their reading materials. Show them how the cloze procedure works on the board with sample sentences such as "Mary had a little lamb; its fleece was white _____ snow." Explain to the students that they can get many clues from the context that will help them determine words that fit, but that they are not to use their books.

6. Allow the students as much time as they need to complete the test. (It will take less than a period.)

7. When the students have finished, count as correct every *exact word* they have used. Do *not* count synonyms.

8. Multiply the total number of exact word replacements by two in order to determine the students' percentage score.

9. Record the scores in the following broad score bands. (See Figure 4–A.)[2]

> Below 35%: Frustration Level
> Between 35% and 55%: Instructional Level
> Above 55%: Independent Level

Figure 4–A

CLASS RECORDING SHEET

Student	BELOW 35% *Frustration Level*	BETWEEN 35 AND 55% *Instructional Level*	ABOVE 55% *Independent Level*
1.			
2.			
3.			
4.			
5.			
6.			
7.			

[2] The percentages follow the general standards developed in the work of John Bormuth.

10. You will now probably have at least three reading instructional groups identified in terms of their ability to deal with the actual material you are using. You can now determine whether you will need different reading strategies within the class and which students will require additional assistance with the material. You will also discover whether the material is too difficult for too many students to be a realistic instructional tool.

4.2 BUILDING VOCABULARY FOR READING AND THINKING

The extent of students' interest in expanding their vocabulary will depend on their need for new words, and this in turn depends upon the opportunity they have to express themselves for various purposes. By junior high school the students usually have developed what the Russian psychologist Vygotsky called "verbal thought," and since their words represent concepts, they provide the means for this thought. As the students encounter an increasing number of concepts, they must be assisted in learning the words and the language of those concepts so that they become their own.

How does a student come to "claim" or "own" a wide vocabulary?

Only through ongoing vocabulary study and emphasis will it be possible to do an adequate job of assisting students with vocabulary development. Despite the claims of the popular "instant" reading and vocabulary clinics, large vocabularies cannot be had in six easy lessons. While some short term increase in word identification certainly is possible, the students will come to know or "own" large numbers of words and meanings for those words only as they and the teacher note, clarify, and work with words on a continuing basis.

How do we aid vocabulary learning?

At the secondary school level, probably the most popular and time-honored method of formal vocabulary instruction has been teaching Latin and Greek root words and prefixes. While generally this is helpful as students learn the more common and consistently used roots, some research would indicate that this may not be the most productive methodology to follow.[3,4] It certainly should not be the only methodology employed.

How do we help students use past experience?

The most effective vocabulary strategies are ordinarily those that assist the students in fitting the new word into what they already know. As they discover the meaning of the new term, they need to relate it in some way to all the other terms, alike and different, that they already possess. The teacher's task is assisting the students with the process of making a new word a part of their thinking. When the students have found a place for the word among the words and ideas they already know, they can call it into play to assist them in ordering and relating other things they are coming to know. The process the teacher is encouraging is similar to the *association game* or *technique*. In that technique, people must select arrangements (alphabetical, sequential, and so on) to associate with particular names or words, so that when called upon to recite the names or words, they have an association or ordering that will make it easy for them to do so. Anyone who has used the technique will testify to its effectiveness. Teachers who have taught vocabulary by "association" methods are equally satisfied with their results.

How do we create opportunities to learn vocabulary?

Using any technique in vocabulary instruction still is only part of bringing the students to a sensitivity to words. Making students "word conscious" or "word conscientious" is the critical strategy in vocabulary development. Once students watch for new words and feel a need to know them for their own purposes, real vocabulary growth is possible.

In the beginning of vocabulary development, the teacher will be the one who creates the need for the words by arranging vocabulary study opportunities for the students.

*4.2A MULTIPLE MEANING VOCABULARY; SUBJECT-SPECIFIC MEANINGS

Level   Middle grades and above.

Objective   To increase student vocabulary.

Description   In almost every subject area there are some words which have a general meaning that is known to most people and also have a

---

[3] Jenkins, Marguerite, "Vocabulary Development: A Reading Experiment in Seventh Grade English," *Peabody Journal of Education*, 19 (May 1942), pp. 347–51.
[4] McDonald, Arthur S., "Vocabulary Development: Facts, Fallacies and Programs," in E. L. Thurston and L. E. Hafner, eds., *New Concepts in College–Adult Reading* (Milwaukee: National Reading Conference, 1964).

meaning quite specific to the particular content area. "Point" in mathematics, "set" in psychology, and "space" in typing are examples of words with such subject-specific meanings. Students are often unwilling to accept a new meaning of a word with which they are familiar. They are generally unaware of how many meanings or uses most words have. They are reluctant to use familiar words in new ways and as a result really are not getting full use even from the words for which they have some meaning. The following activity should sensitize the students to the many possible uses for the same words and how the context of a word operates to dictate its meaning.

1. Put examples of different uses for the same word on the board and discuss them. Select words from your own subject area and compare them with the use of the same word in another subject. For example, "space" is a word almost everyone recognizes, yet "space" is used in science in one way, in home economics in another, and in typing in still another.
2. Point out how the context tells the reader which meaning to use. Discuss the control context has on meaning and what a help it is in deciding what even an unknown word may mean.
3. Ask the students to select a given number of "search" words for the week (probably five per week unless the class is an accelerated one). Direct them to select words used in your subject area.
4. List the words on the board.
5. Ask the students to find as many meanings for each word as they can by the end of the week.
6. Suggest that the students use the thesaurus as well as the dictionary in their search. Remind them to be alert also to the different uses of the words that they find in their own reading.
7. When the students have completed their search, record their findings on a large chart that can remain posted. Allow space to add new meanings if students locate them later. You could also write only the words on a chart. Then, under each word attach three-by-five note cards each of which has a different meaning for the word written on it. Two straight pins will attach several cards to the chart, and the cards can be removed and replaced easily if students wish to use them. (See Figure 4–B.)
8. In addition to the general posting, have the students keep a notebook of the different meanings they find.
9. In your study of the subject area, as you encounter the words the students have searched, call their attention to those words. You might even have the students star each meaning in their workbooks as they find it in their reading. You might also want them to add the page number of the text on which that particular meaning is found.

10. Continue to search five to ten words weekly. It will require very little time once the students and you have established a system, and it will become a process that they will enjoy and profit from using.

Figure 4–B

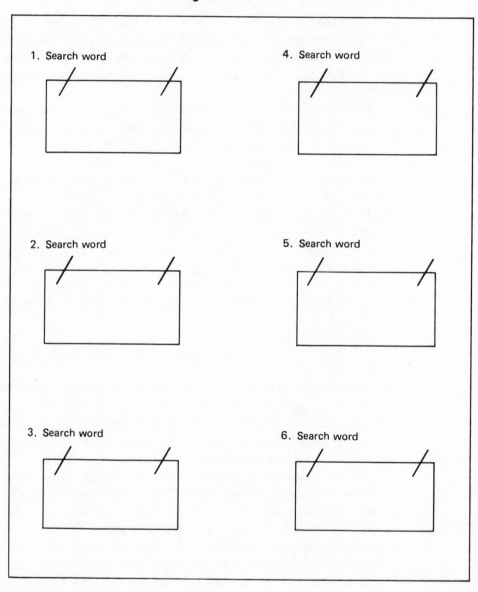

1. Search word

2. Search word

3. Search word

4. Search word

5. Search word

6. Search word

*4.2B EXPANDING VOCABULARY

Level   Middle grades and above.

Objective   To increase student vocabulary.

Description   1. If you have the typical class size of thirty, divide the class into six teams of five students. Make certain that weak and strong readers are in each group. If your class size is larger or smaller you can adjust your teams accordingly.

2. If you have the typical six-week grading period, each team will have an opportunity to present words once during each grading period. If your time frame is different, you can adjust the assignment time accordingly.

3. Arrange your schedule to allow for fifteen minutes of vocabulary work on Mondays and ten minutes on Fridays.

4. On Monday, use the fifteen-minute period for the group to make its new word presentation.

5. On Friday, use the ten-minute period for a short quiz on the use of the new words presented on Monday.

6. Ask each team to introduce five new words. They are to find the words in sources other than their textbook, but the words must be *a.* related to the subject (for instance, "sociogram" in sociology) or *b.* useful in discussing the ideas of the subject (for example, "probability" in mathematics).

7. Allow the teams to make their word presentations in any way they like, but ask that each team type a three-by-five note card that lists the word, its definitions, and examples of its use in sentences.

8. Keep the note cards in a card file in the room where all students have access to it.

9. On Friday, dictate the sentences the students prepared using the words. Leave out the new words and have the class put the correct word in each sentence.

10. Grade the work and record the scores.

11. As the students come across the "new" words in their textbooks, have the sentences they find and the page numbers from the text added to the cards. Each team would be responsible for adding to its own word cards.

12. Continue the use of the system throughout the school year.

*4.2C VOCABULARY GROWTH; INTEREST IN WORDS

Level   Middle grades and above.

Objective   To increase interest in vocabulary.

Description   There has been a great deal of discussion lately of a popular book called *The Book of Lists*. Lists of all sorts are simply presented. They range from the serious and important to funny and trivial ones. You can capitalize on the student interest in the book by having the students follow the same format used there to produce their own word book of lists. You may or may not have the words subject-area-specific.

1. Briefly describe *The Book of Lists* by David Wallenchinsky, Irving Wallace, and Amy Wallace in case some of the students do not know about it.
2. Suggest that the students write their own *Book of Word Lists* for their subject area or for words in general as you decide.
3. Give them examples of the kinds of word lists that could be developed. You could use these obvious ones as examples. Select from the examples, of course, the ones most suited to your subject area if you want the book to be subject-specific.

   a. synonyms
   b. antonyms
   c. homonyms
   d. rhyming words
   e. words that describe quiet things
   f. words that describe ugly things
   g. words that describe pretty things
   h. words that describe exciting things
   i. "hip" words
   j. funny words
   k. words to describe men
   l. words to describe women
   m. strong words
   n. weak words
   o. words that are hard to say
   p. words that are hard to spell
   q. words I didn't know before this class
   r. words I didn't know before tenth grade

   The possibilities are endless, and the best ideas will come from the students themselves.
4. Determine the length of time the students will be given for the project. Probably two weeks will be sufficient for a "Volume I" of the book. If the interest warrants, you could consider putting out other volumes later.
5. Students may not want to work in teams on this project. As a rule of thumb indicate that no team should be larger than two people and there should be two lists for each person in the class.
6. You should plan to make duplicate copies of the lists and bind them to look like books. Credit each student with his or her production. Present at least one copy of the book to the library for the class to share with their friends and classmates.
7. While the majority of the work will be produced outside of class, you should allow time for class sharing of the lists, challenges about meanings, and discussions of the words. For many students, this will be the first opportunity they will have encountered to have fun with words.

*4.2D WORD MEANINGS; WORD GAME

Level   Middle grades and above.

Objective   To increase student vocabulary and interest in it.

Description   This activity is a variation of the spelling bee only it utilizes the newspaper and works with the meaning of the word rather than the spelling of it.

1. Determine which newspaper or newspapers are readily available to all or most of the students.
2. Direct the attention of the class to the section of the newspaper that is most related to your subject area (that is, food page for home economics, business page for mathematics, editorial page for government, and so on).
3. Reserve the last thirty minutes of a class period each week for the activity. Friday is usually best, particularly if you have an afternoon class. Friday afternoon is a time when enthusiasm for school ordinarily lags, and it is nice to have a high-interest activity underway.
4. On Thursday have the students bring the newspaper for every day of the previous week (this would be the Wednesday newspaper through Wednesday). They would not bring the entire paper. They would bring only the sections you designated as related to the field of study and particular articles you may have identified during the week as related to their study.
5. Each student should be directed to circle every word that is new to him or her, interesting, or important to the subject area.
6. You then take the circled articles and either make a list of the words or work directly from the clippings themselves. You can expect a great deal of duplication in the words circled, so the task is not a difficult one. If you have a student assistant or some clerical help, you could utilize their services to have the list made for you.
7. On Friday you simply arrange the class into two teams. Since you must find some unobtrusive way to balance the groups with weak and strong readers, it will be better *not* to have students select the teams.
8. Use the words the students have located and ask for *a*. the definition, and *b*. its use in a sentence. Allow the teams to challenge each other on the basis of either answer.
9. As the students advance into the subject and become more informed about its language and concepts, ask that the sentence be made about something they have studied or are studying.
10. Keep a master list of all the words for yourself and ask the

students to keep one. Keep the list posted in the classroom in a place where all students have access to it.

11. Consider having championship rounds and even challenging other classes.

*4.2E VOCABULARY DEVELOPMENT; INTEREST

Level   Middle grades and above.

Objective   To increase student vocabulary.

Description Sentence games, crossword puzzles, and other word games are very popular with students. The problem of only relying on these commercially produced materials is that ordinarily they are not directly related to the work the students are doing. The words in the games or puzzles only indirectly reinforce or expand what the students are learning in the particular content area. Word games and puzzles directly related to the area will add to the associations the students are making with content words and concepts while providing the same appeal as the commercial games.

1. Determine whether you want to develop a puzzle or a game. Puzzles are easier to construct.
2. Until you have made several of either form, use an existing game or puzzle (the newspaper is always an excellent source) as a model.
3. Substitute words and definitions from the content being studied for words and definitions in the model you have selected.
4. You will have to make adjustments in spaces to fit words from your content area. When this creates a problem with the model you have chosen, simply black out the extra spaces which are causing you difficulty. Your first few puzzles and games will probably have a great many black spaces. This is not a problem. You will be better able to fit words as you have practice.
5. Do *not* use the puzzles or games for grading purposes because they are almost impossible to score in a completely fair way. For example, the student may insert the wrong word, but may have enough letters of that word correct to make the adjoining space correct except for tense or number. Is the second word then correct? There are endless questions raised, none of which is easily answered.
6. Work toward having the students develop their own puzzles so that they begin to search their reading for definition statements and synonyms and have additional practice putting the words and the concepts of the subject into their own existing vocabulary terms.

Crossword puzzles

For regular crossword puzzles you can use graph paper to simplify construction. Take a sheet and write the words you wish to teach. Limit the number of crossovers if you want to make the construction easier. Then transfer your puzzle to a ditto sheet or photocopy machine for duplication. (See Figure 4–C.)

Figure 4–C

					1.B									
				1.L	U	N	C	H						
					F									
					2.F	R	E	S	H		2.S			
					E						I			
					3.T	A	3.B	L	E	C	L	O	T	H
							R				V			
							E				E			
							A				R			
				4.N	A	P	K	I	N	S				
							F							
					5.P	L	A	C	E	4.M	A	5.T		
							S				I		E	
							T				L		A	
											K			

4.3 BUILDING SUBJECT-SPECIFIC VOCABULARY

If they are to be successful in a content area, the students must learn the words that are specific to that subject. They must also learn the particular ways in which those words are used in that field, and the unique ways words already familiar are employed in that content area.

One of the recurrent complaints of the middle school/secondary school teacher is that the students did not learn to read in elementary school. Nobody disagrees that a great many of the reading skills and a large vocabulary should be taught in the elementary grades. However, in the area of subject-specific vocabulary, the task must be that of the middle school/ secondary teacher. For example, it is unreasonable to expect the elementary teacher to teach the terms specific to a biology class. In the first place, he is not trained specifically in biology. In the second place, the students would have no real reason to learn them if they were not going to be applied immediately.

There is a basic subject-specific language for almost every content area. Some of it is new terminology, and some of it is new uses for words already familiar. Everything that has already been said about associating meaning with the terms to be learned and providing a real need for the student to use the words applies to teaching subject-specific vocabulary.

Any inclination to have the students "just memorize" all the necessary terms in isolation so that the teacher can get on with the instruction should be firmly resisted. Even if some students were able to remember the words, the terms taught in isolation would be harder to remember because there would be no context or real understanding that would support or reinforce the meaning and assist the students in finding a place for it in their own mental scheme of things. For some, perhaps for most students, the task would be impossible without the other supports.

As an example of the futility of the "memorize, since you must know it eventually" approach, we will describe the experience of one of the authors in an experimental college French class. One class section of first-year French students, all of whom had previously taken a course in another foreign language, were not allowed the use of a text. Instead, they were given words, phrases, and sentences to memorize, and all instruction for doing so was given in French. Until mid-term all the students went around saying longer and longer sentences in French with little or no notion of what they meant. At mid-term student progress was so unsatisfactory that texts were introduced. The texts were written entirely in French, and students were then instructed to commit to memory specific parts. At the end of the term, student progress was still so poor, the project was abandoned.

Most of the students in the experimental group were academically strong and highly motivated to be successful with the project, so there was at least a superficial need to learn the words. There was just not enough association or context or frame of reference to make any real learning payoff possible.

Experiments like the one in French exaggerate what would happen in memorizing vocabulary in the typical classroom. Certainly, in learning the vocabulary of a subject there will have to be drill, but the drill should be done after the students have some context or association for the word being learned. It can also be accomplished in a way which we referred to earlier as making the student "word conscious" or "word conscientious."

*4.3A CONFUSING WORDS

Level   Middle grades and above. It would be particularly useful in science, vocational areas, and social studies.

Objective   To provide students practice in distinguishing differences in the meanings of difficult words as they develop subject-specific vocabulary.

Description   This is a variation of a popular syndicated puzzle called the *Little Fooler*, which runs in newspapers periodically. In this activity the player is given a definition or description and two possible word choices. The objective is to select the one which is the more exact term for the meaning provided. It is a surprisingly difficult and fascinating task and requires a thorough understanding of the words in order for the students to do the work.

1. Begin with the construction of a crossword puzzle using the terms you are teaching in the subject area. (See 4.2E for detailed description of the construction process.)
2. Until you have had some practice with this activity, you may need to simplify the construction. Do so by telling the students that there will always be enough blank spaces for each word, but there may also be *too* many spaces. This way you do not have to spend a great deal of time finding forms of words that will have exactly the same number of letters.
3. Make the first puzzles relatively simple so that the students have an opportunity to practice with the technique in a situation that promises them some likelihood of success.
4. This is a sample from English grammar of how your puzzle space and words might look:

Words Across

1. Word meaning "belong to them":
   a. their
   b. there
2. Word which joins a phrase to the rest of the sentence:
   a. as
   b. like
3. Correct word for the following sentence:
   Everybody brought _____ lunch to the picnic.
   a. their
   b. his

Blank

Completed

○	1. T	H	E	I	R	○	○
2. A	S				○	○	○
○	○	3. T	H	E	I	R	○
○	○	○	○	○	○	○	○

5. The following pairs of words will provide you with examples of words that are either close in meaning or whose meaning is frequently confused. There are similar confusing and difficult words related to almost every topic we teach. These kinds of terms are ideal for this particular activity.

inferred	prescribe
implied	proscribe
epic	unlettered
epoch	uneducated
detached	borne
disinterested	born
barbarous	climactic
savage	climatic
allude	godly
elude	godlike

6. As quickly as you can, you will want to begin having students develop their own puzzles and exchange them with each other. They will then have the opportunity to work with the words in two situations.

7. You should keep copies of all the puzzles developed so that eventually you will have enough to use more than one for each unit or set of concept-related terms to be learned.

*4.3B WORD AFFIXES: PREFIXES, SUFFIXES, ROOTS

Level   Middle grades and above.

Objective   To increase student awareness of the prefixes, suffixes, and roots that are particularly useful to learning the vocabulary used in a specific unit or subject area.

Description Since this is a time-honored secondary school vocabulary approach, one caution seems appropriate. This should *not* be the only instructional strategy used in teaching the vocabulary specific to your subject. It should be regarded as only one of many useful means for such instruction. It will be most effective if you work only with the prefixes, suffixes, and roots that are used frequently in your subject area rather than to attempt to teach a lengthy list.

1. The prefixes, suffixes, and roots you elect to teach will depend on your content area. First you must determine which ones are necessary or beneficial to student progress in your subject. If you do not have a good list available (a partial one is used here as an example), ask an English teacher for one. Lengthy lists can generally be found in the language arts texts and workbooks. You could also check other reference books that deal just with vocabulary instruction. *Techniques of Teaching Vocabulary* by Edgar Dale and Joseph O'Rourke, published by Field Education Publications, Palo Alto, California, 1971, is a good resource book of this kind.

2. Once you have determined the parts that will benefit your students, discuss with the class the ways in which we have built words or changed their meanings by adding or subtracting meaningful parts. Almost every native English-speaking student will be familiar with the prefix *un*. Begin with it to demonstrate your point.

3. Encourage the students to make up their own words or alter the meaning of the ones they know by changing a part of the word. Allow some nonsense words also if the students enjoy them.

4. Have the students experiment with changing the meaning of a paragraph or a crucial sentence in an assignment by altering the prefixes, suffixes, or roots of a few words.

5. Instruct the students in the kind of format you wish them to use to develop their own word list. One is suggested in Figure 4–D along with some of the more commonly used prefixes, suffixes, and roots.

6. Since most secondary students have a notebook for each class, you will probably want to have the students use their notebooks for recording their word lists. This conveniently keeps the word lists with the students' class notes. The lists should be developing ones that the students will continue to build throughout their study of the subject. Space should be allotted with that in mind. Starting at the back of their notebooks and building forward will solve the mechanical problem of spacing.

7. Before assigning reading that introduces a major new root, prefix, or suffix critical to the vocabulary of your area, you should discuss it with the class and have them add it to their lists.

8. After any reading assignment, you should also ask the students to report any words they came across that they added to their lists.

9. Continue the discussion and recording throughout the year.

Figure 4–D

(NAME OF SUBJECT) WORD LIST			
Root, *Prefix,* *Suffix*	*Meaning*	*General* *Word*	*Subject-* *Specific* *Word*
ab	away from	absent	abcess (science)
ad	to, forward	addition	add (math)
ante	before	antecedent	antebellum (history
anti	against, opposite	antidepressant	antibacterial (science)
aqua	water	aquatic	aquamarine (art)
astro, aster	star	astronaut	astronomy (science)
auto	self	automobile	automatic (vocational)
bi	two	bicycle	bicep (physical education)
bio	life	biology	biochemical (science)
chlor	green	chlorophyl	chloroplast (science)
frater	brother	fraternity	fraternize (sociology)
hexa	six	hexagon	hexameter (literature)
in	not	incomplete	invalid (math)
inter	between	interscholastic	intercept (math)
intra	within	intrastate	intramural (physical education)
itis	inflammation	tonsillitis	arthritis (health)
logy	study of, science of	sociology	cardiology (science)
magni	great, large	magnificent	magnify (science)
meta	change, beyond	metaphysical	metatarsal (physical education)
micro	small	microscope	microwave (home economics)
multi	many	multiunit	multilith (business)
photo	light	photography	photosynthesis (science)
poly	many	polygram	polyester (home economics)
post	after	postponed	post (vocational)
psycho	mind	psychology	psycholinguistic (literature)
thermo	heat	thermometer	thermocouple (vocational)
tri	three	triangle	trimeter (literature)
trans	across	transport	translation (foreign language)
un	not	unattractive	uncentered (business)

10. For further emphasis, you could also make a large word list chart for display in the classroom and rotate among students the responsibility for keeping it up-to-date as new words and parts are encountered in the reading.

*4.3C ASSOCIATING WORDS AND ILLUSTRATIONS

Level   Middle grades and above.

Objective   To enlarge the students' subject-specific vocabulary through association.

Description   In many content areas when we use a term new to the students, we are asking them to associate meaning with something they know only from our description of it. It is certainly well enough that they learn terms such as "murder" in that way. However, for many terms, particularly those which are not highly abstract, their learning can be assisted by simply providing them with a picture of the new term. Elementary teachers have long used this technique for assisting instruction. Secondary teachers can also profit from it. Any reluctance the teacher might have about using the technique should be dispelled if he or she considers how many adults work from some form of graphic representation all the time. Builders use models, physicians use charts, architects use blueprints, designers use patterns and sketches, and so on. Even modern direction signs include a picture to clarify the meaning of the printed message. Vocational, home economics, business, and science classes can make excellent use of the technique of supplying a picture along with a new word, since in those areas the functions and names of several pieces of unfamiliar equipment must always be learned.

The teacher would not follow any special step-by-step plan in this activity, but would simply seek to add a graphic illustration of the meaning each time he or she introduced a new word. The teacher could do so with teacher-made, student-made, or commercial pictures, charts, or cards. It would be important to have the printed word on the visual aid. If it is not there in commercial pictures or those cut from magazines or other printed material, you could simply print the word in large letters on a piece of mystik tape and attach it to the aid.

When you make your own picture cards or charts, check illustrated dictionaries and subject manuals for ideas for illustrations. They are usually simple and well-done and will give you good ideas for illustrations of your own.

*4.3D DEFINING WORDS

Level   Middle grades and above.

Objective   To provide students practice with subject-specific vocabulary.

Description   This activity is a reverse crossword puzzle. You provide the students with a puzzle which has words filled in in each of the spaces. The students are then asked to write the descriptor for the word. Another variation is to provide two sentences from the content reading in which the given word has been used. In one sentence the word should be used incorrectly. The students must then select which one of the sentences has used the word correctly.

The teacher should not always develop these puzzles. Students should also be given opportunities to work with such development. The student-designed puzzle is ideally suited to serve individual differences within the reading levels in the classroom. Even the weakest readers can be successful with it because they can work out their own word references at a level they can comprehend. Weaker readers are also well-served by the teacher-made puzzles because the word given provides a clue from which the students can start their search in their textbook or other sources.

Only one caution is necessary. It is usually better to disallow the use of dictionaries when you are working with subject-specific words. Insist that the students rely only on the printed materials related to the subject so that they are practicing with the glossaries and indexes used in the particular subject area. If increasing the students' general dictionary skills is part of your objective with this activity, then such use of dictionaries would, of course, be in order.

*4.3E CONTEXT CLUES; WORD MEANING

Level   Middle grades and above.

Objective   To provide students with an explanation of the contextual means of determining word meaning.

Description   For most students it will come as a surprise to find out how many means for determining meaning exist in the print surrounding a word. The students who are working from contextual hints are operating largely on an intuitive basis rather than in any awareness of the skill being employed. The other students are realizing no contextual vocabulary support at all. Figure 4–E provides examples of various types of contextual clues.

1. On the chalkboard write a sentence which contains a nonsense word or a blank space. (You may want to use one of the example sentences in Figure 4–E and insert the blank or nonsense word for the one underlined.)
2. Have the class decide what the nonsense word probably means or what should be placed in the blank space.
3. When they have agreed on the meaning, have them discuss how they arrived at that meaning.
4. List the clues they used on the chalkboard.
5. Go through the list of sentences (your own or the examples given) until all the kinds of clues given have been listed. The students may also think of others to add to the list. Encourage them to do so.

Figure 4–E

KINDS OF CONTEXTUAL CLUES

BACKGROUND OR EXPERIENCE:	The meaning of the unknown word can be determined from the students' own experiences or awareness of the topic.
	Example: Santa's sleigh is always drawn by eight *reindeer.*
COMPARISON OR CONTRAST:	The meaning of the unknown word is known to be opposite of the known word.
	Example: Sally was a dull companion, but Martha was always a *vivacious* one.
DEFINITION OR DIRECT EXPLANATION:	The meaning of the unknown word is defined or provided in the print before or after the word.
	Example: She brought a *piñata,* which is a decorated papier-mâché object filled with toys and candy.
EXAMPLE:	The meaning of the unknown word is clarified through the use of an example.
	Example: Harry was a *ne'er-do-well.* In the past he had failed in three different schools, and now he would not even hold a job.
FAMILIAR EXPRESSION:	The meaning of the unknown word is recognized as a part of a commonly known pattern of words.
	Example: The energetic, healthy old man was as fit as a *fiddle.*
MOOD, TONE, OR SETTING:	The meaning of the unknown word reflects the situation described or can be inferred from it.
	Example: As the firefighters fought the fierce flames, the family watched their blazing home in *dismay.*
SUMMARY:	The meaning of the unknown word is summarized in the words that precede or follow it.
	Example: Billy was an *energetic* child. He seemed to be constantly running, jumping, skipping, and romping around.
SYNONYM:	The meaning of the unknown word is restated in a synonym.
	Example: The problem was a never-ending, *perpetual* one.

6. Ask the students to take their textbooks and find two or three examples of clues that they find in the context.
7. Share and discuss these with the class.
8. Do *not* have the students memorize the list, but from time to time have them cite examples of clues they could or did use to identify an unknown word. Point out sentences that you find that had helpful clues.

4.4 WORKING WITH WORD IDENTIFICATION

There are some secondary students who have not yet mastered some of the basic sound skills which help to unlock words. If they are going to become better content readers they will be assisted by attention to these skills.

The content area teacher is neither an elementary teacher nor a reading specialist, although he or she must be a teacher of reading in order to be successful in his content instruction. He has not been trained to work with time-consuming word identification skills. He has also been charged with providing instruction related to a large body of content material. As a result of all these givens, he will not be able to provide extensive instruction in sound/word identification skills. He should, however, be aware of some of the generalizations in this area so that when either time or opportunity presents itself, he has some information with which to aid students.

Many secondary students will be aided by refresher information related to the sounds and emphases in words. Once able to say or hear the unfamiliar word correctly, the students recognize the word itself or are better able to relate the combination of sounds to a meaning associated with them. Such information can be provided to the students throughout the year. Even if the teacher did have the time to teach them, sound identification skills taught in isolation would not be a highly productive enterprise.

GENERALIZATIONS
The following are generalizations. They do not apply in all cases.

Consonants
1. Most consonants represent just one sound.
2. These consonants do not have their own unique speech sound:

> c (cat, city)
> q (quick)
> k (kick and cat)

3. A consonant digraph is two consonant letters that represent one speech sound. The most commonly used ones are:

ch (chug, chemist, chic)
ph (physician)
th (that, method)

4. A consonant blend is two or three consonant sounds blended together. Some examples are:

bl (blend)
br (bread)
fl (flow)
sm (small)
str (stripe)
thr (three)

Vowels
1. Each vowel letter in English stands for more than one sound.
2. A vowel that is the last letter in a syllable usually has the long sound.
3. A vowel that is not the last letter in a syllable usually has a short sound.
4. The vowel before a final *e* is usually long, and the *e* is silent.

Syllabication
1. Each syllable contains a vowel sound.
2. When the first vowel is followed by a double consonant (except for blends and digraphs) the first syllable ends with the first consonant.
3. When the first vowel is followed by a single consonant, the consonant usually is a part of the second syllable.
4. Prefixes and suffixes are separate syllables.
5. When a word ends in *le* preceded by a consonant, the consonant is a part of the *le* syllable.
6. When a word ends in *ed* preceded by *d* or *t*, the *ed* begins a separate syllable.

5 SHARPENING RECALL

It would be wrong to suggest that the secondary school reader will want to recall all the print that he or she processes as he or she reads. Some of the reading, for example, is done simply for escape. However, students do need to remember some parts of assigned reading. Recalling all of it in detail would be impossible, so the students must learn to employ searching, selecting, and relating techniques that will enable them to hold as much of the material in their memories as is required. The Teacher can assist this retention process by instructing them in how to locate and identify the critical points and what categorization, association, and organization are most useful in retaining what must be recalled.

All of us have had the experience of desperately trying to remember something that we wanted or needed to know. Sometimes it comes as a surprise that we cannot recall, and we wonder "How could I have forgotten *that?*" Other times we have a different response and find ourselves saying "I *knew* I'd forget that!" From the differences in our responses, it is clear that we are consciously aware that some things we are reading we will recall at a better rate than others. Let us briefly explore some of the reasons for the differences.

In remembering, as with other aspects of learning, there needs to be operating both *1.* motivation to remember, as well as *2.* a technique to assist the process.

For most assigned reading selections the students have, at least, an extrinsic motivation to remember. The students must recall some portion of the material in order to pass the test, work the problems, answer the questions, write the report, and so on. If the students are also intrinsically motivated to remember the material, they will come to the task with a decided advantage over the students without such concern for remembering. The teacher, then, must take into account the students' motivation to remember when he or she expects recall from them. This means that adequate motivation should always be part of the teacher's instructional strategy. Chapter 2 deals extensively with this topic.

In addition to being motivated or wanting to remember, the students need some instruction in basic memory assistance techniques. They must learn how to break great amounts of material into meaningful, manageable pieces so that they can be sorted and stored in their memories in ways that make it possible for them to retrieve the material on demand.

5.1 LITERAL COMPREHENSION

The students' literal comprehension of their reading material is necessary for any retention at all to be possible. If the students received no information from the print they processed, there simply is no information to be retrieved. The teacher's first concern here must be a determination of whether or not the students are able to read at a literal level the material which has been provided. The teacher's second most important concern must be assisting those students who cannot read at this level. Finally, the teacher must keep the amount of literal comprehension work in proper proportion to the rest of the reading instruction. When instructors never "get beyond" the literal level of reading comprehension, another set of problems is created.

Literal comprehension centers in obtaining facts and details from the print. It is the primary way of getting information from reading material. Particularly in middle and junior high school we are likely to find students who are still having some difficulty in literal comprehension. They are unable to gain enough information from the print to be successful in the recall task required for the class work. For these students it is necessary to provide some reading activities and instruction in the literal comprehension skills. Once the students are competent in the literal skills, all the memory techniques are applicable to what they are comprehending. The literal skills to which the teacher should be alert for difficulties are:

1. following directions;
2. recognizing and recalling dates, places, names, facts, and so on;
3. recognizing and recalling the main idea (Section 6.2);
4. recognizing and recalling the pattern or order of the ideas (Section 6.3A).

While the literal skills do not require some of the more complex thinking operations that are demanded in analytic and evaluative skills, they should not be thought of as always being *easy* . As more information and more detail are added, even literal recognition and recall of it become quite difficult. Since the level of difficulty here can be varied by such things as the length of the material and the amount of detail, the teacher can easily adjust the tasks so that every student is sufficiently challenged.

There is also another dimension to the difficulty of literal skills. When the students are asked to *recognize* a piece of explicitly stated information, they are being presented with an easier task than when they are asked to *recall* that same piece of information.

The easiest informal assessment of the students' skill level in this area is to assign the students some material to be read in class and then ask literal questions based on it. You would first want them to use the reading material to help them to complete the exercise so that you could be certain you were evaluating their ability to obtain literal information from the print and not just their ability to recall. You could then add some literal questions to be answered without the material in order to determine the level at which they recall. You could assess their ability to follow directions by giving quite specific ones for the arrangement of their papers. For example, direct them to write their names in the lower left-hand corner of the paper, the date in the upper right-hand corner, and so on.

Once you have established the need level for the class, you can select the number and kinds of activities appropriate. If you find students who have severe problems in literal comprehension, you may want to supply them with some of the commercial materials that are available for addressing this problem. They are designed as drill books and provide scores of selections from which the students are asked to supply answers to literal level questions. Ask your school reading specialist for the names and addresses of the publishers.

Finally, be alert as an instructor to the need to urge the students beyond the literal level of comprehension once they are able to advance. A recurrent criticism of secondary school instruction and testing is that the attention to and demand for recall of literal information is far too often the primary thrust. Research studies bear out the validity of such criticism. The literal level is the lowest level of thinking operations, and our goal must always be to lead the students beyond this point when it is possible to do so.

5.1A FOLLOWING ORAL DIRECTIONS; ATTENTION TO DETAILS

Level   Middle grades and above.

Objective   To provide students practice in attending to and following directions.

Description   One of the problems which students encounter when they attempt to read directions is that they do not pay close attention to the task. One reason they attend so poorly to reading directions silently is that someone almost always reads the directions aloud to them as well. If the students are simply listening to directions, they attend even less well because most teachers repeat everything a number of times. The first problem related to directions, then, is one of attention to the detail being presented. This point can be made dramatic to the students by the listening activity which follows. In it you will have the students produce a picture from your oral directions which you will give them only *once*. (The picture you will be asking them to produce will be a treble clef sign.)

1. Explain the importance of attending to detail when reading or following directions.
2. Invite students to cite instances when problems have resulted from failure to do so. They will have many stories to tell of fudge that was ruined, dates that were confused, and so on. When the point of the necessity for attending to detail has been made, move along or the activity will get lost in their recitations.
3. Ask the students to take out a pencil and sheet of paper.
4. Give them the following directions:

   a. Draw a single vertical line that slants slightly to the left side of your paper
   b. At the bottom of the line attach a large comma.
   c. To the right side of the top of the slightly slanted vertical line attach another line that curves outward from the line enough to make an oval when it is brought back across the original line at the midpoint of that original line.
   d. At the point where the two lines now intersect begin another line to the left of the slightly slanted vertical line and draw this new line in the shape of the numeral six, *except* that the small circle of the six should not be tightly closed.
   e. The bottom of the line forming the six should rest at the top of the comma which was previously drawn.

5. Have several students put their versions of the figure on the board.
6. Since you may certainly anticipate several different figures, go through each with the words of the directions and discuss what the causes of the differences were.
7. Follow that discussion with a reemphasis of the necessity of careful attention to the detail in directions.
8. You can also develop content-specific directions: for example, in mathematics, a geometric figure; in art, a scene; in physical education, a tennis racquet; in science, a piece of lab equipment.

*5.1B FOLLOWING WRITTEN DIRECTIONS

Level   Middle grades and above.

Objective   To provide students with practice in attending to and following directions.

Description   1. Duplicate a set of directions for a newspaper construction project and supply them to the students. Craft books, simple project books such as Robert Lopshire's *How to Make Flibbers* (Random House), and activity handbooks will supply you with a wide variety of such projects. Select one that you feel will appeal to your particular class. An example of such a direction-following project is found in Figure 5–A on p. 93.

2. Provide each student with two sheets of newspaper. Experience suggests that supplying the papers yourself is better than asking students to do so because they will forget or bring so many that you will have confusion and clutter even before you get the project underway. Since the project in the example requires some space for construction, there will be activity enough.

3. Grading of this project is not necessary since the students have direct feedback about their success or failure from simply viewing their products.

*5.1C RECALLING DIRECTIONS; SEQUENCE

Level   Middle grades and above.

Objective   To provide an individualized experience in attending to and following directions.

Description   By the time students are in middle or junior high school, they have developed some specialized interests. For example, the boys generally like cars, the girls often like jewelry, and so on. If the students are having a difficult time in literal comprehension, their interests can be tapped to work with their problem. (See Chapter 2.) Students who have no interest in improving their reading to "learn" more may be strongly motivated to improve their skills in order to accomplish something associated with their particular interests. Instead of providing these students with the usual free reading period or extra reading time or other time slots in which you use books to attempt to encourage work on reading skills, use this time for a hands-on activity related to the students' own concerns. You must, of course, be certain that the activity you select is rich in reading dimensions. One group of tenth-grade students with whom one of the authors worked were virtually nonreaders. They spent several highly productive and happy sessions constructing model cars from very complex written directions, which they were able to comprehend with some dictionary help, some ditto word sheets, and the teacher's guidance. At the end of the project they were enthusiastic about working more, and some reported they had been *reading* the boxes of models at the nearby discount stores to find other such projects to do. The instructor took pictures of the students with their completed projects, the dictionaries, and the other books they had used. The school librarian then made a display

Figure 5–A

MAKE A HAT!

1. Lay out two full sheets of newspaper on your desk, if it is large enough; if not, on the floor or a table.
2. Fold the top left corner down to the center of the sheets.
3. Now fold the top right corner down to the center of the sheets.
4. Fold up the edge of the top sheet of paper to the bottom of the triangle that was formed by your first two folds.
5. Fold the edge a second time so that it looks like a hat band.
6. Turn the papers over.
7. Fold the right edge one-half inch past the centerline. Fold the left side in the same way to the right edge.
8. Fold the lower right and left corners to the bottom of the hat band.
9. Fold the lower flap above the hat band.
10. Fold the top of the flap down and tuck it into the hat band.
11. Fold the peak of the hat down to the bottom of the hat band and tuck it under the band.
12. Open up the hat.
13. Flatten out the top.
14. Tuck the side peak into the band.

Good for you!

of the photographs, models, and the books, and the students enjoyed some recognition as they were attacking a very serious reading problem. Besides purchasing commercial activity kits, you could write your own directions for students to follow in order to develop projects related to your course work and of interest to them. Some ideas you might consider are:

English:	stage sets
	story settings
Mathematics:	geometric figures
	measuring devices
Social Studies:	replicas of housing
	relief maps
History:	replicas of historic sites
	three dimensional time lines
Science:	inventions or gadgets
	three dimensional representations of concepts, and so on

One caution is in order when using a hands-on activity approach to working with literal comprehension skills like following directions. *Do not confuse the ends* (improved willingness and ability to read) *with the means* (the product itself). Sometimes teachers and students become so caught up in the construction process that they lose sight of the purpose for which it was undertaken, and many of the opportunities to work with reading are lost or not developed as fully as they could have been.

*5.1D LOCATING SPECIFIC DETAILS

Level   Middle grades and above.

Objective   To provide students practice in locating explicitly stated information.

Description   There is something almost instantly appealing about a brightly colored catalogue and, luckily, if you ask well in advance of your need, most large mail-order houses will provide a class set for you at no cost. Ordinarily, even the most reluctant readers will happily accept a catalogue and will usually begin to turn through its pages with interest. The activities described here capitalize on this interest. The task for the students will be to search out the information from the print and select what they need to report to you to fulfill your assignment. Since the catalogue offers such a variety of topics, you can select those that are the most appealing and appropriate to your class.

1. Prepare a wardrobe list for a particular season. Ask the students to shop for it from the catalogue and report their purchases, page number, and purchase number. See Figures 5–B and 5–C.

Figure 5–B

SHOPPING SPREE FOR SPRING! (FOR GIRLS)

Directions: Please select all the following items for a stylish spring wardrobe. Price is no object! List the page number and item number for each purchase.

	Catalogue Page	Catalogue Number
1. a red full-length washable coat	_____	_____
2. a white purse that has a coin compartment	_____	_____
3. a pair of white shoes that are on sale	_____	_____
4. a red-and-white washable scarf	_____	_____
5. a pair of pre-washed jeans	_____	_____
6. a pair of jeans with a matching jacket	_____	_____
7. a cotton shirt that has polyester cuffs and collar	_____	_____
8. a sweatshirt that is reversible	_____	_____
9. a gold-filled bracelet with a synthetic stone	_____	_____
10. a pair of green flameproof shorty pajamas	_____	_____
11. a pink raincoat with a zip-out lining	_____	_____

Figure 5–C

SHOPPING SPREE FOR WINTER! (FOR BOYS)

Directions: Please select all the following items for a stylish winter wardrobe. Price is
no object! List the page number and item number for each purchase.

	Catalogue Page	*Catalogue Number*
1. a gray wool sweater with a hood	_____	_____
2. black slacks with a sewn-in belt	_____	_____
3. a washable solid red necktie	_____	_____
4. a storm coat with a zip-out lining and six pockets	_____	_____
5. a plaid shirt that is 100 percent wool	_____	_____
6. a brown cardigan sweater that has extra buttons	_____	_____
7. a pair of pre-washed jeans that weighs less than two pounds	_____	_____
8. a brown leather wallet with picture compartments that is on sale	_____	_____
9. a pair of green flameproof pajamas	_____	_____

---

2. In class discussion report the purchases and verify by page and
item numbers.
3. You can adapt the purchase list to your own subject area. Some
suggested ways follow:

English: a list of books (by description, not title)
a list of costumes needed for a play or appropriate for a story or setting

Mathematics: a list of books (by description, not title)
a list of equipment for the mathematician
a list which required mathematics operations for
comparing prices

Science: a list of books (by description, not title)
a list of animals, their food, and supplies needed
for a laboratory
a list of seeds, special commercial soil, and food for
plant experiments
a list of science equipment
a list of science supplies
a list of laboratory clothing (that is, fireproof
jackets, gloves, and so on)

Business: a list of secretarial supplies
a list of appropriate secretarial clothing
a list of business machines
a list of duplicating supplies

Vocational Education:	a list of books (by description, not title)
	a list of automotive repair supplies
	a list of automotive equipment
	a list of electrical equipment
	a list of electrical supplies
	a list of carpentry equipment
	a list of carpentry supplies
Home Economics:	a list of books (by description, not title)
	a list of large kitchen equipment
	a list of small kitchen appliances
	a list of table, bath, or bed linens
	a list of sewing equipment
	a list of sewing supplies
	a list of home nursing supplies
Fine Arts:	a list of books (by description, not title)
	a list of painting supplies
	a list of musical equipment
	a list of craft equipment
	a list of craft supplies
Social Studies:	a list of books (by description, not title)
	a list of supplies, equipment, or clothing generally found or associated with a particular situation (that is, American Indian reservation, urban apartment, rural community, and so on)
	a list of status symbols associated with a particular socioeconomic status in the U.S. or elsewhere

4. You can also order specialty catalogues that are directly related to your particular teaching area. These will give the students even more search and select experience with the vocabulary, measurement, and equipment of the particular field.

5. After the students do well with this level of searching for detail, you will want to increase the complexity of their literal-level work. You can do so by adding any of the following dimensions:

   a. Give fewer items in an exercise and ask the students to report them to you in a recall situation. You would, of course, do this only when they were working with subject-specific materials that were important for them to remember for success in the content area.

   b. Ask for more specific detail in the students' search. For example, add the dimensions of size, weight, fabric, and so on to the present details.

   c. Put the class on a budget so that they must not only find the narrative detail, but they must also watch for the cost details as well.

*5.1E RECALLING FACTS; LOCATING SPECIFIC DETAILS

Level   Middle grades and above.

Objective   To provide students with practice in recalling facts and in locating explicitly stated information.

Description   One of the oldest instructional techniques used in the secondary school is the reading guide. It generally is a list of questions that direct the students' thinking to the information they need to retain from their reading. Sometimes these guides are teacher-made; sometimes they are simply questions found at the end of a chapter or section of the textbook. In textbooks ordinarily these questions focus largely on literal-level information (*who, what, when, where*) and for that reason many secondary teachers simply do not use them. If, however, your classes have difficulty with recalling facts, details, and so on, these can be a boon to you. You should read the questions carefully prior to assigning them to determine if they are clear and well-written and ask for detail that is significant. If so, they should be used to provide practice for students who need this kind of skill building.

   If you are dealing with material that does not have such questions prepared, you can produce such questions quickly by simply following the list of *who, what, when,* and *where* and asking as many questions as you feel are required in each of those categories.

5.2 CATEGORIZING

One of the means by which we strengthen the recall of those pieces of information we encounter in print is by coding them in such a way as to make them fit into the information that we already possess. An assistance or clue we rely on heavily in recall is categorization. It is a means of 1. relating what is new to what is already known by placing it with like pieces of information, and 2. reducing the whole of the material to a more manageable size for remembering.

In some ways retaining new information is a process not unlike adding another item to an already full closet. If we take the time to classify the new item and put it with other items similar to it, there is a far greater likelihood that we can find it when it is needed than if we simply "dump" it in and close the door.

   Almost everyone has had the personal experience of putting an item in a place it is not usually kept and not being able to locate it later. As we try to recall the location, we generally say, "I knew when I put it in the wrong place I'd forget!" What we mean is that in order to recall very often it is necessary to have an assistance of some sort in the process. In the case of the forgotten item, *place* was the assistance on which we had relied. When we failed to put the item in the predictable place, we had lost the memory clue that we usually received from such locational information.

   Categorizing can be simply defined as a *placement scheme*. It is a means of placing, classifying, or sorting ideas into a regular arrangement. The teacher can aid the students in the development and improvement of this placement system by identifying kinds of categories they can use for sorting their information, encouraging them to develop categories of their own, and providing them with some experience in doing so.

It is very important, once the students have a good understanding of a category system, that they work toward their own categories. It is into their own mental frameworks that the students must incorporate the new material they hope to remember. As long as they try to remember a "superimposed" category—plus the new information—they probably will not really be assisted a great deal; they may just have been given one more item to recall.

*5.2A CATEGORIES FOR REMEMBERING

Level   Middle grades and above.

Objective   To clarify to the students some of the ways in which they use categories.

Description   1. Define *category* and discuss the term.
                   2. Ask the students to provide some examples of categories they use frequently. Ask them to concentrate on categories that everyone generally uses in the same way. You can prod their suggestions with categories like the following:

> fat people
> friendly people
> tall girls
> short girls
> new cars
> old television programs

3. As they list, discuss the categories' characteristics.
4. Ask the students to suggest some categories that might have more individual meaning to them. Start the suggestions with ones like the following:

> things I will tell at home
> things I won't tell at home
> hard teachers
> easy teachers

5. As they suggest different categories, discuss the ways in which the categories might vary from person to person and why.
6. Ask the class to list and discuss some of the categories they use in thinking and remembering school material. Begin the suggestions with categories like the following:

> things Mr. Jones will ask on a test
> things Mr. Jones won't ask on a test

7. Have the students determine categories that would help them remember material in your content area. For example, in art,

periods of art; in physical education, contact and noncontact sports; in music, reeds, woodwinds, and so on.

8. Conclude the activity by discussing again why we use categories and the ways in which they are helpful to us in remembering.

*5.2B GENERAL CATEGORIES FOR MEMORIZATION

Level   Middle grades and above.

Objective   To identify some of the most generally used categories for remembering.

Description   1. Write on the chalkboard any of the following:

Where will you remember a green gorilla?
Where will you remember a duck-billed platypus?
Where will you remember three fat frogs?
   (or any other item you might elect)

2. Ask the students to list on their papers as many categories as they can think of into which to place the item you selected.
3. After they have finished their lists, have the students report their categories.
4. Begin a list on the chalkboard of some of the possible systems one might use for categorizing information. (This could also be a homework project.) Lead the students to an awareness and discussion of at least the following general systems into which they can fit the new information they find as they read.

   a. Interrogative Categories
      Who?
      What?
      When?
      Where?
   b. Language Function Categories
      Nouns (kinds)
      Verbs (kinds)
      Descriptive words (kinds)
   c. Information Sequence Categories
      Enumerative (one, two, three)
      Chronological (early, middle, late)
      Spatial (near, far)
      Narrative (classification is around ideas and facts)
         i. causes and effects
        ii. questions and answers
       iii. specifics and generalizations
        iv. examples
         v. conclusions
        vi. principles

> d. Physical Appearance Categories
>   Size
>   Shape
>   Weight
>   Height
>   Strength
>   Ornamentation.

*5.2C CATEGORIZING INFORMATION

Level   Middle grades and above.

Objective   To provide students opportunities to practice categorizing with feedback as to their category decisions.

Description
1. Ask the students to write down in any order the contents of their locker.
2. After they have written a list of every item in the locker, ask them to put the items in categories. Allow them some creativity in their classification system, such as listing a moldy sock under "growing things," but be certain that they know they must be able to defend their category as a classification system.
3. After they have classified their items individually, arrange the class into groups and have the students defend their classification schemes to each other.
4. Ask each group to select the three most defensible categorization schemes in their group to present to the class. Remind them that the criteria for a good category is that it will enable the thinker to remember and recall more easily the information when he or she requires it.
5. Particularly in classes of upper-grade or accelerated students, encourage creativity in their categories. This will make the activity more enjoyable to them and make them better able to remember the advantages of using categories. In this way a book for an experimental physics class could be classified under a category like "Things that will change the world" rather than under something quite literal like "textbooks."

*5.2D CATEGORIZING FOR TEST TAKING

Level   Middle grades and above.

Objective   To assist students in test preparation with the use of categorization of the material to be recalled.

Description
1. Instead of the usual review for a quiz or test, work with the students with categories of information that should be known or recalled for a high score.

2. In class discuss the best categories into which to divide the information for recall. Those categories will, of course, depend largely on the material that was covered and the subject area. The most general and inclusive system would be the simple "who, what, when, and where" system. Other systems might be "early, middle, late"; "persons, places, things"; and so on.
3. Begin the discussion by inviting students who generally use categories as a study technique to explain the ones they use.
4. If necessary, point out the problem or limitations that may exist with the reported systems.
5. Work toward class agreement as to the most beneficial categories for classifying the material to be covered in the examination. For example, for a test in physical education, the students could use the categories of "directions, scoring, and rules."
6. Have the students arrange their study notes or review sheets following the system accepted.
7. Throughout the year try to spend some time associating new material with categories that will be helpful to the students in recalling it, and whenever possible review their material in this way before examinations.

*5.2E CATEGORIZING WITH CONCRETE OBJECTS

Level   Middle grades and above.

Objective   To provide students who have difficulty with abstractions an opportunity to study categorizing in a concrete way.

Description 1. Provide the students with sets of items that have easily determined similarities. They should be small enough for easy classroom storage and for arrangement on the students' desk. They should also be inexpensive enough so that several different sets can be used for drill and practice before you ask the students to deal with the concept in more abstract terms. Plastic or paper lunch bags provide excellent storage containers. Old envelopes from the school office could also be used. Do not hesitate to involve the students in the collection of the items to be used, for many of them enjoy being of assistance. Some suggestions of items you might consider for the students to practice with follow:

> *Color as a category:*
> strips of different colors cut from construction paper
> commercial color chips from a paint store

alike items cut from a catalogue
buttons that are the same size but different colors

Size as a category:
strips of the same color paper that differ in size
buttons
stones
alike items cut from a catalogue that differ in size
small containers (pill bottles of varying sizes)
candies

Function as a category:
small plastic objects (for instance, a whistle (to blow), a drum (to
  hit))
items cut from catalogues
items in the room.

2. As soon as the students are able to sort the physical objects (or pictures) with some understanding, work with the concept using only the words for the object themselves. Simply type the words on a ditto and cut them apart for sorting by the students.
3. As the students are able to accomplish the categorizing of items in these concrete ways, begin to move toward more abstract categories with them. Whenever possible, introduce any new category with at least a pictorial representation of the concrete object before you begin your abstract discussion.

5.3 ASSOCIATION

Associating new ideas and information we wish to recall at a later time with ideas and information with which we are already familiar is a technique that is highly effective. By this means we expand what is known by relating something new to it. We also increase the likelihood of remembering that increased information base because the new is not something distinct but something securely anchored in what is already there.

As the students encounter new ideas and information in the print they are assigned, they *first* must be certain that they have understood it clearly. They *then* must find a means of safeguarding that understanding by storing it in their memories. We know from research that part of successful remembering is a function of *how many* new things we must recall. We also know that the *general understanding* of material is retained longer than the *specific points* or details. We know too that relating or associating that new understanding with what is already known provides a strong assistance in recalling it, for it is then part of an expanded knowledge base and not something separate.

MNEMONIC DEVICES

The *mnemonic device* is probably the best-known and one of the oldest association memory techniques. Mnemosyne was the Greek goddess of memory, and memory systems were employed as far back as ancient Greek civilization.

While "mnemonic" only means "memory," the mnemonic device is generally thought of as an association technique. The students associate what they want to remember with a rhyme, an expression, or some other device. For example, students learning to spell the word "surprise" are often told to remember that "there is *no* prize in *surprise*." Using the same method, beginning musicians generally remember the treble clef notes spell "F A C E" as an attempt to aid their recall of the names of each space interval.

To be effective, the mnemonic device needs to be simple and clear. If the association device is so complicated it is difficult to remember, then no purpose is served by using it.

A second effective association technique is to provide an image for oneself of what must be recalled. There are several approaches to the image association process. Sometimes one tries to develop an image of the letters of the word or words to be recalled. This is an approach often suggested in spelling instruction. The students are asked to "see" the printed word in their minds so that this picture can provide them the information they wish to remember.

USING IMAGES

Another approach to associating material to be remembered with an image is the exaggerated or absurd one. The student tries to picture a situation related to the material that is so outrageous or unlikely that the intensity of this association will evoke the recall required. Many of the popular "how to remember" books, clinics, and experts rely heavily on this technique. Using this aspect of imagery association you would, for example, encourage the class to visualize hundreds of pigs going swimming as a key for the recall of the "Bay of Pigs."

Another way of using imagery association to assist recall is to suggest an image directly related to the idea or information. This is the one that is most used in reading instruction. Everyone has seen the picture/word cards that are used with elementary school readers. Equally familiar are graphics to represent numerical information provided as pictures or images for secondary school students.

A caution is in order. With any technique used for enhancing recall, the teacher must be certain that what is to be recalled is really served by the technique. The following true story illustrates the point.

Conrada Roszkowski was a former student of one of the authors. When she began her career, she was a substitute teacher in elementary schools. She found her name was difficult for the students to remember, so she would aid them by drawing a picture beside her name. The picture was of a cow wearing skis. Above the cow she would print the name "Roz." Then she would explain that this was a cow named Roz who could ski. Then she would relate the picture to her name, *Rosz-kow-ski.* It seemed to be an effective association image that assisted the students' recall. She continued to use the technique until one day in a hallway she passed a youngster she had taught a few weeks before. He recognized her, and after a moment of thoughtful hesitation said with great confidence, "Oh! Good morning, Mrs. Dogsled!"

An image and an association were clearly in the student's mind; however, they were not sufficiently sharp or related to serve the recall purpose for which they had been designed. To prevent confusion and to ensure the correctness of the association, the teacher needs to seek some fairly immediate feedback from the students. The strength of the recall will also be improved if some early opportunities for practice in the recitation of the material are provided.

5.3A ACRONYMS FOR RECALLING INFORMATION

Level   Junior high and above.

Objective   To provide students information about and practice with using acronyms.

Description   1. Discuss the usefulness of association techniques for recall purposes.
2. Invite the students to share some of the association techniques they employ to help them remember particular things.
3. Define *acronym* (a pronounceable word made up of the beginning letters or groups of letters in words that make up a title or phrase). Point out that the acronym is used not only for abbreviation purposes but also as an association technique to enhance recall.
4. On the chalkboard begin a list of some of the most widely known and used acronyms. Invite the students to contribute ones with which they are familiar. You could begin with any of the following:

   MASH   Mobile Army Surgical Hospital
   CARE   Cooperative American Remittance (to) Everywhere
   SALT   Strategic Arms Limitations Talks
   NATO   North American Treaty Organization

5. After the students are clear about the meaning and uses of acronyms, ask them to take out the material they are presently studying in class. Have them work as a group to develop an acronym that could assist them in recalling this material.
6. If there seems to be a need for further assistance with the technique, spend some time prior to the next examination

determining if there may be some helpful acronyms that could be developed. For example, in health class you could work with ones like BAT (Basic Aid Training).

7. You can also divide the class into rotating committees that would be charged to look through all new material that the class is expected to recall to determine and report useful acronyms to their classmates.

*5.3B DEVELOPING ASSOCIATIONS; REMEMBERING IMPORTANT PEOPLE

Level

Middle grades and above. It is also a useful activity if persons are to be discussed in mathematics and science areas.

Objective

To demonstrate to students ways of associating unfamiliar personalities, their characteristics, and their importance with familiar ones to increase the likelihood of recalling the characteristics of the new ones and to provide them some practice in the technique.

Description

1. Most literary and historical figures have modern-day counterparts in at least some aspect of their personality and importance. The first task is to search out and select the characteristics and details about the figure that the students would be able to recall. Obviously, the height and weight of Copernicus or of Martin Luther are of little consequence. Their relationships to changes in scientific and theological thought are what are important.

2. After the consequential characteristics have been selected for the figure, search for a modern-day counterpart who is *well-known* to the students. It will not help the students for you to identify a figure who is unfamiliar to them; that simply provides another piece of information to be remembered.

3. When you have determined such a person, discuss the ways in which the two can be associated in their thinking.

4. Invite the students to make associations of their own. Once they understand the process, they will be brilliant at finding relationships and making meaningful associations. They are even sensitive to the status changes of the present-day famous, and you will find that the associations they develop will indicate that. In a school with which the authors are familiar, the teachers often used this association technique for teaching the plays of William Shakespeare. John F. Kennedy was a great hero among the students in this school, and, after his death, the widowed Jacqueline Kennedy was frequently cast in lofty roles. However, almost immediately after her remarriage to Aristotle Onassis the former Mrs. Kennedy began to appear in classes all

around the building cast as Hamlet's mother. The students had changed their perceptions of what her characteristics were.

5. Employ the association technique at any time the persons, their contributions, or circumstances make meaningful associations possible. Direct your questioning to prod the students to looking for such meaningful associations.

5.3C DEVELOPING ASSOCIATIONS FOR EVENTS AND SITUATIONS

Level   Junior high and above.

Objective   To demonstrate to students ways of associating unfamiliar situations and events with familiar ones to increase the likelihood of recalling the details of the new information and to provide them some practice in using this technique.

Description
1. Very often an event that students are asked to remember from their reading has a modern-day counterpart. For instance, some of the early European struggles for confederation have aspects that are similar to present-day struggles for independence or unity. The present-day events are well-known to most of the students. Situations about which students are asked to read and remember also have parallels in present times. A classic example of this is the romantic dilemma of Romeo and Juliet which was played out again in *West Side Story*. The first task is to search out and select the characteristics and details of the situation or event about which the students are reading that are most crucial for recalling.

2. After the consequential characteristics have been determined, search again for a modern-day situation or event that shares these primary characteristics. Be certain that the association selected is one with which the students are really familiar or the relationship will not be a helpful one for them.

3. When you have determined the event or situation, discuss the ways in which the two can be associated in the students' thinking. In addition to providing the students with an association clue for recall, this step may also help some students come to a better understanding of the event or situation.

4. Invite the students to make associations of their own. Once they understand the process, they are very good at finding relationships and making meaningful associations. Do not neglect local situations or events as possible associations—they may also find these useful. Encourage them to look about their classes and the school for such relationships.

5. Employ the association technique at any time the situation or event makes significant and meaningful associations possible.

Direct your questioning to encourage the students to look for such meaningful and helpful associations.

*5.3D DEVELOPING IMAGES TO IMPROVE RECALL

Level   Middle grades and above.

Objective   To provide students an explanation of and practice with images for improving their recall.

Description   1. Begin the discussion with the students by reminding them of the word with a picture clue card they used as beginning readers.
2. Ask for examples of how images are also used in adult reading to clarify or strengthen a point or stimulate a response. You may want to help them get started with some of the following:

    graphs in math books
    diagrams in language books
    overlay drawings in science books
    pictures in advertising, books, and periodicals
    sketches in cartoons and comic strips

3. Explain to the students that being able to "see" something they are reading often helps the readers organize their thinking better and consequently increase the likelihood of their correct recall of it.
4. Ask the students to share any of the experiences they have had with image creation related to their own reading and learning. There are virtually always students who will volunteer that they "diagram" difficult sentences in their head in order to help themselves understand the word relationships or clarify the meaning of the material. Others will follow with examples. Since some image creation is highly idiosyncratic, you will want to encourage this aspect to emerge from your discussion also.
5. Call students' attention to mental images suggested by the material they are currently using.
6. Ask the class to search through the material they are currently using for parts about which they could form helpful mental images that would assist in their recall of the material.
7. As opportunities will invariably arise for directing the students to obvious images or image production, continue to encourage their use of the technique throughout the course.

*5.3E USING MNEMONIC DEVICES TO IMPROVE RECALL

Level   Middle grades and above.

Objective   To provide students a description of and practice using mnemonic
                     devices.

Description   1. Explain to the students that while a mnemonic device is actually
                        any memory device, it is generally thought of as an *association
                        trick* or *gimmick* related to the information to be remembered.
                     2. Remind the students that this device, like all others related to
                        recall, requires a *searching out* of the new information for the
                        purpose of *selecting* the important aspects to store in the
                        memory and a determination of the best way or ways to
                        accomplish the goal.
                     3. Ask the students to share any mnemonic devices they may use.
                        You can initiate the discussion by reminding them of some of
                        the more familiar spelling ones like the following:

                        a. The princi*pal* is a *pal*.
                        b. There is a *lie* in be*lie*ve.
                        c. Use *i* before *e*
                           except after *c*
                           or when sounded like *a*
                           in neighbor or weigh.

                     4. After the class has shared any devices they have developed, you
                        can describe three of the popular mnemonic systems which
                        many of the "how to help your memory" experts suggest. All of
                        the systems operate from the same theoretical basis (described
                        in the beginning of this section), which is the importance of
                        helping the students relate what they hope to remember to
                        something that is already known. The systems are sometimes
                        called *hook systems* or *link systems*—a new piece of information
                        is "hooked" or "linked" to an existing piece of information.
                        Sometimes the systems are also called *peg systems* since an
                        existing information base is a "peg" on which new information is
                        being "hung" or supported. We prefer to label the systems
                        collectively as the *thumbtack theories*.
                           One obvious and major difficulty with such mnemonic
                        systems is the lack of a "meaningful" relationship between the
                        new material and the system clues themselves. In this regard
                        they are more organizational than associational devices, al-
                        though successful users and sellers of the systems would not
                        agree that this is completely true. A description of three ver-
                        sions follow:

a. *Alphabetical System*

The students are asked to use a specified number of alphabet letters—for example, the first five letters of the alphabet. They would then "link" or "hook" the new material they hoped to remember to one of those letters. As they read they would:

1. search out the material for what was of importance;
2. select what part or parts of the material should be recalled;
3. "link" or "hook" each piece of information to one of the alphabet letters they have designated;
4. practice so that the letter itself would elicit the recall of the material they had "hooked" on to it

Example of Alphabet System:

key letter		information attached
A	←——————→	battle was fought in 1942
B	←——————→	general was Smith
C	←——————→	losses were 800
D	←——————→	Red side won
E	←——————→	consequence was loss of strategic bridge

b. *Numerical System*

The students are asked to associate or "link" their new material to a number scheme. As they read they would:

1. search out the material for what was of importance;
2. select what part or parts of the material should be recalled;
3. "link" or "hook" each piece of information to one of the numbers they have designated;
4. practice so that the letter itself will elicit the recall of the material "linked" to it

Example of Numerical System:

key number		information attached
1	←——————→	battle was fought in 1942
2	←——————→	general was Smith
3	←——————→	losses were 800
4	←——————→	Red side won
5	←——————→	consequence was loss of strategic bridge

c. *Object System*

The students are asked to determine a specified number of objects. For example, a fish, a duck, a chair, a color, and a boat. As they read they would:

1. search out the material for what was of importance;
2. select what part or parts of the material should be recalled;
3. "link" or "hook" each piece of information to one of the objects designated;
4. practice so that the object itself will elicit the recall of the material "linked" to it

Example of Object System:

key object		information attached
fish	←————————→	"fishy" battle fought in 1942
duck	←————————→	"ducky" general was Smith
chair	←————————→	"chairman" had to face losses of 800
color	←————————→	"color" red won
boat	←————————→	"boats" could pass now because bridge destroyed

5. Many mnemonic devices do not have a sound basis in learning theory and because of their gimmicky nature can sometimes bring unpredicted results. (One student remembered "Thirty days hath September, All the rest I can't remember!") Consequently, the mnemonic device should be used only when it is helpful and should be disregarded when it is not.

5.4 ORGANIZING

One necessary aspect of promoting maximum recall of new material encountered in reading is to develop appropriate organizers to relate the new material to the existing knowledge base. Organization in this broad sense must be directed toward more than just a simple arrangement of the parts of the new material. It should attempt to cause the new material to become truly "organic," or in other words, have a necessary interrelationship between itself and what is already known. An "organizer" is a means of clarifying such an organic interrelationship, and it can take any number of forms.

Organization as a means of improving recall is the most basic and encompassing of the memory-assisting approaches. As the students understand new information, they must find a way to interrelate it to what is already known. Learning theory tells us that (1) the fewer separate "blocks" of information the students must recall, the better they are likely to do so, and (2) the more meaningfully the students can relate or fit the new information into a system or order of like information that they already possess, the better they will remember it.

The extensive work of learning theorist David P. Ausubel gives great support to the validity of organizational approaches to improve learning and retention. His meaningful learning theory stresses the students' use of meaningful hierarchies to subsume the new information they encounter in order to increase their learning and retention.

Using *search, select, and relate techniques*, the students attempt to decide upon the appropriate "blocks" and fit them into those "frameworks" meaningful to them.

There are many different meaningful relationships that will exist between the students' own thinking structures or systems and new information they will encounter in their reading. Consequently, after they have read, there are many ways to organize their new information meaningfully. Any particular student might profitably approach the task as an outline, categorization, noting, or a highly idiosyncratic process.

Students may also use outlines, summaries, and similar devices to sort their information. They do not need to develop highly complex or sophisticated techniques. General purpose-setting questions, for example, can serve as such organizers since the students are then reading with a framework of the information they should receive in mind.

One caution is warranted. Students are oftentimes confused as to what "organization" really means and, as a result, operate as though "organization" and "orderly" were synonymous. It is important to assist them in making the distinction. A simple example should clarify: A youngster is capable of keeping the toys in his room in a tidy arrangement long before he can make an organized arrangement of those same toys. Organization requires the existence of a relationship—a truck and a drum neatly placed on the same shelf is an orderly arrangement; trucks placed with other wheeled toys and a drum placed with other musical instruments is an organized one.

5.4A PURPOSE SETTING

Level   Middle grades and above.

Objective   To demonstrate some ways of setting the purpose for reading and to provide the students some practice in doing so.

Description In purpose setting the students are working with an advance organizer. They are given or asked to develop a question or a framework before they begin their reading. As they read, they will build on to that framework as they find the materials that belong with the various parts. The nature of the framework must necessarily differ for different types of material. For example, if the students wanted to know and recall the details in a piece of fiction, they might work with a framework of journalistic questions like *who*, *what*, *when*, *where* as they began their reading. If the students wanted to know and recall the details of a piece of argumentative exposition, they might begin with the categories of *pro* and *con* as they started to organize their reading. In each example, the nature of the material would determine what kind of advance framework would be most meaningful.

1. In order to direct student thinking toward the helpfulness of a framework for understanding and recall, you might write on the board something like, "go in with a question to come out with an answer." Ask for a discussion of what a statement like this

means. Many of the students would remember having been given this advice as elementary school readers.

2. When it is clear that the students have a good understanding of the usefulness of a framework or direction as they read, ask them to discuss what kinds of directions or frameworks one might use.

3. List their suggestions on the chalkboard and discuss them. You could help them begin their listing with one of the following:

    a. questions
    b. study guides
    c. topic outlines
    d. topical listings

4. After all the students have had a good opportunity to contribute and discuss, ask them to suggest what kinds of reading would be best served by each of their suggestions. Pair the material they identify with the framework they indicate as appropriate.

5. Provide the students with several short and different reading selections (four is about the right number) or identify specific selections and pages in their texts. Vary the selections on the basis of the kind of information the readers would seek when they read it. As minimum you would want to include *a.* a narrative, *b.* a process, *c.* an argumentation, and *d.* a description.

6. Organize the class into as many groups as you have selections.

7. Assign each group one selection.

8. Direct the groups to take the selection they were assigned and develop an appropriate advance framework for helping a reader effectively understand and recall it.

9. Have each group present and defend its organizational framework.

10. Prior to reading assigned throughout the course, discuss appropriate organizers and provide some suggestions and direction to the students in formulating and using them.

*5.4B SUMMARY AS AN ORGANIZATIONAL SYSTEM

Level   Middle grades and above.

Objective   To demonstrate some ways of summarizing material and to provide the students some practice in doing so.

Description
1. Most secondary students will understand the term "summary." However, it is well to begin the activity with a discussion of the definition.

2. Invite the students to share times in which they find

summarizing useful. You can prompt their discussion with suggestions like when writing a postcard, a lab report, test notes, and so on.

3. Explain to the students that a summary can exist in several forms, and that the appropriate form is determined by what information the reader needs to know.

4. Ask the students to suggest some summary forms. You can begin the list with any of the following:

Material	Possible Summary Form
a. character sketch	a list of personal traits
b. report of math data	a graph
c. description of legislative process	a flow chart
d. story	identification of setting, characters, and theme
e. expository paragraph	a précis

5. In the text material the students are using, identify different pages or sections that represent different kinds of material. Ask the students to read and decide on the appropriate summary form. Identify a purpose for each summary. You could use any of the following as suggestions of purposes for which the students might want to summarize.

   a. a test
   b. to remember something for a long time
   c. to tell a friend what the information was
   d. to write a paper or report

6. When the students are able to do this, ask them to take one of the selections and summarize it for several different purposes. This will, of course, require several different summaries in some cases.

7. Discuss the differences.

8. On a continuing basis assign various summarizing activities to the students and discuss the value of those activities with them.

5.4C OUTLINING

Level   Middle grades and above.

Objective   To provide students practice with using the outline to organize their thinking and recall of the material they read.

Description   1. Most secondary students will have had some experience with outlining as a means of organizing their writing. It will be helpful to assess what they already know about outlines before you begin. Their answers to the following questions should give you an indication of the level of understanding at which they are operating:

    a. What is an outline?
    b. Why do we use an outline?
    c. What kinds of outlines can be made?

2. If the students indicate a good understanding of the outline as a means of *logical* and *consistent* ordering of ideas, then you may go to item 8 in this section. If they do not indicate that kind of understanding, use the following steps.

3. The aim of the next steps is to help the students overcome the notion that the outline is just a mechanical or cosmetic framework. At this point you should avoid extensive discussion of parallel form, indentation, and so on in their work, as your goal here is a much broader one.

4. Discuss the steps one takes in developing an outline. You can have the students fill in additional material, but begin with the following:

    a. determine the major points;
    b. list those points;
    c. determine the minor points;
    d. decide to which of the major points each of the minor points is most closely related;
    e. arrange those minor points under the major ones;
    f. determine if there are significant supporting details;
    g. arrange those under the points to which they have provided support.

5. Select a piece of material the class has already read and have them outline that material using the directions.

6. Write the outline they develop on the board as they decide the appropriate location for each of the parts.

7. As a check for comprehension of the purpose of outlining, provide the students with an incorrect outline and have them make the appropriate changes. The first time they do this, use a simple one like the following:

    Hunting Rabbits
    I. Places to hunt
        A. Woods
        B. Traps
    II. Equipment needed to hunt
        A. Fields
        B. Guns
        C. Fresh air
    III. Advantages of hunting
        A. Exercise

      B. Outdoor clothing
        1. Boots
        2. Warm jacket

8. When the students can quickly spot logical flaws and inconsistencies in exercises like the one above, they should begin to develop their own simple outlines from the material they read.
9. At this point, you will want to instruct the students in some of the manuscript conventions used in outlining. Any grammar or language book will provide you with such rules, or you may begin working from these:

   a. Use a consistent plan for numbers and letters;
   b. use a regular system for indenting for minor headings;
   c. use the same form throughout your outline. It could be topics, sentences, or paragraphs;
   d. place all the items in the outline in parallel grammatical forms;
   e. make all headings as clear and informative as possible. (Do not use terms like body or conclusion.)

10. Provide students opportunities to practice with and to use outlines throughout the year.

5.4D NOTE-TAKING AS A MEANS OF ORGANIZATION

Level   Junior high and above.

Objective   To give students direction in the use of note-taking for organizing their reading for better comprehension and recall.

Description   Note-taking is a difficult skill for many students to acquire. Often even students who report that they "take notes" are not recording information in a way that makes it helpful to them at a later time. Secondary teachers seldom collect and mark student notes, but it is a good idea to do so. Any grade involved would be unimportant, but the feedback to the students would be very helpful to them indeed. The only direction required for this activity is to provide the students with a great deal of directed practice and feedback. The following guidelines for note-taking will serve the learners well and should be carefully covered with them.

Guidelines for Note-Taking
1. Determine the purpose for the notes: to clarify? to recall? for others? for self?
2. Determine what systematic arrangement of the information to be noted will most "organically" relate that information for your best comprehension and recall of it. (Thus, if the purpose was to take the notes to prepare for a test, in one classroom alone the

teacher should expect that a wide variety of personal learning backgrounds and styles be reflected in the note system determined in this step.)

3. Limit a note or entry to one "piece" of information. This may be a synthesis or "chunk" of several pieces of information, but each item recorded should be discrete.

4. Write the note in your own words except when it is necessary to record figures or when a direct quotation is required.

5. When the collection of notes come from more than one source, always include bibliographical data. When using note cards, it should be placed directly on the card. In notebook notes, the information should be recorded at the end of the entry immediately preceding the change of sources. In taking notes from a single text, bibliographic data need not be reported except at the beginning of the notebook.

6 TEACHING HOW TO ANALYZE

One of the readers' tasks is to analyze what has been read: *1.* to ascertain that they have clearly understood the message and *2.* to enable them to manipulate the information for various purposes. Thus the readers variously determine the author's purpose, main idea, and line of reasoning in order to catalogue information, compare it with other experiences, or organize the information for making judgments.

As readers mature, they find themselves processing a more sophisticated and wider variety of reading. Through analytical techniques they sort out the messages and test their purposes and validity.

Analysis of written material is a complex operation and needs to be taught systematically. Readers must first have understood the material at the literal level before successfully undertaking any analytical processing of the print. See Chapter 8 of Smith, Smith, and Mikulecky for teaching strategies for analytic reading.

6.1 DETERMINING THE AUTHOR'S PURPOSE

The writer produced the print for a purpose. The stated or implied purpose may be an honest or a dishonest one. It is dishonest if the writer deliberately attempted to mislead the readers with wrong information or propaganda techniques. While the readers need to understand the message the writer hoped to communicate, they also need to protect themselves from unfair manipulation by the writer. For these reasons it is critical for the readers to try to determine the writer's true purpose in writing as they interact with the print.

It is well to point out to the students that all writers are manipulating their readers in the sense that they consciously try to select words and word arrangements that will bring the readers to the thinking they wish to share. The analytical task becomes increasingly necessary where writers do not do this accurately and honestly.

The author's purpose usually is honest and obvious. He or she is trying to direct, to instruct, to convince, to clarify, to entertain, or to influence some other particular behavior in the readers. Sometimes the author will even announce his or her purpose at the outset. In novels of the past century the author would actually enter into the story at various points with such remarks as, "Now gentle reader, I will show you the benefits of virtue (or the dangers of vice!)" While the literary convention of directly interrupting what is being said to clarify the author's intentions to the "gentle reader" has passed from vogue, many writers still use direct means of notifying the readers of their intent. The huckster's "Now I'll tell you what I'm going to do!" is familiar to all the secondary readers as they have encountered it even from pre-reading days as television watchers, and they continue to do so as they read advertising for record clubs, motorcycles, job training, and so on.

As a result of their experiences, generally with the reading of advertisements, some secondary readers have become alert to the difference in the writer's announced purpose ("I'm going to tell you how to make $500") and his real purpose (getting the reader to purchase a sample case for $50). The less sophisticated reader will need instruction in determining when the writing has been purposefully misleading.

Language in Thought and Action by S. I. Hayakawa (3d edition, Harcourt Brace Jovanovich, Inc., 1972) is a classic in the area of language study and is written so that teacher and student alike can find its discussion of semantics useful. Another classic that treats language manipulation is Vance Packard's *The Hidden Persuaders.* It goes beyond the language aspects but can be easily and enjoyably read by most secondary students. Both books provide good material related to the writer's purpose and how he or she uses print to further it. Both books will generally be available in any secondary school library.

6.1A AUTHOR'S PURPOSE

Level   Junior high and above.

Objective   To provide students with a format to determine whether a writer's probable motive for producing the material should alert the reader to peruse cautiously his or her text.

Description   While present-day students are more sophisticated in some ways than were their predecessors, in other ways they are not. Most of the students continue to have great respect for information they find in print. Most of them have had little, if any, training in rhetorical devices or logic. As a result there is generally an acceptance of what is read with little or no critical examination. For many students there is even an uncertainty as to how one might proceed with such scrutiny.

What the teacher needs to do is alert the students to 1. the influence the author's purpose has on the writing he or she produces, and 2. some easy ways to examine the work for writing tactics that should be examined. Effort should be made to make the students understand that a critical analysis is in order even if they believe the author's purpose is a fair and worthwhile one.

The following questions can be used as (1) a discussion guide for the teacher, (2) a study sheet for the students, or (3) number 11 could be used as a separate analysis sheet to be applied in any number of ways. The list of questions is not intended to be exhaustive. It should, however, be sufficient to alert the students to the necessity of some critical appraisal of print. The teacher should review or teach any unfamiliar terms which appear on the sheet, since not all students will be familiar with terms like those in number 11.

1. Why do you think the writer produced this material?
2. What evidence do you have to support your reasons?
3. Was the writer a qualified person to have done so?
4. Where or how can you verify the writer's qualifications if it is necessary to do so?
5. How important is it to the writer to have the reader agree with him or her? (Place a mark along the line.)

probably of no   very
importance   important
L_____J

6. Do you have any means of verifying this opinion if it is necessary to do so?
7. What are they?
8. Would the writer's need for you to agree likely motivate him or her to: (Place a mark along the line.)

be completely   tend to distort   be
honest   or exaggerate   dishonest
L_____J

9. Do you have any means of verifying this opinion if it is necessary for you to do so?
10. What are they?
11. Is there any evidence to suggest the writer may have resorted to any of the following devices to serve his or her purpose? (Place a check in column that applies.)

	None	*Some*	*A Great Deal*	*Example on Page, Line*
Inaccurate Sources				
Exaggeration				
Distortion				
Propaganda Techniques				
Oversimplification				
Over Generalization				
Faulty Reasoning				

12. Does the evidence in number 11 suggest that you need to read this material cautiously or can you proceed with trust?

*6.1B SLANTED WRITING

Level   Middle grades and above.

Objective   To give students some experience in producing and reacting to slanted writing.

Description

1. Write a purpose for writing on the chalkboard. "To convince the reader that Local High School was unfairly treated in a recent ball game" could be used for this purpose.
2. Write the opposite position beside the first. Using the example in number 1, you would write "To convince the reader that Local High School was fairly treated in that same ball game."
3. Divide the class into writing teams. No more than four students should be assigned to a team. Pair weak readers and writers with strong ones.
4. Assign each team either position one or position two.
5. Assign each team the task of developing a paper that tells the story according to their position.
6. Tell the students they are to slant their facts to convince the reader their position is the correct one, but that *nothing* can be written that is inaccurate or incorrect.
7. Ideally the teams should plan and write the paper in class. However, if that much time is not available, at least have the teams do their planning in class.
8. When the papers are finished, they should be read and discussed in class.
9. A good follow-up would be to list on the chalkboard each device the writers used to "slant" their writing. Invite the students to clip examples of those devices they find in their reading and post them next to each item listed.

6.1C IDENTIFYING PROPAGANDA DEVICES

Level   Middle grades and above.

Objective   To identify the more common propaganda devices to students so that they are aware of some of the means of manipulation with which the reader must cope.

Description   Propaganda techniques are so common in contemporary writing that students need to be alerted to the more commonly used ones. They must also be reminded that such techniques are used for worthwhile causes as well as suspect ones. The most generally used ones follow:

1. *Name Calling*

   The words used have bad connotations that the writer hopes will become associated with the person or ideas he wishes to discredit.

   Example: The woman was *skinny*. (*skinny* instead of slender)
   He looked *un-American*. (*un-American* instead of Oriental.)

2. *Glittering Generalities*

   The words ordinarily have a pleasant connotation, but are used in a way that makes the meaning vague.

   Example: The mayor's plan was *inspired*! (But what was it?)
   This house has *splendid* options. (But what are they?)

3. *Card Stacking*

   The writer attempts to make his point by telling only the points that support his position and only the points that discredit the other side. He attempts to convince by ignoring all evidence contrary to his position.

   Example: Working women spend less time at home. (But what evidence do we have that this is a problem?)
   Passage of the ERA will destroy sex differences. (Changes in employment and compensation are not mentioned.)

4. *Testimonial*

   Someone who is likely to be admired (a glamorous movie star or a sports hero) or someone with whom the reader enjoys identifying (bright young executive) endorses the writer's idea. The writer's hope is that the reader will want to emulate the person testifying and thus support his ideas.

   Example: Six famous movie stars all believe we should read this book.
   Miss Teenage America always reads this book.

5. *Bandwagon*

   The writer hopes that the reader will want to be a part of the crowd or like some group of people with whom he ordinarily identifies. The writer wants the reader to feel he will make a mistake if he does not accept his position, since those people "like" him are doing so.

Example: The speaker said that all real Americans were voting for Smith. (Certainly, one wants to be a real American.)
Intelligent people will immediately see the value of supporting Candidate Jones. (Certainly, one wants to be considered intelligent.)

6. *Transfer*

The writer attempts to associate a symbol which enjoys high regard with his idea or a symbol with derogatory implications with opposition to his idea. The writer hopes to transfer to the reader's mind the implications associated with the symbol.

Example: The idea is as patriotic as the American flag. (What could be more patriotic than the flag?)
The good old country doctors always suggested this in times of crisis. (Who would dispute as venerable a symbol as he?)

7. *Plain Folks*

The writer attempts to convince the reader that his is a common or ordinary position with which everyone can associate himself.

Example: This idea has always been accepted by people like you and me.
Every man on the street agrees that this is true.

6.2 GETTING THE MAIN IDEA

Before any advanced critical judgments can be made, a reader must identify the main idea. In a paragraph the task is sometimes referred to as determining the topic sentence, or in a longer work as identifying the thesis. The length of the work or the label given the task are not consequential. What is consequential is that the reader is able to recognize the writer's central thought. This requires the reader to distinguish the main idea from supporting statements or details.

Almost everyone has had the experience of listening to a highly excited person who was trying to describe something alarming that had just happened. The task for the listener was not only to recognize the words the speaker was saying but also to determine what really did happen—or what the speaker's main idea was. That task is an exaggeration of the task of determining the main idea in printed material, but it requires the same process. In both cases the receiver of the language message must determine what statement, combination of statements, or implication from all the statements was the central thought that the sender of the language wanted him or her to understand. It is a task of sorting out for the purpose of clarification or verification. In most secondary school reading getting the main idea requires only literal comprehension of the writer's statements. In some literary forms that the students will study, however, the task will require an understanding of inferences and applications. Most of that kind of reading will be confined to classes in literature.

*6.2A IDENTIFYING MAIN IDEA

Level   Middle grades and above.

Objective   To give the students practice in identifying the main idea in a paragraph or selection.

Description   1. Provide the students with three or four different paragraphs or selections in each of which there is a clearly stated main idea or topic sentence. (You could simply identify such paragraphs in the text they are using.)
2. Ask the students to write titles for each paragraph or selection.
3. Discuss and agree upon an appropriate title for each selection.
4. Have the students then search the paragraphs for the statement or statements that are most like the title. (In some cases the words of the title will have come directly from the print.)
5. Encourage discussion throughout the activity so that all the students have opportunities to explain and clarify how one determines 1. the central thought and 2. the clues that one can expect to obtain from the title in regard to that central thought.
6. For more advanced students encourage a discussion of the differences between "labels" and "titles" for print selections. They could consider when each is best used, which requires the more sophisticated processing of the print, and so on.

*6.2B LOCATING A MAIN IDEA

Level   Middle grades and above.

Objective   To familiarize students with the typical placements of the main idea or topic sentence in print.

Description   1. Explain to the students that the style of most textbook writing is highly regular or predictable. Since the author's purpose in most of this writing is to inform, he or she seldom resorts to stylistic surprises or innovations.
2. Show the students the form in which they are likely to find the main idea presented. (Figure 6–A)
3. Discuss the advantages and disadvantages of each arrangement.

Figure 6–A

LOCATION OF MAIN IDEA

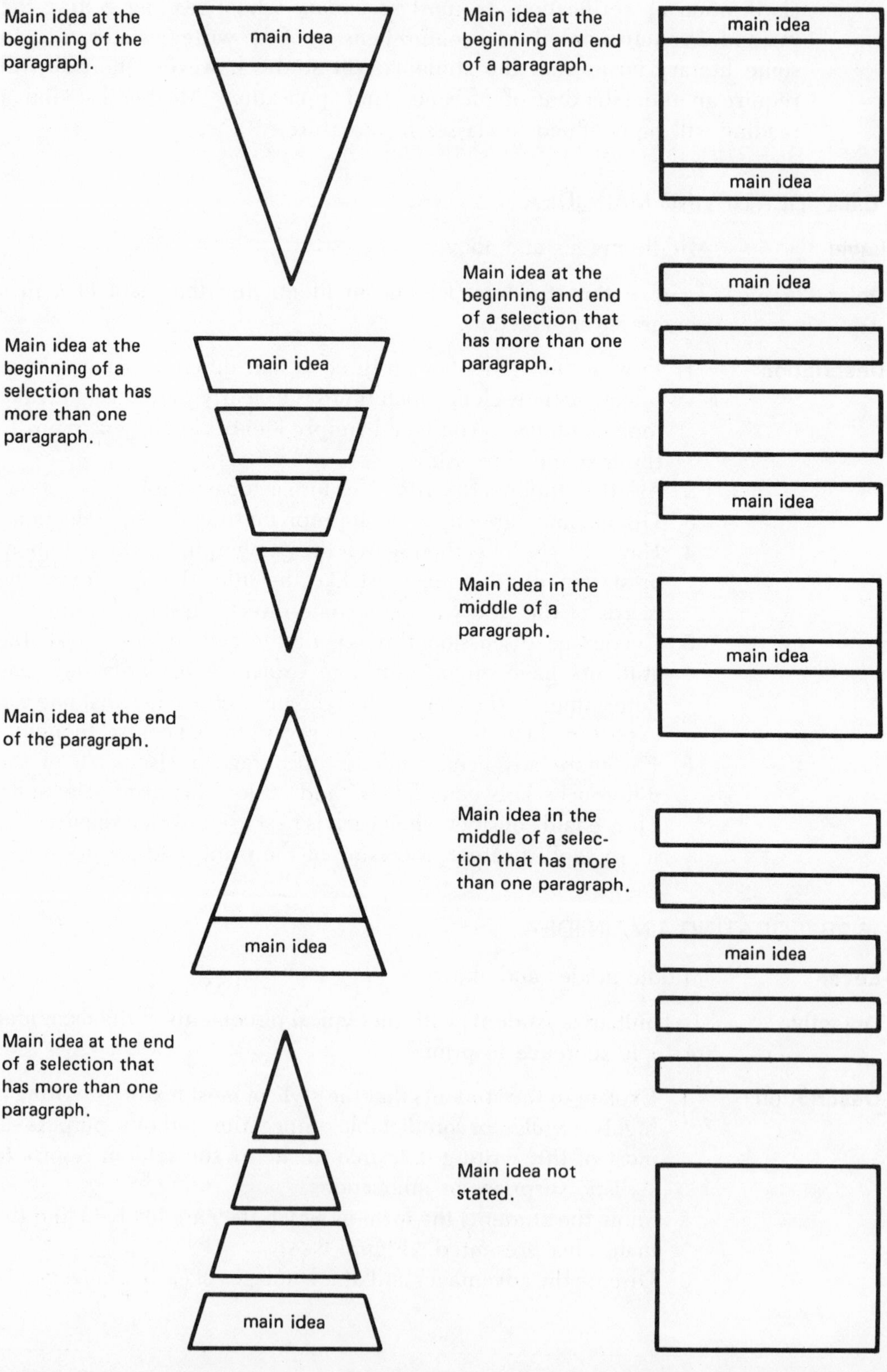
Main idea at the beginning of the paragraph.
main idea
Main idea at the beginning of a selection that has more than one paragraph.
main idea
Main idea at the end of the paragraph.
main idea
Main idea at the end of a selection that has more than one paragraph.
main idea
Main idea at the beginning and end of a paragraph.
main idea
main idea
Main idea at the beginning and end of a selection that has more than one paragraph.
main idea
main idea
Main idea in the middle of a paragraph.
main idea
Main idea in the middle of a selection that has more than one paragraph.
main idea
Main idea not stated.

4. Have the students search their textual material for examples of each arrangement.

(In lower grades or highly technical subjects it is better to work with one form at a time.)

*6.2C SUPPORTING DETAILS FOR MAIN IDEA

Level   Middle grades and above.

Objective   To give students practice in checking support statements against the main idea.

Description   1. In list form put the series of sentences that make up a paragraph on the chalkboard or provide a ditto sheet for the students to follow.

   Begin the activity with a paragraph that has a good topic sentence. Any textbook chapter will provide suitable examples.
2. Have the students identify the main idea. (There will be a topic sentence in this case.) As a guideline have the students ask *1.* does the meaning of this sentence encompass the meaning of all the other sentences around it, or *2.* does this idea state what all the sentences in this paragraph or selection are saying in total, or *3.* from the words used, is this the idea that those words tell me the writer wanted to communicate? Work through some practice exercises with the students.
3. Rewrite this sentence beside the list of sentences that is already on the chalkboard. (See Figure 6–B)
4. Have the students "test" each sentence in the paragraph against the one identified as the main idea. The test will be determining if the sentence supports the identified main idea statement by either *1.* expanding, *2.* clarifying, *3.* providing an illustration or example of the idea, or *4.* restating the idea in some form. Indicate on the chalkboard what the sentence does. (See Figure 6–B)
5. This process will require some time, but it will be time well-spent. This is a valuable exercise in print analysis and provides the students with some guidelines for doing such analysis inde-

Figure 6–B

Sentence 1, which is identified as the main idea	1. Sentence # 1 of the paragraph 2. Sentence # 2 of the paragraph 3. Sentence # 3 of the paragraph 4. Sentence # 4 of the paragraph 5. Sentence # 5 of the paragraph 6. Sentence # 6 of the paragraph	1. main idea 2. example of the idea 3. more of the example 4. more of the example 5. application of idea 6. restates the idea

pendently. From time to time the students may find they have identified the wrong sentence or idea. Allow this kind of error to happen and guide them into the discovery that they have been incorrect. They will almost always find their mistake if you carry the testing through rigorously.

6. Work with this activity periodically until the students are all able to do this kind of testing with paragraphs that have clearly stated topic sentences.

7. After they are adept with main ideas that are stated, provide them with material in which the main idea is not directly stated.

8. On the chalkboard have the students write the main idea in their own words and put it where they had previously listed the topic sentence.

9. Proceed with the testing as before.

Note: This activity is far more difficult than it may appear to be. It is ideally suited for a variety of grade levels since the only adjustment required is in the difficulty of the material, but it is much better to underestimate the difficulty of the material required for a particular class than to overestimate it, especially when you are first beginning to use the activity.

*6.2D SUPPORTING STATEMENTS FOR MAIN IDEA

Level Middle grades and above.

Objective To provide the students with some graphic means of demonstrating the relationship between the supporting statements and the main idea.

Description For some students the graphic representation of an idea is the best assistance they can have in grasping a concept. This activity will be very helpful to them and thus *should* be provided. It should *not* be seen as the only system to be used to develop the concept of supporting statements and main idea, however, because for other students the task of relating the graphics to the idea makes the concept *more difficult*. The graphic design you use to demonstrate the idea is not consequential so long as several suggestions are made. Use a variation of any of them.

1. Begin the activity by reminding the students that they should use the same guidelines for determining whether a sentence is a main idea or a supporting statement as they used in 6.2C.

2. Invite the students to suggest ways the relationship between supporting statements and the main idea could be pictured.

3. Use any of the following as suggestions to get the students underway in their thinking. Remind students in mathematics, science, music, and vocational education that sometimes their supporting material is presented in graphic form or symbols rather than in words alone.

a.

MAIN IDEA (OR TOPIC SENTENCE)			
1. Supporting statement	2. Supporting statement	3. Supporting statement	4. Supporting statement

b. The trunk of the tree is the basis of the tree . . . the branches enhance the tree.

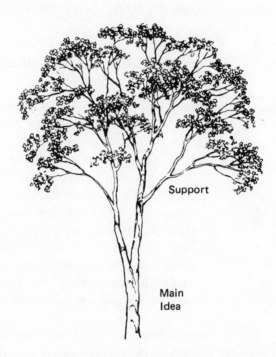

Support

Main Idea

c. The blossom is the main idea and the stem and leaves support it.

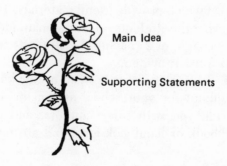

Main Idea

Supporting Statements

4. When the students have decided on a graphic form or forms they like, use it with several paragraphs or selections from their textbooks.
5. Repeat the activity throughout the year if your class finds it helpful.

6.2E OUTLINING MAIN IDEA AND SUPPORTING STATEMENTS

Level   Junior high and above.

Objective   To provide students with an outline format for indicating main ideas and supporting statements.

Description   Students very often need a good deal of practice in identifying main ideas. The two suggestions that follow would provide a variety of ways for them to practice.

1. Have the students each bring to class two felt tip markers of different colors. Have them indicate the main idea with one color and the supporting statements with the other color. This, of course, would only be done on consumable materials.
2. Have the students underline each main idea, or if it is implied, have them write the main idea beside the paragraph. Then ask them to number each support statement. When they can do this easily, they could then be asked to rank the relative strength of each of the supports. (1 = strongest point, and so on)

Even after you have discussed main ideas and supporting statements and have worked through several activities, there will be junior high and secondary students who will still need a great deal of practice in determining what the main idea is. Fortunately, there are many activity books on the market which provide useful materials. The books consist of activities such as 1. having the students select the main idea from a list of statements following the passage, or 2. having the students select the best title for the selection from a list provided.

If you find students in need of this kind of material, a call to the reading consultant for your school system or an educational book publisher will provide you with titles, authors, and costs. Ordinarily the books are in workbook or handbook form and are not expensive.

6.3 CHECKING THE LINE OF REASONING

When the readers react to what the writer has put into print, they must respond to more than the meaning of each word. They must also consider whether the order of the writer's ideas is an acceptable one and attempt to follow that arrangement as they process the print. The readers must also be aware of the line of reasoning presented in the reading and be able to determine if it has been honestly presented and has followed the rules of logic.

Students are assisted if they are aware of the predictable arrangement of ideas in print. The knowledge that particular sequences and words signal predictable presentations of information alerts the readers to use these clues to help themselves more easily process the print.

Elementary school children are often given exercises in which they identify "what is wrong with the picture or story." When they find a rosebush that is growing bananas or a mailman who can turn himself into a kangaroo, they identify the combination as a "mistake" because that is not the logical order of things. Or, they recognize the material as fantasy and enter what Coleridge called the "willing suspension of disbelief." There is no question that fantasy enriches our lives, but that kind of writing should not be confused with what represents itself as informational writing. Since for a variety of reasons some writers do fail to follow the rules of logic even in informational writing, students must also be alerted to the logical fallacies that are the results of such failures.

6.3A ORGANIZING IDEAS

Level   Junior high and above.

Objective   To direct the students' attention to some of the more usual systems of ordering ideas.

Description   There are four patterns for ordering ideas that are generally used in the kind of informational writing that the students will find in secondary textual material. These organizational patterns for presenting ideas are:

1. number sequence
2. time sequence
3. comparison and contrast
4. cause and effect

You may elect to work with all of the patterns at the same time, but we do not recommend that you do so except possibly with an upper-grade accelerated class.

*6.3A1 ACTIVITY FOR WORKING WITH NUMBER SEQUENCE

1. Discuss with the students the advantages the reader has when there is a predictable pattern with which to follow the writer's ideas.
2. Provide the students with a passage in which the ideas are arranged in enumerative order. You can also simply identify such passage in the textbook.
3. After the students have read the selection, have them identify the pattern they found and indicate how it was helpful to them in understanding the reading.
4. Discuss with the students what kinds of information may most advantageously be presented in this particular organizational pattern. List their ideas on the chalkboard and discuss. The list should at least include:

   a. directions;
   b. instructions;
   c. material in which each idea must build on information found in the previous ideas;
   d. events that occur in a time sequence.

5. Have the students suggest and then list on the chalkboard the signal words the reader would expect to find when such an order is being used. Some of the obvious ones would be:

one	first	firstly	initially
two	second	secondly	finally
three	third	thirdly	

6. Have the students find examples from their textual material of each of the situations they listed as appropriate for enumerative order. Discuss as many as time permits.
7. As exercises, have the students:

   a. write something in this pattern for others in the class to read;
   b. rewrite something from the existing reading material so that it is in this pattern;
   c. cite examples from their general reading of effective use of the pattern;
   d. on consumable materials, color-code with felt tip markers or underline the signal words that indicate that such a pattern is probably being used.

6.3A2 ACTIVITY FOR WORKING WITH TIME SEQUENCE

1. Discuss with the students the advantages the reader has when there is a predictable pattern with which to follow the writer's ideas.

2. Provide the students with a passage in which the ideas are arranged in a time sequence. You could also identify such a passage in the textbook.
3. After the students have read the selection, have them identify the pattern they found and indicate how it was helpful to them in understanding the reading.
4. Discuss with the students what kinds of information are most advantageously presented in this particular organizational pattern. List their ideas on the chalkboard. The list could include:

   a. historical description (retelling of events);
   b. most fiction stories;
   c. material which requires an understanding or knowledge of past events to clarify present ones;
   d. biographical writing;
   e. argumentation based on a sequence of events.

5. Have the students suggest and list on the chalkboard the signal words the reader would expect to find when the pattern being used was time sequence. Some of the obvious ones are:

once	later
then	now
in the meantime	while
finally	at first
at last	meanwhile
until	next
after	before

6. Have the students find examples from their textual material of each of the situations they listed in number 4 as appropriate for the time sequence pattern. Discuss as many as time permits.
7. Have the students do these exercises:

   a. write something in this pattern for others in the class to read;
   b. rewrite something from the existing reading material so that it is in this pattern;
   c. cite examples from their general reading of effective use of this pattern;
   d. on consumable materials, color-code with felt tip markers or underline the signal words that indicate that such a pattern is probably being used.

6.3A3 ACTIVITY FOR WORKING WITH COMPARISON AND CONTRAST

1. Discuss with the students the advantages the reader has when there is a predictable pattern with which to follow the writer's ideas.
2. Provide the students with a passage in which the ideas are

presented by using comparison and contrast or identify such a passage in the textbook. You may wish to provide some time for discussing the definition of comparison and contrast.

3. After the students have read the selection, have them identify the pattern they found and indicate how it was helpful to them in understanding the reading.

4. Discuss with the students the kinds of information most advantageously presented in the comparison/contrast pattern. Their definition should be similar to the following:

> *Issues and ideas that have distinct opposing dimensions* (for example, good/bad, new/old, valuable/worthless) *and some shared dimension* (for example, useful/useful, easy/easy, inexpensive/inexpensive).

5. Have the students suggest and list on the chalkboard some of the signal words the reader would expect to find when the pattern of the reading was comparison/contrast. Some you would expect are:

but	on the other hand	however
still	rather	likewise
on the contrary	in comparison	in contrast

6. Have the students suggest specific issues which would be best presented in the comparison/contrast pattern. Have the students locate the use of this pattern in their textual reading and cite its location to class members. Discuss as time permits.

7. Using the following format have the students take passages identified from their reading and list the comparisons and contrasts on the board:

PASSAGE A, PAGE 7

Comparisons	*Contrasts*
1.	1.
2.	2.
3.	

8. On consumable materials, have the students identify the comparisons and contrasts with either two different colors or underline the comparisons and circle the contrasts. The items which related to each other could then also be coded with letters or numbers to indicate their relationships to each other. (See the example in Figure 6–C on page 133.)

6.3A4 ACTIVITY FOR WORKING WITH CAUSE AND EFFECT

1. Discuss with the students the advantages the reader has when there is a predictable pattern with which to follow the writer's ideas.

Figure 6–C

John and Sam were both in the third grade. John *liked the third grade,* but Sam *did not.* John and Sam both liked Mrs. Adams, the teacher, very much though. They both also enjoyed the field trips their class took.

Comparisons	*Contrasts*
1. in the third grade	1. John liked third grade, but Sam
2. liked Mrs. Adams, the teacher	did not
3. enjoyed field trips	

2. Provide the students with a passage in which the ideas are arranged in a cause and effect pattern. You could also simply identify such a passage in the textbook. You may also want to spend some time discussing the definition of cause and effect.

3. After the students have read the selection, have them identify the pattern they found and indicate how it was helpful to them in understanding the reading.

4. Discuss with the students what kinds of information are most advantageously presented in this particular organizational pattern. List their ideas on the chalkboard and discuss. The discussion should emphasize the importance of validating the result (effect) as a true result generated by the stated cause. (See 6.3E for material related to logical fallacies in causal relationships.) Some of the situations the students could suggest would be:

   a. reporting experimentation;
   b. discussing events;
   c. most analytical writing.

5. Have the students suggest and list on the chalkboard some of the signal words the reader would expect to find when the pattern being used was cause and effect. Some of the usual ones are:

as a result	therefore
it follows that	because
consequently	since
for this reason	so that

6. Have the students cite and discuss examples of the use of the cause and effect arrangement in their textbooks. They will find in this search that very often the effect is listed first. They should discuss why this may also assist the reader in understanding the writer's main idea.

7. As exercises have the students:

   a. write something in this pattern for others in the class to read;

b. rewrite something from the existing reading material so that it is in this pattern;

c. cite examples from their general reading of the effective use of this pattern;

d. on consumable materials, color-code with felt tip markers or underline the signal words that indicate that the cause and effect pattern is being used;

e. using the following format have the students list the causes and their effects as the writer presents them. Initially, use the chalkboard for this purpose so that there can be class discussion. Later, students could simply do such an exercise with pencil and paper.

Cause Presented		*Effect Presented*
1.	⟶	1.
		a.
		b.
2. both causes resulted in ⎱	⟶	2.
3. one identified effect ⎰		

6.3B COMPARISON/CONTRAST: SOCIAL STUDIES

Level   Middle grades and above.

Objective   To help students become critical consumers of print and current issues.

Description   These three activities provide students practice in comparing the various points of view surrounding many issues, with the goal of intelligent analysis and decision making.

1. Warm-up exercise: Select an article which presents two sides of a question. Newspapers and magazines commonly carry side-by-side editorials by different people on the same topic. Or, videotape the "Point/Counterpoint" portion of the television program *60 Minutes*. Ask:

   What is the point of view of each side?
   What are the major arguments for each?
   Which arguments seem most valid to you? Why?
   What arguments would you add to this whole discussion?
   Is one opinion "right"? Can both be "true"? How?
   What accounts for the different conclusions these writers draw about this topic? (for example, lies, ignorance, different vested interests, different criteria, frames of reference, and so on.)

2. Select an interesting issue with printed data only covering one side of the issue. Ask students to analyze this without benefit of a rebuttal right beside it, using questions similar to those above. Ask students to write and present the opposing viewpoint. Take a poll of the class to see which is the most widely held view.

3. Study a locally hot issue from several points of view. Using a subject that is likely to provide a range of opinions, ask students to write privately their stance on the matter and stick it away for future reference. Then, comparatively study the issue:

   a. Ask students to list the various groups with vested interests in this topic.
   b. Divide the students into groups to cover each of these interest groups and ask them to study in the newspapers and library resources to determine exactly what their group thinks about this issue, why they believe this way, and what are they likely to do about it.
   c. Present the various vested-interest viewpoints in class.
   d. Ask students to again write their personal opinions since hearing these reports.
   e. Compare new position papers to the original opinions for evidence of change.

6.3C COMPARISON/CONTRAST: LANGUAGE ARTS

Level   Junior high and above.

Objective   To establish student habits of scrutinizing language arts experiences critically.

Description The following are projects that may be introduced early in the year and provide an on-going lesson throughout the term. In each the students are asked to analyze some aspect of their media consumption and report findings to their classmates in some regular format. In each, too, the students are to evaluate by comparing and contrasting.

1. Compare and contrast several versions of the same narrative. This is an old saw, but never before has it been so easy for students to encounter the same story in several media: news article followed by television feature; film followed (or preceded) by paperback; classic novel followed by film; older film followed by contemporary remake; poem or song expanded into novel or film; bestseller book followed by television special. Whenever students have such an experience they can receive extra credit by reporting to the class orally or in bulletin board displays their evaluation, which could include such points as:

   What are the similarities and differences of each version?
   What are the natural advantages and disadvantages of each medium?
   How does each version build upon the time era in which it originates?
   How was the story altered by the medium or personalities involved in each version?

Perhaps a whole-class experience will get the ball rolling. The exciting and ever-popular *Dracula* is a natural. It is currently available in dozens of versions, the best of which are the full-length or abridged novel by Bram Stoker, comic books by many different publishers, the first movie release, which is a silent film called *Nosferatu*, the early Bela Lugosi films and the newest public television film starring Louis Jordan.

2. This progression of activities aims at students' establishing a classroom movie-review station in the school which will be maintained and used all year. To set the skill in the students' minds, select a movie soon to come to town which is likely to be of student appeal. Gather as many diverse reviews and advertising releases of the film as possible. Ask students to compare the views expressed:

   What criteria were the respective reviewers following to make their judgments?
   How do the reviews differ on specific points?
   What controversial aspects based on these differences interest you?

   After someone has seen the movie, ask him or her to write or orally report to the class how the reviews did or did not match the actual viewing.

   Ask students to agree on a standard format and set of criteria for judging films which meet the interests and limitations of their movie-going. This might be a checklist or a rating system. As any student throughout the year becomes the "first on the block" to see a new movie in town, let it be his or her extra-credit responsibility to post a review and give it a rating for the other class members. A special wall or portion of the bulletin board should be designated for these reviews. Other students should feel welcome to post opposing reviews as long as the same agreed-upon criteria for the class are used.

   Similarly, television can be used in this manner. Frequently a special series or a one-time show is advertised and reviewed in advance of its presentation. Students can be on the lookout for upcoming shows which may be of student interest and post notices of the topics, times and stations of the shows. This may be followed up with written or oral discussion of how well the show met its advance promises.

3. To encourage students to be critical consumers of words, this lesson asks students to evaluate the relative effects of common language behavior.

   To get students thinking about weighing the words they see and hear, present at least the first chapter of Edwin Newman's

book *A Civil Tongue*, Warner Books, 1976. In it is an explanation of how he feels the English language is mistreated and
people are misled, accompanied by examples of these acciden-
tal and deliberate language abuses.

Mr. Newman's first book, *Strictly Speaking: or, Will America
Be the Death of English?*, is a examination of why he believes
sloppy diction, corny advertising, overtechnology, and slang
have corrupted the otherwise beautiful language into an impre-
cise, substandard medium of exchange.

Begin with a general discussion of language: its purposes,
roots, and fluctuations. Included here, too, might be debate
over whether Newman has a valid point or is merely spouting
needless erudite gibberish. Ask students to produce examples
of how the language has grown or changed in their lifetimes:
how did it happen? who does it? is it good, bad or neutral?

Study Newman's examples of misused language as well as
common political or advertising slogans. Where is evidence of
what Newman is saying? Does it really matter? How are you
affected by this misuse of language?

Establish a permanent place in the classroom where throughout the year students can post examples of uses of language—
examples which they feel make for particularly effective communication; misleading language; rich and expressive slang or
new words; and cheap, vacuous slang or uses.

*6.3D COMPARISON/CONTRAST: MEDIA STUDY

Level   Middle grades and above.

Objective   To help students develop critical reading skills in literature and to
help them become wary consumers of the electronic media, this
series of activities aims at teaching them to make clear, judgmental
distinctions between fact and fiction.

Description Distinguishing between fact and fiction in legends and ballads is a
fun way to begin this critical reading skill. This activity, designed to
span parts of several weeks of class time, is divided into four parts:

1. Discuss the typical legend or ballad, perhaps playing any one of
many available recordings:

> Where did it come from?
> How was it passed along?
> What likely happened to it en route?
> What useful purpose does it present?
> What danger does it present?

Read aloud (or play) a short, particularly fanciful legend. As students listen, ask them to make note of potential points of error or exaggeration. Compare.

2. Select an interesting legend for which the factual account of the incident is available. Ask students to compare the versions and speculate why and how the differences came to be and what effect they have had. An excellent, simply written example can be found in the January 26, 1978 *Scholastic Scope* magazine, which presents first the "Legend of Gregorio Cortez" followed by a short article revealing the facts about him.

3. Search for local legends and follow the same skeptical reading (hearing) and fact-finding invetigation. For example, the Morgan-Monroe State Forest in Indiana abounds with stories about headless hunters roaming in the night, a black witch who rocks dead babies, and the like. Direct students to recall and write down any stories they know about their area and help them find library or community resources which will shed light on the real stories behind the fantasies.

   For an international flair, direct students to the Nova Scotian legends about the giant Angus MacAskil. It is a delightful story based upon a real man; more can be learned about him by writing to The Angus MacAskill Museum, Englishtown, Cape Breton Island, Nova Scotia—a museum featuring his giant-sized clothing and furniture. Other sources of information about Angus may be found in records of the Barnum and Bailey Circus with which he toured.

4. Create "new legends" from old facts. Check out of the local library the book *The Super Athletes* by David P. Willoughby, A. S. Barnes and Co., Inc., 1970. This volume has hundreds of factual stories of super-strong people who have lifted trains and pianos and performed similar amazing feats. From the documented information and photographs, have the students select one figure who catches their fancy and write a legend about this person. Urge the students to note the legends they already know to see what kinds of things happened to the facts to make it a great tale.

   This story could be written and passed around, performed on video with costumes and music, or made into a live readers' theater performance for elementary children. It might be illustrated and published for the school library.

6.3E LOGICAL FLAWS

Level   Junior high and above.

Objective   To identify some of the more typical logical flaws that students will encounter in their reading.

Description   Flaws in logic are so common in contemporary writing that students need to be alerted to the more typical ones. They must be reminded that even honest writers make such mistakes in presenting their ideas and that therefore the reader's task must almost always be an analytical one as he or she reads. The analytical task is particularly important in the students' reading of argumentation, as it is in that kind of writing that the writer is most likely to "get carried away" with an idea at the expense of sound logical thinking. The most typical flaws follow:

1. *Argument to the Man*

   In this fallacy, the writer tries to win the support of the reader by attaching an idea to a particular person. If the person is in disrepute, the writer hopes this will cause the reader to discredit the idea. If the person is highly regarded, the author hopes the approval for the person will extend to the idea being presented.

   Example: (in attempt to discredit):
   The tax evaders all supported that legislative bill, and we know what kind of dishonest efforts *they* stand for.

   Example: (in attempt to enhance):
   The most loyal public servant of all is President Brown, and he strongly supports the new legislation on governmental procedures.

2. *Authenticity of Sources*

   In this fallacy, the writer either simply presents a view as absolute and admits no possible qualifications, or presents sources that are inaccurate. Most secondary readers do not have the background in a field to determine when this has happened, so the burden falls to the teacher to inform the students when this flaw exists. It is very important for the students to be aware of their need to check sources because they generally approach the print with a built-in attitude that encourages their belief of it.

   Example: (the writer as the absolute authority):
   Despite contrary claims, theory X is the correct response to the problem and requires no further discussion.

3. *Begging the Question*

   In this fallacy, the writer *assumes* the truth or proof of what he or she is trying to prove and uses it to advance those arguments. It is a deduction from a generalization which may or may not be true.

   Example: Lazy people don't earn much money.
   He doesn't earn much money.
   He is lazy.

Example: He failed the course because he is dumb; only dumb
people fail courses.

4. *False Analogy*

In this fallacy, the writer compares two things which are
different in an area which is critical to the meaning of the
analogy. Just because two ideas or situations are alike in some
ways, they are not necessarily alike in all ways.

Example: A successful businessman will always make a good
statesman because he understands how to spend our tax
dollars. (It is likely to be true that a successful businessman
has learned to manage money well, if he did not just inherit
his successful business. However, statesmen must do more
than spend tax money.)

5. *Hasty Generalization*

In this fallacy, the writer draws a conclusion from too little
evidence.

Example: Girls are much smarter than boys. Both of my daughters
made better grades than my son.

6. *Ignoring the Question*

In this fallacy, the writer changes the real issue at hand to
another in order to win support for the second point, sidestep-
ping the critical one. The students will enjoy being reminded
how often they see this device employed by classmates who are
unprepared to answer classroom questions directed to them.

Example: **Question:**   Where do you stand on the Equal Rights
Amendment?
Answer: When we discuss ERA, we are discussing one
of the finest aspects of the United States, its
lovely women. Women enhance all of American life.

7. *Limited Alternative*

In this fallacy, the writer suggests that there are only two
possible solutions to a problem, when actually there are probably several. It is an "either–or," "yes–no" approach to the issue.
It is sometimes called the "all or nothing" fallacy or the "false
dilemma." The reader is expected to believe that there are
only the *writer's* way and the *wrong* way from which to choose.
This is also called oversimplification.

Example: Only people who wish to encourage irresponsible behavior
support welfare funding. If you believe adults should exercise personal responsibility, then you cannot support welfare payments for them.

8. *Mistaken Causal Relationship*

   In this fallacy, the writer attributes effects to suspect causes. The most common problem here is when the writer indicates that one event is the result of the other simply because it follows it in time.* Another common mistake in causal logic occurs when the writer uses an inference for a logically sound conclusion. (This is called a *non sequitur*, which means "it does not follow.")

   > *Example:*   She was a hard-working girl before she went to college; going to college must be the reason she has become so lazy. (*post hoc, ergo propter hoc*)
   >
   > This is the best book I have ever read; everyone should read it. (*non sequitur*)

9. *Overgeneralization*

   In this fallacy, the writer attributes far greater generality to his or her facts than they warrant. It is similar to the hasty generalization, in which the writer generalizes too soon. In this fallacy, the writer generalizes too widely. Both mistakes are usually the result of trying to reach a conclusion without going through all the necessary steps. Words such as *always, all, none, never, absolutely,* and *certainly* must be examined carefully by the reader to determine if the writer is overstating the case.

   > *Example:*   *Every*one has done something wrong sometime so we should *never* allow ourselves to trust anyone.

10. *Statistical Fallacy*

    In this fallacy, the writer uses figures to support a point in either a dishonest or incorrect way. Since many people do not understand the ways in which partial reports from graphic and statistical data can be misleading, this fallacy is commonly used to mislead the reader. Secondary students cannot be expected to complete a course in statistics for the purpose of reading such data with understanding, however, they *must* be alerted to the need to completely understand the terms being used and to know what each number stands for before they accept conclusions drawn from them.

---

* This is called *post hoc, ergo propter hoc*, which means "after this, therefore because of this."

Example:

Graph A
(report of
student
progress over
nine months)

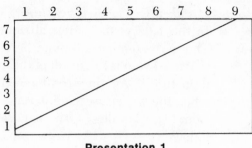

Presentation 1.

Graph B
(same report
of student
progress
over nine
months)

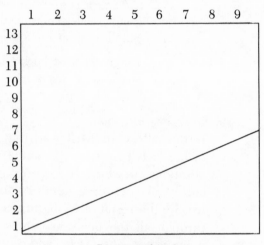

Presentation 2.

The same information is presented but the appearances of student progress seem to be quite different.

11. *Stereotyping*

In this fallacy, the writer tries to win the support of the reader by appealing to generally held beliefs whether they can be validated or are simply unfounded generalizations or prejudices. The students must be alerted to ask if the statement is true in *every* case or if *all* individuals or cases can be described as the writer has described them. If the writer has stereotyped, the students will not be able to answer in the affirmative.

Example: College professors are never well-rounded individuals. Smart students are always lacking in some other aspect of their development.

The specific strategy used in teaching each of the items listed above must, of course, depend on the circumstances under which the students encountered the problem, or were likely to encounter it. In general, however, the logical flaw needs to be defined and discussed, and the students given opportunities to work through a number of examples as a group. It is also important to follow up the introduction of each problem so that the students are aware that their encounter with it was not an isolated instance and that they must be aware of it in all their reading. Some follow-up activities you might consider are listed below:

a. Have the students bring examples of the fallacy they have found in their general reading. Share these with other members of the class as time permits.

b. Ask the students to watch newspapers and magazine writing for examples of logical flaws; ask them to clip those, and to bring them to class for posting. (You may want to begin a color code: red underlining for hasty generalization, blue for faulty causal relationships, and so on.)

c. Begin a posting board that all the students can see and use for displaying their "finds."

d. Suggest that the class give awards on a regular basis for illogical writing. Some things they might want to cite would be:

   i. Illogical Book of the Month
  ii. Illogical Idea of the Month
 iii. Illogical Story or Article of the Month

If they elect to do this, arrange for the school newspaper to provide coverage about each of their awards and have the students write explanations accompanying the award to explain why it was "deserved."

7

PRODDING CRITICAL THINKING

Reading and thinking go hand in hand. To read critically is to think critically while reading. One of the mistaken notions many students have is that critical reading means saying negative things about the selections read. That idea can be dispelled if critical thinking is described as evaluative thinking, that is, making judgments and asking questions about the information and the concepts that appear in a reading selection. Critical reading, then, means using one's knowledge of the selection being read, analyzing the information through questioning and logic, and then deciding or acting on the information in light of one's analysis. Students can be taught to be evaluative in their reading by being asked to identify the criteria or the standards they use in applying or in using the information that is in the text.

One of the major tasks in fostering critical thinking/critical reading is to foster the students' self-esteem, a sense of their ability to make the judgments that are a defined part of critical reading. At almost any age children can tell a teacher that they have likes and dislikes. Those preferences or those judgments for the most part are the result of submerged standards or criteria. In the early stages of developing critical reading, students need regular practice in searching for the *reasons* for their preferences as they become selective in their reading and in their ideas. That is the reason the teacher asks, "*Why* do you like it? *Why* do you dislike it?" after receiving an unexplained judgmental statement. From that early base of trying to recognize the hidden criteria which all students use, the teacher can take major steps to advance the students' critical skills.

Some means the teacher can use to help the students are:

1. Direct the students to establish criteria and make judgments from them.
2. Help the students to identify when they are using personal standards and to understand their limits in content reading activities.
3. Teach the students to use external criteria for making judgments, that is, criteria that are taken from a source other than the personal beliefs of the readers.

4. Insist the students develop a questioning attitude about ideas in all subject areas so as to prompt inferences, hypotheses, and logical analyses before taking action or making a value statement about what is read.

EVALUATIVE THINKING

The basic operation of critical thinking/critical reading is making judgments. The mind ends a process by saying, "This is good; it is enjoyable; it can be used for x but not for y; on a scale of one to ten it ranks four" and similar statements indicating a decision about the value, goodness, or utility of an idea. In every subject area teachers want students to make those evaluative decisions. Those decisions probably determine more than anything else whether the students will develop an interest in the topic and will continue to explore the ideas surrounding the subject. But that kind of evaluative decision-making thinking does not come easily. Even though people make daily decisions about what is good for them, very few know how to make judgments systematically. From subject to subject, students need to know what the criteria are and how to apply them to the information and the conditions peculiar to each individual subject.

In each subject, then, teachers need to show students how to establish criteria for making judgments about various aspects of the subject; how to use personal standards in some cases and how to use objective or external standards in other cases, depending on the topic and the kind of interaction the teacher wants at that moment. Perhaps one of the most valuable activities that students can engage in is one that reminds them that they should consciously maintain a questioning attitude about what they read and hear. For practice, for example, the students could stop after every paragraph and make a brief judgmental comment—or at least raise questions which will prompt judgments later.

7.1 ESTABLISHING CRITERIA

Since most daily life judgments are made quite matter-of-factly, very few people consciously draw up criteria or standards for making those decisions. If we have to select a movie for our entertainment, we review available offerings to see what strikes our mood, our taste, or which one stars the actors and actresses we like. Even though we do not consciously call on criteria, the very listing of mood, taste, and stars indicates that there *are* criteria operating. If we used the ratings that the movie industry places on films to indicate their acceptability for children, adolescents, and adults, our standards would be more obvious. In dressing to go to school or to go on a date, a person once again employs a set of criteria which guide the choice of clothing to wear. In critical reading it becomes beneficial to establish clear criteria that will guide judgments about the value and use of the information.

When it comes to making judgments about ideas in courses and in books, a complex process of thinking and weighing circumstances must occur in a manner not dissimilar to that of selecting a movie or of choosing clothes for a particular occasion. But there are several differences: *One*, the students may not be accustomed to judging the ideas they are now reading—they have little or no precedent to guide them. *Two*, students do not know how to establish standards or criteria for academic content. They have a sense that they must memorize it and hold it rather than make evaluative decisions about it.

A classroom teacher, then, can help students by:

1. making them aware of the need for judging information, opinions, and hypotheses in what they read;
2. helping them establish criteria or standards for making judgments about a particular subject matter; and
3. helping students to apply internal and external criteria to content materials.

*7.1A STANDARDS OF UTILITY

Level Middle grades and above.

Objective To help students see that they make judgments in their everyday lives—judgments based upon usefulness.

Description
1. To raise students' awareness of their use of criteria in making daily decisions, have them bring in a wide variety of newspaper and magazine ads for products used in daily life—soaps, lotions, deodorants, shampoo, and so on. Ask them to bring all the soap and cosmetic ads they can find, including those for the common products which they use personally.
2. The ads should be stacked in categories. Each group represents a list of products from which they must make a single choice for their personal use. Put all the face soap ads together, for example, and choose the one which they will use. Follow the same routine for each of six or eight categories: shampoo, acne lotion, mouth wash, and so on.
3. Have the students make a list of the products they choose for each category. Next to each item they should give the reason why they chose it. If the reason for their choice is not written in the ad, they should write the source of their reason.

Product Chosen	Ad/Product Choice Reason	Source of the Reason
1.		
2.		
3.		
4.		
5.		
6.		

4. In the discussion that follows, put these terms on the board:

Reasons (standards)

convenience				
achieves effect				
general knowledge				
	soap	deodorant	mouth wash	other

Products

As each student gives a reason for his choice, place a mark next to the term that matches the reason. A tally through the chart above will demonstrate the commonality of standards most people have for reading ads, at least at one level of appeal. There certainly are others and they should be listed and categorized as students mention them. For many people their standards for choosing a product are criteria of usefulness: "It's easy; it gets the job done; my family has used it successfully for years (common knowledge)" and so on. Sometimes those reasons are taken from experience and sometimes the ad promises that use of the product will make one's life easier, as in the case of household cleaners of various kinds. The desire for efficient, effective, secure products guides the decisions of many of us. We often use these standards of utility without even realizing we are applying them.

5. And that is part of critical reading/critical thinking of advertising. The same thing would be true of extended reading of subjects that seem to have practical implications in our lives—subjects like home economics, vocational arts, health, child care, and others, depending on our focus. The teacher helps by

asking students to check their standards to see if they are clear enough and sufficient for the judgments to be made. That is where transfer of learning occurs between this exercise and reading books in all content areas. Discuss with students how their practical judgments can be employed when reading the subject textbook. By using the practical aspects of many subjects, the teacher could pose critical reading questions (problems) for students. The products now become things like muscle tone, cleanliness, efficiency with a sewing machine, and so on. But the reasons for choosing certain activities will be similar to those used in selecting household products: convenience, achieves effect, enables me to achieve a personal goal. In other words, a similar chart could be used to help students see how to use standards in content area reading. Take health as an example. What are the reasons or standards for reading (learning) about exercise, diet, and so on?

Reasons (standards)

good looks				
happy life				
sound body				
general knowledge				
	daily exercise	balanced meals	cleanliness	positive attitude

Products

7.1B MAKING JUDGMENTS ABOUT UTILITY; CONSUMERISM

Level   Junior high and above.

Objective   Examine the persuasion techniques of media advertising and decide how they affect personal judgments. Assessment, motivation, and practice activities.

Description   Today everyone is bombarded with television, newspaper, and billboard advertising. Intellectually we all know that the ads are pressuring us to buy their products, but we probably do not examine our judgments to see how they are affected by the ads. This is a two-part activity: the first part asks students to examine their awareness of how they judge advertised products; the second part asks them to use their awareness to influence judgment. These activities could be used in any secondary class where consumer reading might be an issue, such as social studies, consumer economics, health, vocational education, and journalism.

Deciding What to Buy: A personal assessment

1. Tell students to make a list of familiar ad phrases, such as, "You deserve a break today," and "the quicker picker-upper." They can list them on the chalkboard or work in small groups and then combine the items on the board (or turn them in to be reproduced). Each phrase must be from a popular commercial for an easily recognized product. If they have difficulty, point out the advantages of listing them by categories: fast food, paper towels, beer, dog food, cosmetics, and so on.

2. Either distribute a form or have students copy one from the chalkboard as shown below:

IF YOU COULD HAVE ANY OF THESE PRODUCTS, CHECK THE ONES YOU WOULD WANT AND TELL HOW THE ADS HELPED YOU MAKE YOUR DECISION.		
Ad Phrase and Product	*Which Would You Buy?*	*For Those Items Checked, Explain How the Ad Phrase Helped You Decide.*
. . . . (McDonald's)		
. . . . (Big Boy)		
. . . . (Burger King)		
. . . . (Meow Mix)		
. . . . (Levi's)		
. . . . (Coca-Cola)		
. . . . (Close-Up Toothpaste)		
. . . . (Others)		

3. Collect the forms and review the reasons given. Discuss the reasons with the students. See if they can analyze some of the ways their decisions were guided by the words or the retained images of the ads. What were the ads doing to influence the students' judgments? (Ads often suggest a criterion for a choice or create a sense of need for the product.)

Making Judgments: Practice

1. Pass out a list of identifiable commercials, such as Figure 7–A, and have students designate categories for the commercials—entertainment, jingle, slogan, informative, comparison, and so on. Compare the designations among the class and discuss which categories seem to be the most effective. Have students estimate which would most successfully sell the product. Generate ideas about the type of commercial appropriate for a specific type of product. Discuss the way types of ads influence the buyer's opinion and judgment.

2. Have students copy from television and elsewhere the entire commercials for several popular products. Include samples of various types—catchy jingles (noting the importance of the music written for the words), informative, amusing, and irritating.

3. After reading the commercials aloud, have students write down whether they would be inclined to try the product or to avoid it, based on the ad. Make a tally of the responses. Then discuss the ways they think the ads convinced them to buy or to avoid.

4. Present students with several hypothetical products and point out their attributes—for example, a twenty-five-cent hamburger which has a secret sauce, a do-it-yourself pizza parlor, beer made from Alaskan snow, pink cosmetics made from rose petals, foot powder from a secret South American formula. Have individuals or groups of students create a commercial for each one. (If possible, videotape one selection from each stu-

Figure 7–A

SAMPLE AD PHRASES

Home of the Whopper.
Have it your way at _____.
It's fluffy, not stuffy.
You can see yourself right through to the shine.
_____, the beer that made Milwaukee famous.
_____, the Uncola.
It's finger-lickin' good!
Sometimes you feel like a nut, sometimes you don't.
Incrediburgerible!
Let your fingers do the walking.
I'm a pepper, you're a pepper, wouldn't you like to be a pepper too?
Fly the friendly skies.
Keeps babies drier.
Here comes Miller the Spiller.
Nervous is why, there's new _____.
I was flat till I went fluffy.
Melts in your mouth, not in your hand.

If you've got the time, we've got the beer.
I'd like to teach the world to sing, in perfect harmony.
He really got stroked this morning.
No pouring out. Goes right through the water to the clog.
A man is going to get on a plane and beer cans drop out of his pockets.
You get more to like at _____.
_____, where America shops.
Oh, I wish I were an _____ wiener.
Love that squirt.
It smells as clean as it looks.
_____ wants to be your car company.
Got a date with Denise—but the dentist . . .
Takes a lickin' and keeps on tickin'.
Please don't squeeze the _____.
Stops bugs dead!
Not the greasies.
They get good checkups.
Thanks, I needed that.
The orange juice astronauts drink.
Makes your mouth smell clean, not medicine-y.
Six paper towels gone, one _____ going strong.
Get your teeth their whitest.
You, you never looked so good.
Works like a white tornado.
I can see myself!
It's not nice to fool Mother Nature.
Come to the Florida sunshine tree.
How do you spell relief?
Mm-mm good.
Price and Pride.
Mrs. Olsen.
I'm cleaning my oven while I sleep.
I dare you to try that with your panty hose.
Snap, crackle and pop.
A dog chases a wagon into a cabinet.
Let's get Mikey to eat it!
Don't your Charlies deserve the best?
It's us or rust.
From one beer lover to another.
It's good to the last drop.
Strong enough for a man, but made for a woman.
It's stroft.
Mountain grown.
We try harder.
Get a piece of the rock.
Sorry, Charlie.
You asked for it, you've got it, _____.
Get the red out.
A sprinkle a day keeps the odor away.

dent.) Pass out copies of all the commercials and have students decide which items they would buy and why.

5. Make a corresponding tally of which products would be purchased and see how well the created commercials sold the new products. Have the originators of the most frequently selected commercials discuss the language, images, and music used to affect the buyer's judgment.

7.1C VALUES AND DECISIONS

Level   Secondary grades.

Objective   To create an awareness of criteria used to make value judgments about hot current issues.

Description   1. Hot current issues are written and discussed in the public press. Most high school students will have sufficient acquaintance with those topics to venture an opinion. For example: "Should jobs or protection of the environment come first? Should we use nuclear power for electricity while we still have fossil fuel? Should you vote for a candidate in a government election when you are not acquainted with the candidate's qualifications?"

2. List three or more of those issues on the chalkboard. Ask the students to make a decision about each and to write their decisions on a piece of paper.

Issue	Decision	Reason
1.		
2.		
3.		

3. Tally the yea/nay decisions on each of the issues and provide time for the students to clarify their decisions on the issues, if they care to.

4. Then ask them to write their reasons for each of their decisions. If the issues (questions) have been properly posed, there will be no correct answers. Judgments will be made on the basis of certain values (for instance, that the environment must be protected at all costs). In these issues people make decisions based on what they think is most important—to themselves or to the nation. In some instances students may use the word of an authority. That too represents a value—the authority speaks and that authority is their standard.

5. The students should privately examine and categorize their reasons for their decisions. Point out that these are value is-

sues, and their reasons indicate the values (standards) which guide their judgments. As with any standard, the decision-makers should decide whether or not their standards are well-informed. Perhaps they see the need for clarification or for some additional reading to help them shape their values.

6. Hot issues requiring value-based judgments can be found in social studies (voting without knowing candidate's qualifications), science (nuclear power for electricity), home economics (should the buyer be warned of possible ill effects of additives in foods?), and in vocational subjects (should every trade have a timed apprenticeship program?), and so on.

7.2 USING PERSONAL STANDARDS

Whatever the subject matter, students have attitudes which color the statements they make about a subject. They consider it quite appropriate for someone to ask them whether or not they liked a television program. And after some prodding, they can usually give a vaguely positive or negative response. Some vague standard within them prompts their responses. All of us have hidden in our minds and feelings some personal standards which guide the judgmental statements that we make about our likes and dislikes—even about esoteric subjects such as physics, mechanical drawing, and sex education. By asking for the reasons behind the students' judgmental statements, the teacher can draw out these personal standards and establish them at the conscious level.

Using personal standards to make judgments about academic subjects is a starting point, not an epitome, of judgment. Once the teacher and students have brought a personal standard out into clear view, the adequacy of the standard itself is open for discussion. It is legitimate for the teacher to say, "That is your judgment based on the experience you have had. How reliable do you think your background with that subject is?"

Some topics lend themselves to the use of personal standards more than others. Adolescents have experience with interpersonal relations, vicarious adventures through television, a minor sense of government and the laws regulating society, and a few experiences with the basic laws of physics and chemistry (water boils into steam). But it is primarily in the areas of literature and government where their generalized experiences help them form personal standards which they can use in class activities. "Yeah, I know some people who are lonely and that was a good description of how a lonely person acts." "The Democrats come up with all the good ideas. Lincoln must not have had many good ideas because he wasn't a Democrat." It is easy for students to make judgmental statements about lonely people and Democrats, but not easy at all to make specific judgments about physics, ancient history, geometry, and so on, unless, of course, someone has forewarned them, and then they overgeneralize: "I hate it."

The teacher should elicit those personal judgments, however, in order to bring to consciousness the standards that stand behind them. "What makes you say you hate it? Who told you it was bad, or valueless, or too difficult? Is your standard for making that judgment clear? Is it yours—from your experience? Based on your personal standards, what else can you say about the topic?"

By placing personal standards on the chalkboard or on a sheet of paper, the teacher helps the students develop a critical sense of how the mind works in making judgments, and that personal standards sometimes are quite adequate for making judgments and sometimes they are quite inadequate. To find out, one must list them, and then apply them. The following activities provide opportunities for this.

*7.2A FREE READING STANDARDS

Level   Middle grades and up.

Objective   To encourage students to establish standards that will guide their free reading.

Description   1. One obvious criterion for selecting free reading is personal interest. But students need to think about expanding selection criteria to help them grow beyond their immediate interests. First have them list their standards for selecting free reading material. The students should put their standards on one side of a sheet of paper. That list may take the form of "I would select books about . . . ."

2. All the lists should be put in a pile, anonymously. An identifying number, such as a social security number, could be put on each paper if desired. Then have the lists distributed at random among the class, and have the students write on the backs of the sheets what they think the person is like, based on the standards for free reading listed thereon.

3. The lists with the character analyses should be placed on a table or desk and retrieved by their initiators.

4. Ask the students to consider the old adage: "You can tell what kind of man he is by the books that he reads." Or, "Reading is food for the mind." Then let the students examine their standards to see whether they included: recreational reading, current events, hobbies, personal development for school or future occupation, citizenship, personal development for spiritual values, and so on.

5. The class may want to thrash out the accuracy of the character analyses and whether their reading habits do in fact reflect the persons they are.

*7.2B FREE READING STANDARDS

Level   Middle grades and above.

Objective   To apply standards to real situations.

Description   1. In the order of importance to the individuals, the students should list the standards they would use for selecting free reading material.
2. Using the standards they have listed, students should decide what they would read in the following circumstances:

   a. *Doctor's office:* You are in a doctor's office and are told that there will be a long wait. As you look over the magazine rack, you see these types of magazines: news, sports, general health, new baby, house and garden, and a business weekly. You will have enough time to read two or three. In order of preference, list the three that you will look at.
   b. *Bookstore:* You were left at a fairly large bookstore and told that you would be picked up in an hour. As you browse through the magazines and books, which ones will you look at for possible purchase?
   c. *Hospital:* An accident puts you in the hospital and out of school for two weeks, and there is no television in the room. A nurse's aide says he will go to the library for you and bring the books that you request. Make a list of the books or the kinds of books that you want.

3. Most students will want to exchange their lists with their neighbors just to see what the differences are. That would give them an opportunity to discuss their criteria and how they applied them in each situation.
4. In the end, the teacher has the opportunity to point out that developing personal criteria for selecting reading helps make the choices in each situation a little easier. Without these personal standards the choices are random or are guided merely by the interest of the day.

7.2C EVALUATING PEOPLE; USING PERSONAL STANDARDS

Level   Junior high and above.

Objective   To identify personal standards as they relate to other people.

Description   1. Judgments about people are made in everyday life and are also made in English, social studies, science, child development, and health courses. Those judgments can be refined, but they probably must start with an identification of how we use standards to judge the people around us. To give practice in identifying and using those standards, ask students to suppose they are planning to go to an important dance, and they have to decide whom they are going to ask.

2. On a slip of paper the students should list the characteristics they would look for in a date for this big dance. List at least three or four characteristics in their order of preference, for example, "has 160 IQ."

3. Then distribute on a sheet of paper or write these four choices on the board. The students are to choose their dance date from the four listed.

Choice W: Good looking. Athletic. Popular. Cannot dance.
Choice X: Arty type. Plays in concert band. Talks a lot. Dances well.
Choice Y: Quiet and shy. Reads a lot. Average dancer.
Choice Z: Comedian. Wild looking and acting. Jokes while dancing.

4. Get some volunteers to explain how they used their criteria to make a selection among the choices. Even though the final choice may not have had all the characteristics found in the list of criteria, the process represents the way most decisions about people are made. The criteria guide our choices among imperfect human beings.

5. To transfer this activity to reading, remind the students that they can begin any character analysis by lifting out their personal standards for the type of person in question and applying them—to people in history and government, for example, or to characters in a story. Once personal standards have been applied, then other standards can be brought out for review: "Do they fit the job? or, Did they have the moral fiber to tackle the assignment given them?" All evaluative thinking implies the use of standards or criteria in determining the eventual decision.

7.3 USING EXTERNAL STANDARDS

While personal standards are based on the individual's experience, the objective use of external standards requires the individual to withhold his or her personal judgment and follow the logic of external criteria. It is like placing oneself in another person's skin to see how he or she would evaluate an issue. For example, "If I were the Republican Congressman from our district, how would I vote on a bill that provided for an expansion of the federal welfare system?" To answer that question I must make explicit the criteria which I think the Congressman would use and apply them to the provisions of the proposed bill. My judgment of the value of the bill and how I would vote are now dependent on the external criteria rather than the personal criteria that I may have built up through my own experience.

In some cases, criteria are determined by the nature of the topic or the form of the literature to be judged. To answer the question, "Is it a narrative poem of literary value?" requires not only that I determine the form of a narrative poem but also that I identify (probably through definition and comparative examples) what I mean by "literary value." Or I can judge the validity of an experiment by noting how well it fits the criteria listed in my science text—hypothesis, control of variables, sufficient number of trials or subjects, appropriate measures, and so on.

In many cases it may be desirable to join personal standards with external standards, but it helps clarify students' evaluative thinking to have them identify external criteria and practice applying them in their reading to decide on the value, the goodness, or the utility of the information and concepts presented.

7.3A ACHIEVING AN EFFECT; PURPOSE AND EXECUTION

Level   Junior high and above.

Objective   To judge whether or not the author achieved his or her purpose; evaluating humor; practice activity.

Description Some types of writing more than others are aimed at achieving specific effects. Humor, horror stories, suspense novels, argumentative and exhortative selections in health and in social studies all fit into the category of writing for effect, as do those works that fall into the literary field, including poetry, narratives, and humor. To make students conscious of these planned effects, they should have practice in identifying the author's intended effect and make a judgment about his or her success in achieving the effect. With writing of that type, then, practice activities first require identification of the special effect intended, then a personal judgment on the part of the reader, and finally a discussion among class members to see how they arrived at their judgments of success or failure.

To take a specific example, have the students work with James Thurber's story, "The Night the Ghost Got In." (Each of the following practice steps could be applied to almost any selection aimed at creating a similar special effect.)

1. Have the students read the first few paragraphs to determine what effect they think the author is trying to establish. What evidence do they cite for the intention they identify?
2. Have them read the story in its entirety.
3. Ask them to recount what they thought was amusing and what they thought was dull. Review the basic line of information: Where did the story take place? How do they know it was near Indianapolis? Can they find signs of regional or unique humor?

4. Do they think the author achieved his purpose? Have several students elaborate on their judgments. How did they reach their conclusions? What contributed to the achievement of the effect? What detracted from the intended effect? Which incident, in their judgment, was the most humorous? What did the writer do to make that incident stand out as the most humorous—for you?

5. There is also a film version of this story. As a follow-up, it might be interesting to show the movie and have the students decide whether the movie or the book version did a better job of developing the intended humor. What made the difference?

More and more, movies and television programs are available for school viewing, and many of them have counterparts in book form, or the scripts from television shows are available from the television networks. This is especially true of programs shown on the Public Broadcasting System. This makes it quite convenient for teachers to ask students to decide whether the book or the television program was more valuable or more effective. In any given case, for example, does the movement, color, and music in television make a stronger emotional impact on the students than do their imaginations working from the printed page? Can they note the differences?

A variety of practice opportunities in different subject areas will reinforce the concept that the more the students watch what the author is trying to do, and the more the students try to interact with the author and the author's techniques, the better their critical reading skills will become.

7.3B JUDGING BUSINESS AND GOVERNMENT

Level   Secondary.

Objective   To show the need for information as part of making critical decisions.

Description   1. It is great public sport to accuse U.S. corporations of making too much money and of gouging the American consumer. In an economics or business education class, conduct a survey of the students to see how much they think corporations make in profits. Begin by discussing the notion of profits in business. A business sells a product to make money, and therefore each dollar of the purchase price has some profit built into it. Usually businesses figure a certain percentage of each dollar as a profit margin.

2. On the chalkboard place the following notation:

American corporations, on the average, make the following percentage of profit:

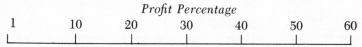

Profit Percentage

| 1 | 10 | 20 | 30 | 40 | 50 | 60 |

Ask the students to draw this figure on a piece of paper and place an *X* on the line to indicate the percentage they think goes for corporate profits.

3. Collect the sheets from each of the students and tally their responses on the diagram on the chalkboard. If their reactions are typical, they will probably guess that profits are above 35 percent.

4. Discuss with them the source of their judgments. They have made a decision about an important institution in the free enterprise system. How did they arrive at their conclusions? Do they think that businesses ought to make as much profit as they think they make? What do they believe is a fair profit rate?

5. After that discussion, have the students read an essay on corporate profits, or, alternatively, read one to them and explain where necessary. They will be surprised that profits for manufacturing corporations hover around 4 to 5 percent. (A good essay is "Corporate Profits," by M. Stanton Evans in *National Review Bulletin,* June 16, 1978.)

6. After reading the essay, ask them what it takes to answer your original question: "What is the percentage of profits made by the average American corporation?" One of the obvious replies should be: "Get some facts." An intelligent decision cannot be made without information. Information is especially critical in matters of economics, science, health, and vocation. Given some reliable information, then a person can think about the second question: "What is a fair profit rate?" And the reader can certainly ask: "Have I been given both pro and con arguments in order to make an intelligent decision?"

7.3C EVALUATING TECHNICAL WRITING

Level   Secondary science and technical subjects.

Objective   To develop objective standards for evaluating technical writing.

Description   1. Students need to realize that there is good and bad technical writing. Ask them what they think makes a technical report, a laboratory report for example, good. They may identify characteristics such as clarity, a well-defined hypothesis, thorough descriptions of the process, accuracy of charts, conclusions that stay within the hypothesis or goal, and so on.

2. Divide the class into groups of four to six students and have each group make a list of at least four criteria they will use to evaluate a laboratory report or some other piece of technical writing.

3. Distribute a report (or have the students use a selection in their text) and ask each group to judge the merits of the selection according to their criteria.

4. A spokesperson for each group should then describe briefly what the group thought of the report that they evaluated.

5. Have each group post their criteria on the bulletin board where they can remain for several weeks as reminders of the need to demand accuracy, clarity, and organization from technical writing as much as from any other type of writing.

7.3D EVALUATING LAB REPORTS

Level   Junior high school and above; science and technical subjects.

Objective   To assess students' ability to judge laboratory reports.

Description   1. Give each student a copy of a laboratory report. Several different reports may be distributed, but there should be no more than four different ones in order to carry on discussions later. It is beneficial to use actual reports written by students in the class.

2. At the top of the sample reports the students should write the criteria they will use in evaluating the report.

3. On a separate sheet of paper, the students should then make a judgment about the report, discussing it in terms of the criteria listed.

4. Collect the evaluations and determine which students know how to establish criteria and use them on this type of writing. Further explanations and demonstrations may be necessary for some students.

5. Return the evaluations to their owners and discuss with them their criteria and judgments. Perhaps listing some of the criteria on the chalkboard will remind the students to use them in their reading and in their own writing of reports. Criteria might include:

   a. clear, simple descriptions
   b. a well-defined hypothesis
   c. step-by-step description of the process
   d. clear conclusions within the bounds of the hypothesis

7.4 A QUESTIONING ATTITUDE

Probably the main reason that teachers ask so many questions of their students is that they hope their students will adopt a similar questioning pattern when reading and thinking about the subject. Related to critical reading–thinking, the teacher wants students to read with a sense of doubt, skepticism, and application. Regarding concepts, opinions, scientific laws, procedures, artistic products, and so on, the teacher asks: "Does it make sense, does it fit, could you use it, would you use it, whom would it benefit, whom would it hurt, is it better than a similar proposal?" and so on. Those types of questions are designed to jar the mind and make the students wrestle with the ideas. As readers, the students are not just to soak up information, but constantly to put it to the test. The teacher's questioning pattern helps the students by reminding them to engage in evaluative thinking while they read.

The burden of developing evaluative thinking should not rest on the teacher's shoulders alone. The students need to become conscious of being active while reading. Thus, for given selections, the teacher tells the students to write in the margins the questions they ask themselves as they read. On a common topic the students and teacher can compare their notations and discuss the manner in which they kept their minds asking critical questions about what the author said. In one sense, the more questions students write, the better critical readers they are. Those who write the most questions might be asked to rethink the selection aloud to indicate the questioning process that took place in their minds.

7.4A DETERMINING AUTHOR'S PURPOSE

Level   Junior high and above.

Objective   Comparison of author's original intention with popular filmed version of work. Motivation and practice.

Description Students need increased ability in determining an author's intention. In the case of ad writers, for example, their words may often veil their intentions. In political and social discourse and in artistic presentations, knowing the purpose of the writer helps the readers understand the message in its proper perspective. Teachers then must alert students to the ways writers use words and techniques to achieve certain purposes. See Chapter 6 and the discussion of slanted writing for additional guidance. This activity is designed to show that the intentions of a writer are not always communicated as the message is delivered in writing and then in film.

    1. Show a rented or videotape version of the original *Frankenstein* film featuring Boris Karloff.

2. Discuss how frightening the monster is. Point out that Boris Karloff was credited for bringing depth to the character and have students point out the displays of human emotion they noted.

3. Have students read the *Frankenstein* novel by Mary Shelley. Discuss the obvious physical differences between the presentations of the two "creatures." Discuss the differences in their degrees of humanity and need for companionship. Again point out instances in the film, such as the girl with the flowers and the man with the violin, comparing them with the book creature's attempts to have a companion creature made.

4. If possible, have students view *The Bride of Frankenstein*.

5. Having viewed the second film, have students work with the differences in the two Dr. Frankensteins. Have them note the descriptions of his "crime" and guilt and determination to rectify it in the book.

6. Have students write their own script for a more literal interpretation of the book.

7. Discuss the film audience that the original films were designed to appeal to. Point out other films made during the 1930s and the need at that time for escapist entertainment. Have students edit their versions to become escapist entertainment and then compare their results with the films they viewed.

8. Some students may have seen the modern spoof, *Young Frankenstein*. This offers another opportunity to show how the author's intention and her use of the language are important factors in reacting critically. The book *Frankenstein* and all these movies operated from the basic idea of a created monster and his interactions with people around him. Considerable differences in effect occur, however, as the author's purpose and language lead the reader–viewer forward.

*7.4B ASKING QUESTIONS WHILE READING

Level   Middle grades and above.

Objective   To encourage students to ask questions constantly while they read.

Description It has been demonstrated frequently that active readers comprehend better than passive readers. The reader who keeps asking questions while reading is more likely to retain information and understand the value of a selection than one who goes through the selection, "absorbing it." The teacher wants to do everything possible, therefore, to promote active reading—to promote a questioning attitude.

1. Distribute the article below, or one that relates more specifically to the subject of the class. Direct the students to write questions in the margins at any point—for more information, for clarification, to satisfy a doubt, to demand proof, to satisfy curiosity, and so on. An article typed in a narrow column, such as a newspaper or magazine column, is useful to promote this behavior at first.

ALLERGY SHOTS AND THE BODY'S REACTION

It is quite common for the human body to develop a sensitivity to substances in the environment, such as pollen from plants, chemicals in foods, and so on. After a while the body's reaction may become severe. It indicates its distaste for the irritant with secretions, such as watery eyes and a skin rash. Hay fever and itching skin are very common reactions to pollen or dust and to hypersensitivity to wool.

When these reactions, called allergies, become strong and are persistent, doctors may recommend that a patient take allergy shots, that is, a chemical solution for hyposensitization. The solution for hyposensitization is obtained by extracting various antigens from their native states. It is standardized according to certain specifications, such as nitrogen content, protein–nitrogen content, or weight of pollen per unit of volume. The initial dosage strength is based on the patient's history and skin test reaction. Each subsequent vial of the solution is more concentrated than the previous one. The goal is to reach the highest dosage and concentration that any particular individual can tolerate in order to impart the most protection against natural offending allergens.

Because the solution injected in the body is concentrated, the body may set up a severe reaction, and precautions must be taken to care for the patient under those circumstances. Here are some routine precautions to be taken:

a. Have the patient remain in the office for twenty minutes after the injection.
b. Observe the site of the injection for any marked swelling or redness: any induration over an inch in diameter is too much.
c. For a severe local reaction (swelling as large as a half-dollar), give an antihistamine: actifed, benadryl.
d. For constitutional reactions (shock, coughing, asthma), inject one-half cc of 1-1000 epinephrine (adrenaline) in the opposite arm; apply tourniquet above site of extract injection; surround the site of extract injection by multiple punctures, using about $-.15$ cc of 1-1000 epinephrine.

When a patient has a severe reaction to an allergy shot, keep him under close observation and hospitalize if it seems necessary.

2. Ask the students for sample questions that they wrote in the

margins. Classify them as need for definitions, additional information, explanation or reason, evaluation. By hand vote, tally the number of questions each student wrote to see what the range is. Generally speaking, the more questions, the more active the reader.

3. It would be helpful to join three or four students into groups to see what their questions were and whether or not they can help each other answer them.

4. In a series of continuing assignments, have the students bring in articles related to the course with questions that they wanted to have answered as they read. A bulletin board display of those articles will keep the idea before the students and remind them to develop the habit of questioning while they read.

7.4C FINDING SOLUTIONS; INFERENCE QUESTIONS

Level   Junior high and above.

Objective   Examination of available information to infer possible solution. Motivation and concept development in asking questions while reading.

Description   Students often do not understand *how* to find solutions to problems they are posed. They have not learned to ask questions and to use clues contained in a selection to infer possible solutions. To help them see the way they are to work with problems in various subject areas, use the example of a mystery story, and how clues are left so the readers can infer the innocence or guilt of several characters.

1. Begin a discussion of popular crime-solvers on television—for example, Columbo and Barnaby Jones—giving students an opportunity to point out their favorites. Add to the list of favorites the unique qualities that students consider important about the characters. Accumulate differences in style and method in reaching the eventual solution. Allow students to point out plot flaws that they noticed in recent episodes they viewed. Add to the list descriptions of characters outside the mainstream of popular television (Hercule Poirot, Perry Mason, Ellery Queen, Sherlock Holmes) and point out the unique aspects of their styles and the methods they used, how they collected and sorted information, and how they discussed or withheld the inferences they were making.

2. Have each student write a summary of his or her favorite recalled episode.

3. Edit and reproduce the summaries. Have students read them and then discuss methods of deduction used by the characters. Look for traits common to detectives. (For one thing, they are

asking questions and making inferences all the time.) Then look for any pattern in episodes chosen. Together, make a quick tally of how many different characters were represented and what the questioning–thinking styles are of those who are most popular.

4. Pass out an unfinished story. (Ready-to-use examples can be found in *Solve a Crime, More Solve a Crime, Bananas,* and *Scope,* all published by Scholastic Books. Any episode of an old rerun can also be used easily in this activity.) Have students read the given information and complete the story.

5. Reproduce or exchange the finished versions and have students read the solutions and select the ones they think are most in keeping with the situation. Have them look for and note the previously listed methods of deduction. Clues and inference-making play similar roles in science problems, social studies problems, and even in math.

6. For enrichment, have students expand an ending, writing the whole story as they think it might appear as an episode of their favorite detective show. Pass out the reproduced versions to be read during a class period.

   Or, have each student set up a situation generating a mystery to be solved and finished. This can be done either with created characters or as a possible script for one of the detectives on television. Have the solutions written separately and make the mysteries into a class version of *Solve a Crime.* In classes other than English, challenge students to create problems which require inference-making and the use of clues in order to develop reasonable solutions.

7. Though mystery stories are usually the province of the English class, the same technique can be applied to other subject areas. Clues to outcomes or conclusions can be found in social studies, health, most science courses, career education, business education, and so on. In science or math, for example, the teacher could create this mystery:

   A spaceship from Earth lost its navigational instruments and did not know where it was when it landed on a planet. The captain estimated they had traveled approximately fifty million miles since leaving Earth. Some of their equipment told them that the atmosphere of the planet was composed of nitrogen, carbon dioxide and water. Where do you think they were?

8. Following the teacher's model, students could then construct mysteries with answers available in their books. The mysteries could be exchanged and solutions discussed in the class.

USING AND EXTENDING READING

Just as the skills of art and science are tools to accomplish something in the real world, so is reading a tool. Teachers need to remind students constantly that reading books enables them to reach out into the real world of ideas and things. To develop a sense of how to use reading, students need practice in extending information from books by predicting, concluding, applying, and using it for problem solving. In a more personal sense, students should also learn to use their emotional responses to reading as a projection of what they read. Thus music, art, dance, and other personal creative activities are legitimate expressions of feelings stimulated by reading. The teacher directs students beyond the printed symbols to extend both the understanding and the richness of a reading experience.

Once the teacher sees that students have a literal grasp of the message in a book or journal, he or she can then ask them to apply or transfer the message to aspects of life beyond that described in the book.

In some ways the teacher will be attempting to help students discover very idiosyncratic information, such as finding out what kind of reading gives them personal pleasure. In other ways the teacher will help students discover general principles about information, for example, how to examine data presented and draw valid conclusions. Both tasks, different as they are, are based on thinking that goes *beyond* the printed symbols.

Good learning situations are structured so that the possibilities for extending that learning are enhanced. Certainly, the thinking of some students will be more divergent than that of others, but this is not an acceptable reason for failing to encourage all students to reach their highest level of use and extension of what they read.

8.1 PREDICTING

Much of our behavior is based on what we predict about a particular situation or outcome. We dress in a certain way because of what we have predicted about the weather. We plan our spending in a certain way because of what we have predicted about our income. Most of our predictions are based on information we collect from print. Readers must be guided in learning to read carefully and analytically so that they will learn to make accurate predictions from their reading.

Since having information about what is likely to occur makes us better able to deal with that event, prediction has always been an important part of people's lives and thinking. Great honor and reverence have been awarded to prophets or those who predicted well. In ancient times this ability to predict well was held in such awe that it was usually believed that such skill must have come from a supernatural force. Today the desire for predictions continues to be strong as seen in the great interest in astrologists and futurists. At high business, educational, and governmental levels we find people who use sophisticated statistical and data collection systems to forecast trends in every area of our lives. Prediction even enters the arena of recreation—Jimmy the Greek's predictions on the outcome of sporting events determine how thousands of dollars are wagered every week.

If we are unwilling to accept the ancient notion that some people simply have direct contact with the gods, or the science-fiction theories of informational encounters with outer world sources, we must look for reasons why some people are able to predict better than others.

REASONS FOR ACCURATE PREDICTING

Obviously, some people are older than others and thus have the advantage of time. Yet not all older people predict better than younger people. Some people are smarter than others and thus have the edge provided by superior intelligence. Yet not all people whom we believe to be intelligent make good predictors. Some people read faster than others and thus process more information. Yet not all fast readers are perfect predictors. The list could go on, but the fact that some people are able to use information more effectively emerges clearly from any list of this kind that we can make.

What teachers must do is provide the students with guidance and practice in the effective use of the information they have so that they can employ that information to foretell other information or events.

Students need to learn to make informed guesses (trial hypotheses) about possible solutions or outcomes. Then they need to learn systematic means of selecting the best choice or choices from those alternatives. The teacher's emphasis should be directed to assisting them with the thoughtful development of alternatives and careful analysis of the data presented.

*8.1A PREDICTING OUTCOMES AND SOLUTIONS

Level   Middle grades and above.

Objective   To give students practice in an organized analytical process for predicting outcomes and solutions.

Description   1. Select a piece of material that leaves the solution in doubt or the question raised unanswered. Social studies and science classes may want to select materials that are not highly controversial for the first attempt to work with this activity. After the students understand the process, it is well-suited for controversial issues, but to use such issues first would likely put excessive emphasis on the content rather than on the process.
2. Ask the students to read the material prior to the class.
3. Briefly discuss the material with the students to determine that they understood the selection.
4. When you are certain the material was understood, distribute the Prediction Worksheet in Figure 8–A to the class.

Figure 8–A

PREDICTION WORKSHEET

1. What is the problem? (What do I need or want to know that I do not know?)
2. Is only one answer, outcome, or solution possible?
3. Is only one answer, outcome, or solution desirable?
4. Was there information in the print that led me to believe my answers to 3. and 4.? If yes, indicate what that was.

Yes _____   No _____

5. If there was no information in the print that led me to the answers in 3. and 4., what *did* suggest the response to me? (Something I'd read before? My own knowledge of such events or things?)
6. What was my immediate or common-sense answer to the question or solution to the problem?
7. What information in the print, if any, would lead me to *limit* or *eliminate* my reliance on first response or common-sense logic here?
8. If there is other information, what responses does that information suggest?
   a.
   b.
   c.
9. In what two ways could I reconcile my answers in 7. and my answers in 8. for a trial solution?
   a.
   b.
10. In which of the two trial solutions in 9. do I have the most confidence?
11. What are the reasons for my choice?
    a.
    b.
    c.

5. Work through the worksheet step by step with the students.
6. Entertain *all* ideas presented, but prod the students to present some logical bases for their ideas. As the students have more practice with the process, you might even consider asking them to preface their ideas with the reasons. For example, "Because X happened, I believe Y is a good prediction here."
7. Continue to use the worksheet for predicting outcomes and solutions either as a homework study director or as an in-class activity.

*8.1B CHARTING OUTCOMES AND SOLUTIONS

Level   Middle grades and above.

Objective   To give students practice in an organized analytical process for predicting outcomes and solutions.

Description
1. Select a piece of material that leaves the solution in doubt or the question raised unanswered. Social studies and science classes may want to select materials that are not highly controversial for the first attempt to work with this activity. After the students understand the process, it is well-suited for controversial issues, but to use such issues first would likely put excessive emphasis on the content rather than on the process.
2. Ask the students to read the material prior to the class.
3. Briefly discuss the material with the students to determine that they understood the selection.
4. When you are certain the material was understood, distribute the Prediction Chart in Figure 8–B (see p. 170) to the class.
5. Work through the chart step by step with the students.
6. Entertain *all* ideas presented, but prod the students to present some logical bases for their ideas. As the students have more practice with the process, you might even consider having them preface their ideas with their reasons. For example, "Because X happened, I believe Y is a good prediction here."
7. Continue to use the chart for predicting outcomes and solutions either as a homework study director or as an in-class activity as the material and student need warrant.

8.1C DETERMINING OUTCOMES

Level   Middle grades and above.

Objective   To help students develop habits of picking up an author's clues and be able to infer outcomes to stories.

Description
1. Select an interesting story which ends with a few "loose ends," that is, a story where the author does not tell what finally

Figure 8–B

PREDICTION CHART

PROBLEM (What don't I know that I want or need to know?)		
A Common-Sense Solution	*An Unusual Solution*	*Another Solution*
Place check by final choice.	*Combination* **TRIAL SOLUTION ONE**	
	Combination **TRIAL SOLUTION TWO**	
REASONS FOR FINAL CHOICE 1. 2. 3. 4.		

happens to the protagonist or does not reveal how the hero actually gets along after the climax. Either read this aloud or assign it as homework and ask students to write a "P.S." to clue the reader in on the ending. Students can compare answers to see which conclusions seem to fit the facts of the story most logically.

2. Read aloud an interesting story and stop at intervals, asking the students to jot down quickly what they think will happen next. A particularly good story for this purpose is "The Final Ingredient" by Jack Sharkey.

3. Extend a favorite story. Using the clues the author has provided

about the setting, plot, or characters, ask students to write follow-up pieces to the literature. An excellent source would be the novel *Acorn People*, by Ron Jones, or the abridged version published in the March 16, 1978 *Scholastic Scope* magazine. After reading, the students might plan a party or reunion for the group in the novel, complete with guest list, logical activities, menu, and so on. Or, ask students to write a letter from one character to another, dated after the time of the book.

8.1D COMPARING FACTS TO PREDICT OUTCOMES

Level   Secondary school.

Objective   To aid students in making real-life decisions and evaluations by comparing the experiences of several similar people, with an emphasis on inferring valuable lessons.

Description This lesson deals with literature about sports. Three stories consider the theme of the aging athlete whose early glory and success on the field were never quite matched in later years.

1. Ask students to read aloud in class the Jason Miller play *That Championship Season*. For some students, the teacher may want to edit the language. Discuss the causes and effects of the victory in these men's lives both as teenagers and as adults.

2. Tell students they are going to read another work somewhat similar to that play, the story "The 80-Yard Run," by Irwin Shaw. Before reading it, ask students to form notions of what to look for in the story, based on the title and the previously read play. Jot down these expectations, perhaps in question form. After reading the story, compare the two presentations of the plot.

3. The Jack London story "A Piece of Steak" offers a slight variation on the theme of the aging athlete, bringing in some sociological and psychological aspects of the role of sports in current times. Based on the two earlier experiences, ask students to decide on some relevant areas of study as they read or hear this story—that is, predict what might happen and why. They might be prepared to pose such questions as:

> What was the scope of the early success?
> How did it affect his lifestyle?
> How do (did) people react to him?
> Was the early success worth the "coming down"?
> What about the lives of the men in these stories caused the unfortunate endings?
> At what points along the way might the protagonist have averted personal disaster?

4. Relate these fictional situations to real-life problems: for instance, should Little League and vigorous high school competition be curtailed, eliminated, or altered in some other way? Should professional athletes make so much money? How would you handle a professional athletic career?

5. After setting the stage with these sports stories, students may want to look at current real-life sports with a new perspective:

> Choose an "old" athlete for study. How has his experience been alike or different from these fictional heroes? Select some whose lives have had poor endings: Jack Johnson, Joe Louis, and Willie Mays are examples of athletes who hit the big-time, but ended up penniless and without any significant role to play in society. Look at their histories, watching for the reasons for their downfalls. Compare them with athletes who ended glorious careers with dignity and professional growth ahead: Bob Mathias, Jesse Owens, John Wooden, Byron "Whizzer" White. What was different about these men, their careers, or their opportunities which resulted in happy endings?

6. Watch over a period of several weeks or months the careers of recently retired athletes or those about to retire. As the students watch, urge them to keep several pertinent points in mind. Students should select their own points, but they might include, for example:

> How does the behavior of the athlete indicate his reluctance about or acceptance of retirement from the public eye?
> What preparations has he made for a new career?
> What can you deduce about the financial, social, or emotional well-being of the athlete?

After reporting on these or other factors, the students should be asked to make a prognosis for the athlete's post-athletic success.

Examples of current athletes at or near retirement are:

Bill Bradley
John Havlicek
Billie Jean King
O. J. Simpson

*8.1E. PREDICTING FROM EVIDENCE

Level   Middle grades and above.

Objective   To provide students directed practice with predicting outcomes and solutions.

Description   1. Provide students with a ditto copy of a detective or mystery story from which you have omitted the ending.

2. After they have read the selection, put the Prediction Chart in Figure 8–B on the chalkboard and have the entire class work together completing it.
3. In the next class, or in another period, if necessary, divide the class into four teams. Pair weak and strong readers on the teams.
4. Provide the students with another open-ended detective or mystery story, but this time have each team of students follow the chart to predict the outcome.
5. Allow each team to report and defend its conclusion or solution.
6. Provide students with a copy of the chart to use on their own for a guide to directed prediction.

Note: Advanced home economics classes would enjoy a variation of this activity. Give them a recipe from which one ingredient is missing and ask them to predict the outcome. Have them work through the chart just as the students did with the mystery stories. Physical education classes might enjoy an article about a sports event that leaves the end of the event in doubt.

*8.1F PREDICTING ENDINGS; COMICS

Level   Middle grades and above.

Objective   To provide students with practice in considering information that will predict outcomes.

Description   Most middle school students read comic strips. Even slow readers can obtain some information and entertainment from the print and pictures found here. Almost all students have one or two favorite strips which they follow regularly and you can begin with those.

1. Ask the students to cut out several comic strips that they have read and to bring these to class. Ask the students to cut the final frame from each strip they bring and to put the two pieces (the first three or four frames *plus* the final frame) into an envelope. The envelope does not need to be a new one, but there should be one for each strip.
2. Collect the strips several days in advance of the time you wish to work with them so that the mechanics of collection and distribution will be lessened on the day you wish to use the activity.
3. Divide the class into groups of four or five.
4. Provide each group of students with an envelope from which you have removed the final frame. (Code each final frame and strip with either a color, a number, or a letter for easy match-up identification.)
5. Ask the students to predict what the final frame was.
6. After they have had a few minutes to discuss and determine their answer, give them a second envelope; then give them a third envelope.

7. After the student groups have finished their predictions, provide them with the final frames which the cartoonist developed.
8. Poll the groups to determine whether any of the groups and cartoonists developed the same or similar endings. *You* can predict at least two or three will be the same.
9. Have the groups which did develop the same ending as the cartoonist describe the comic strip and the ending.
10. Ask the group to tell the class some of the reasons for their prediction of the last frame.
11. List their reasons on the board.
12. Discuss their reasons as kinds of information which one uses to predict outcomes and solutions.
13. Attempt to have the class generalize their application of these reasons to the other print areas in which they would like to predict.

8.2 CONCLUDING

The reader arrives at a conclusion only partially on the basis of the multiple facts and pattern of reasoning presented by the writer. Arriving at a conclusion from reading material presented is an analytical and interpretive process. The readers link together the information found in the print itself with the extended meanings they bring to it and construct meanings from their own ideas and experiences. In aiding students to draw conclusions from their reading, the teacher builds from the operations of analysis and the evaluation of facts and ideas.

There are two kinds of conclusions secondary students are presented in their reading. In one kind the writer *tells* the readers what he or she believes the conclusion to be. The reader must affirm or deny what the writer has decided.

In the second kind, the reader is presented with information and then is asked to *develop* a conclusion.

Both types of conclusions require the students to have a literal grasp of such things as the main idea or ideas, the sequencing or ordering of those ideas, and the details or examples in the text that support the ideas presented. Both also require the students to make decisions based on what the print provides. In the first case, the students must accept or reject. In the second case, the students must select from the alternatives there or those they can develop, and settle for the one which seems to square most with the information the print has provided and their own experience.

It seems reasonable to allow adolescent readers to suggest and support a variety of conclusions. Very often the bases for their conclusions may be as sound as the ones on which the teacher or textbook has rested his/her/its decision. The presidential campaigns waged and subsequent elections held every four years in this country are ample testimony to at least two possible conclusions to be drawn from large amounts of evidence presented.

ADJUSTING TO ABILITIES

In teaching students to draw conclusions, the secondary teacher is faced with a wide range of student abilities. For some students, the teacher will have to begin his or her instruction at quite a literal level. These students are only ready to take the next step after finding main ideas and must be taught to locate and identify the conclusion even when it is stated.

Secondary subject matter presents a second problem in teaching students to draw conclusions. Information presented in a poem and information presented in the description of a chemical experiment provide quite different print signals to the students as they direct them toward conclusions. The subject area teacher must explain how conclusions are generally presented in his or her specific field. Then, with a set of questions, the teacher can guide student thinking through reaching conclusions. Using these questions as a series of steps serves to direct the students' *own* thinking rather than attempting to *control* that thinking to conform *always* to that of the teacher or the author. A sample set of such questions follows:

QUESTION SERIES

(When A Conclusion Is Presented)

1. What did the writer conclude?
   (see Section 6.2 also)
2. Was the writer's information reliable?
   (see Section 6.1 also)
3. Was the writer's reasoning logical?
   (see Section 6.3 also)
4. What exists in my own personal experience, information base, or thinking that can support the author's conclusion?
5. What exists in my own personal experience, information base, or thinking that rejects the author's conclusion?
6. If I must reject the conclusion, what is a source on which I could rely to suggest a way to reconcile my conclusion and that of the author?
7. If I know of no source, where could I find information about locating one? (A librarian, a teacher, a book, and so on.)

QUESTION SERIES

(When No Single Conclusion Is Presented)

1. Is a conclusion about the matter or material presented *necessary* or is it really an issue which should be open-ended at this time?
2. Is a conclusion *possible* with the personal information I presently possess and that which is provided in the print for me? (If the answer here is *no*, locate the other resources before continuing.)
3. If a conclusion is necessary and possible, what are some conclusions the material presented would suggest and support?

Possible *Conclusion*	*Support from* *the Reading*
a. (For instance, "The matter cannot be resolved now.")	(For instance, "A recent national study quoted here says so.")
b.	
c.	

4. If a conclusion is necessary and possible, what are some conclusions my own personal experience, information base, and thinking would support or suggest?

Possible *Conclusion*	*Personal* *Support*
a. (For instance, "The answer is that more sports activity is needed.")	(For instance, "My experience as a camper at three different camps supports it.")
b.	
c.	

5. Is there a conclusion that has *support* in *both* 3. and 4.?
6. Is that overlapping conclusion satisfactory or do I need to explore more alternatives? (If more alternatives are needed, continue to repeat 3. and 4. until a satisfactory conclusion is determined.)

*8.2A VOCABULARY AS A SIGNAL TO CONCLUSIONS

Level   Middle grades and above.

Objective   To identify key or signaling words that alert and direct the readers to the stated conclusions.

Description   1. As an introduction to the activity, ask the students to list some signals they use to help themselves every day. You can prod their discussion with such things as stop and go lights, school bells, traffic signs, automobile brake lights, and so on. (Make your list as subject-specific as possible. For example, in home economics and chemistry you could use the skull and crossbones as the poison symbol.)
2. List the signals on the chalkboard with the responses they evoke beside them.
3. Ask the students to take out their books and identify some signals they follow in their reading. They will likely list capital letters, punctuation marks, and so on.
4. Suggest to the students that certain words can also be signals. If you believe they are at a level where they could locate such words, ask them to find some examples. If they are not reading at that level, begin this step by asking them what such words as "secondly" might signal to the readers. (It would tell them there had been a "firstly" and that they are reading a list or material with a sequence of some sort.)

5. After you have pointed out several signaling words in the students' books, discuss with them how such words can help the readers understand the print.
6. If the students are able, ask them to think of words that would signal to them that they were at the most important part of the print and should read with even more care than they usually do. If you need to identify these words for them, you should begin by calling them *concluding signals*. They should locate in their texts, list, and have some practice using at least the following terms:

as a result	consequently
in the end	therefore
in total	at last
finally	in conclusion

7. You will want to point out the special words related to your field which signal concluding information. For example, in mathematics, *so that* is an important concluding signal; in chemistry, *the results are* is an important concluding signal; in art, a reference to *totality* is an important signal.
8. As you encounter new concluding signal words in the students' reading, particularly if those words are subject-specific, you should call them to the students' attention. Using a continuing chart or a permanent list on the chalkboard would also assist you in making the students aware of these helpful terms.

*8.2B DIVERGENT THINKING IN CONCLUSIONS

Level   Middle grades and above.

Objective   To provide opportunity, encouragement, and practice for students to develop highly divergent conclusions to reading material which has left the conclusion open or in doubt.

Description   1. Choose a reading selection that leaves the conclusion up to the readers. Locate one in the students' textual material if possible. Examples of some topical materials that would lend themselves easily are the effect of food additives in home economics classes, bioethical questions in biology and chemistry classes, problems with more than one answer in senior high mathematics classes, welfare funding issues in social science classes, consumer protection practices in vocational classes, and so on.
2. Ask the students to read the material and develop a conclusion *a.* that they believe no one else will select, and *b.* that can be supported in some way or ways from the material presented.
3. Since many students are used to trying to *anticipate* what the

teacher is likely to *want* them to say, you may need to take some time to assure them that you have not *already* decided anything. If it is an accelerated class, you often will have a number of "grade worriers," so you will probably need to work through an example with them before they will be very comfortable about not trying to "second-guess" you.

4. After the students have each developed a conclusion, put them in groups of no more than four or five and let them share their ideas.

5. After everyone has had an opportunity to share, ask them to build on the most interesting conclusion that emerged from their group or ask them to arrive at a consensus idea by using a collection of the conclusions presented.

6. Have each group share its "super" conclusion and the supports for it.

7. Periodically, present opportunities for students to engage in this kind of divergent thinking activity with material about which several conclusions can be drawn.

8.2C DRAWING SUPPORTABLE CONCLUSIONS

Level   Junior high and above.

Objective   To provide students direction and practice in selecting supportable conclusions.

Description
1. Choose a selection from either your textual material or subject-related articles in a newspaper to which all the students have access. (Having everyone bring the same newspaper from time to time gives some variety to the material, and finding subject-related material in the newspaper adds a dimension of reality to the classroom and study that is very appealing to most secondary students.)

2. Have everyone read the same selection and develop three possible conclusions from their reading.

3. Have the students each write down their conclusions without indicating which one they feel the most confident about.

4. Ask the students to find a partner, exchange conclusions with him or her, and mark the conclusions as *a.* correct, *b.* partially correct, or *c.* not a possible conclusion from the facts and evidence presented in the material.

5. Have the partners discuss their ratings and defend them to each other on the basis of evidence they can point out in the material.

6. After there is some agreement between the partners around the room, put representative conclusions on the chalkboard from

each category and discuss the evidence in the print to support the ratings given each.

7. Next, have each student read a different passage. (Here, the newspaper is easier to use than the textbook.)

8. After everyone has read a passage, have them again develop three conclusions. In this step, direct the students to deliberately write a conclusion that is *not* supported by the material.

9. Have the students again exchange with their partners the passages and conclusions for reading and rating.

10. After everyone has read and rated, have the "developer" check and discuss with the "rater." (You can begin to see that confusion is lessened here if the students are paired as partners rather than passing papers back and forth to several people.)

11. As a follow-up, from time to time ask the students to develop "sets" of conclusions about material they have read and exchange these with members of the class for rating and discussion.

8.2D ARGUMENTATION FOR DRAWING CONCLUSIONS

Level   Secondary.

Objective   To provide students with an awareness that conclusions drawn in formal situations and argumentation follow the same process as those drawn in their regular reading, and to provide the students with some practice in arriving at such formal conclusions.

Description   At some point in most secondary social studies curricula, the process of the formal court case and argument is covered by the students. In most English, speech, and humanities classes, formal argument is also taught. To add another dimension to these two topics, the teacher can take the opportunity to *emphasize* to the students that the conclusion process here (reasoning from known facts and evidence) is only a more formalized case of the operation they perform when they arrive at conclusions in their regular reading. The teacher can do this by using any of the following suggestions:

1. Simply discuss with the students the idea that arriving at a conclusion from regular reading is the same process as coming to a judgment when formal arguments are presented.

2. Have the students act out a particular case and arrive at a conclusion. (They would be functioning as a jury.)

3. Have the students prepare formal arguments for review and discussion by the class.

8.3 EMOTIONAL AND CREATIVE RESPONSES:

One of our most persistent myths is that *feelings* have no place in secondary instruction. Even though we periodically have a round of popular books that implore us to make the school a more sensitive and humanistic place, they surface and disappear with little more permanent impact than waves on the sand. We continue our nonaffective instruction as before without caring much about, or certainly not encouraging, any kind of emotional response to the material we present. Home economics classes respond with no anger when the products they purchase are not what they were advertised to be. We avoid any sensitive reactions students make to battered children when we discuss such problems in social studies classes. In biology classes we seek to make abortion a totally clinical issue. We *even* take poetry and spend entire periods analyzing and critiquing the lines without any attention at all to what the students felt.

Personal emotional responses should be a routine part of discussing reading.

This state of affairs is strange indeed, since when one talks with avid out-of-school readers, they usually report that the greatest percentage of their reading time is spent with print from which they receive emotional satisfaction. Perhaps one reason we have no more avid out-of-school readers than we do could be that they have had so few emotionally satisfying experiences with reading *in* school, they are unconvinced that they can do so on their *own*.

Since the reading attitudes and behaviors that young children see in their homes have a great influence on their own reading attitudes and performance in school, it is important that the school produce readers who will continue with their reading once they are no longer in school. Otherwise, as the children of these former students become students, reluctant readers will continue to plague us.

TIME FOR PLEASURE

For many secondary teachers, allowing students to "read for pleasure" seems to be a waste of "valuable instructional time." The lament is that there is so little time to teach chemistry and verb tenses, how can the teacher *add* on something more? The notion of *addition* is the problem here. We do not ever suggest that the teacher do any of the activities in *addition* to his or her content instruction; they are designed to be used as a *part* of it. Obviously, not every problem-solving session in mathematics will lend itself to escape or delight. However, working through the print explanation of a novel or an exciting proof in mathematics brings a response from the students. "Wasn't it *exciting*? Weren't you *angry* when you saw how the number was manipulated? Didn't you feel *embarrassed* when you saw the way the last figure made it seem so simple?" All of these are legitimate reactions to the mathematics print. By encouraging or allowing such responses, the math teacher is saying that something happens, or can happen, when one reads the print and goes *beyond* simple receipt of information.

CREATIVE RESPONSES

Some of the finest protest music and painting of this century came out of the creator's responses to *reading* about a war, a social condition, and so on. Yet, in most secondary classrooms, creative response to *any* reading is so unlikely that the teacher who said, "Let's draw a picture or make up a song about the new welding regulations, (or anything else)" would undoubtedly be reported to the principal, taken to the nurse, or described throughout the building as "nuts." At the very least, the teacher's colleagues would say he or she "wasted time," "had no academic integrity," and "thought this place was kindergarten." After the shock was over, the "nutty" teacher, however, might also have students who were eager to *read* what he or she assigned because there might be *something* (besides a test) to "do" with it.

The point of all this is that there *is something* for students to "do" with reading besides take a test over it. Maybe another reason more people do not read after they are out of school is that nobody is giving them a test over it. And, just maybe *we* are responsible for making them think that that is the only valid response to reading.

If every content teacher will occasionally provide opportunities for students to respond creatively to the reading assigned, the students will begin to feel different about reading.

*8.3A EMOTIONAL RESPONSE TO BOOKS

Level Middle grades and above.

Objective To provide students with opportunities to identify their feelings about reading material and report them to others.

Description 1. For all the reasons discussed in the introduction to this section, seldom is there an occasion or an opportunity for students to do any sharing about reading they have found enjoyable or satisfying. "Has anybody read any good books?" is unlikely to elicit much of a response from students, since there is a notion that teachers are not going to approve of anything but "classics" anyhow. We would, however, hope that almost every student has had at least one moving experience with print.[1]

Discussion may reveal that the students have identified some *kinds* of print they like, such as happy stories, sad stories, and so on. You are well-served by beginning the discussion with questions directed to *kinds* of ways they feel about certain reading. The students very likely will *not* tell you immediately; remember, nobody talks much about feelings in secondary schools! Consequently, you will probably need to share some of

---

[1] If your students read so poorly you suspect this may not be true in your class, you may want to use movies or television shows from which the students have found satisfaction to begin this activity. You would then be establishing "creative work" as a source of satisfaction, with the hope that this could be expanded to cover print as you progressed with the students.

your own feelings about things you have read to begin the discussion.

2. Suggest that the students list some of the ways they feel after reading. You could prod them with the following:

> bored
> happy
> angry
> sad
> excited
> nostalgic

3. Ask for any material the students have personally read that might go under each category. (Be cautious about being thought judgmental at this point. The students are determining if you *really* want to *know* what they feel and think.)

4. Make a permanent chart of their information and post it in the room.

5. Encourage the students to add everything they read on their own for the class to one of the categories so other students will have the benefit of their assessment and feeling about the material.

6. When the students write the name of the material, have them put their initials beside it. This way others can contact them for further discussion if they would like to do so.

7. If space permits, have a place where the students can post magazine and newspaper clippings, announcements, and advertising under categories also. Ones you might want to set up here could be:

> It Made Me Mad!
> It Made Me Happy!
> It Made Me Laugh!
> It Made Me Sad.
> It Made Me Sick!
> It Made Me Feel Better!

8. Initially, you could post a few items yourself, but be careful not to monopolize the boards. You want student response to their reading, not your own.

*8.3B REPORTING FEELINGS ABOUT READING

Level   Middle grades and above.

Objective   To provide the students with opportunities to identify their feelings about reading material and report them to others.

Description This activity is patterned after the biorhythm charts that the students read in newspapers to chart their biorhythms.

1. Engage the students in a discussion of material they have read recently in your content area. Encourage them to speak freely about their feelings. Be very careful not to be judgmental about their comments. They will initially be testing you to determine if you *really* do think that what they *feel* is consequential.
2. When you determine the students are comfortably sharing their real feelings about their reading, suggest they try to find a quick way to chart their feelings so they can share them with others.
3. Supply them with some biorhythm charts you have clipped from old newspapers. Ask them to think about ways they might construct a "Read-o-rhythm Chart" to chart their real feelings about particular pieces of reading material.

   You might show them the example in Figure 8–C. You could have a ditto copy for them or just draw it on the chalkboard.

Figure 8–C

READ-O-RHYTHM CHART

Title:

		Plot	Theme	Characters	Setting
Intellectual (ideas)	5 4 3 2 1				
Emotional (feelings)	5 4 3 2 1				
Physical (difficulty)	5 4 3 2 1				

Read-o-rhythm Readout:

0–5	Negative	Look For Something Else
8–10	Neutral	Toss a Coin
11–15	Positive	*Get This Book!*

4. Divide the students into groups of four or five and let them work out a group chart along with the meanings of their ratings.
5. Let each group put its chart and rating on the chalkboard and explain it.
6. Determine the Read-o-rhythm Chart the class prefers.
7. Make copies of the chart and ratings and leave an easily accessible supply of them available for the students.
8. Ask the students to fill one out and post it after they have read material that they think others might like to know more about.
9. The Read-o-rhythm Charts will a. create some interest in how the students feel about their material, and b. suggest materials to others.

*8.3C IDENTIFYING PERSONALLY SATISFYING READING

Level   Middle grades and above.

Objective   To assist students in developing a collection of reading resources to which they can go for assistance or satisfaction when dealing with their feelings and problems.

Description   There is a growing body of literature which describes the usefulness of helping students solve their problems through reading about others with similar circumstances and problems. Some excellent annotated general lists of materials exist for directing students to reading which relates to specific problems and concerns. These lists provide helpful information to the teacher who has not read widely in materials related to adolescent development. If you fall into this category, an excellent list with which to begin your reading can be found in *Developmental Reading in Middle and Secondary Schools* by Lawrence Hafner, Macmillan Publishing Company, 1977, pp. 330–341. It is, of course, characteristic of such general lists to be *need–* rather than *content-area–specific*, and teachers will have to select from such lists to make recommendations to students in their content areas. Since such recommendations would be made to students on the basis of their acknowledgment or your perception of some need or problem, it would matter very little whether you were their mathematics or English teacher who was making a recommendation. Since the kind of list we are suggesting should be developed would almost certainly *not* come from a mathematics, vocational arts, or physics class, we would suggest that those teachers who do develop such materials should make every effort to share them with teachers in other content areas. Keep in mind that the following activity is a developing one, and you should not anticipate having an extensive list immediately. It should also be thought of as a list that would never be "finished," as you would want to encourage students to continue to contribute to it.

1. Explain to the students that you would like to develop a list of reading materials that you could recommend to other students to help them with particular problems, feelings, interests, or needs. Tell the students that it is important to both you and the students to whom the material would be recommended that you have real confidence in the quality of the list and its appropriateness for students in *your* school. Explain that you would like to annotate and post it and add to it over the years. Explain further that anything you put on the list would be there *only* as a result of a *student* recommendation.

2. Ask the class to be prepared to "tell about" something they have read that was particularly helpful or satisfying to them. Attach no other official criteria to their choices, but point out that this is not a "shock the teacher" game in which they try to bring in material from sources that they really would be uncomfortable about recommending to their friends. (If you have a class that is likely to bring thirty copies of an X-rated magazine, you may need to make this point strongly. Approaching the assignment in a serious way generally prevents anything like this, but not always.)

3. Ask that anyone who has nothing to report see you. For those students who come to see you, ask them to simply think back about reading material as far as they can and allow them to report something from the past. For those who you honestly believe have never had a satisfying reading experience, simply respect their dilemma and allow them to listen to the rest of the class.

4. Have the students report their selections, engage in a discussion of their recommendations, and begin a list.

5. Post the list and encourage anyone who elects to read anything from the list to add his own comment if he wishes. Leave a large envelope and a package of three-by-five cards near the posted list. The students can then write their comments and drop them in the envelope at any convenient time. You can periodically take the comments from the envelope and add them to the annotations that are already there.

*8.3D CREATIVE RESPONSE TO READING

Level   Middle grades and above.

Objective   To encourage the students to respond to printed material in a medium other than answering questions about it, and to provide the students with the opportunity to experience some delight in their response to reading material.

Description 1. Ask the students to discuss some ways in which they might share information without responding to written questions about the information. Urge them to go beyond "talking about" it or "drawing a picture" of it.

2. Often the students have had very little (perhaps no) experience in creative responses to reading, so they may need to work in pairs or groups initially. This way they can support and assist each other's ideas. If a group idea shared with the class is not well-received, one student does not feel the degree of personal rejection he or she would have as an individual.

3. Provide the students each with a selection to read or indicate particular passages in their texts. The material could be anything you would prefer, but exciting or moving newspaper or literature passages are always good.

4. Since it is unlikely that music or art supplies are available in your content area classroom, ask the students to *describe* how they might give you information about their reading.

5. After the groups have read and made their decisions as to the way they would prefer to provide information to others about the material they have just read, have them share their ideas with the class.

6. As a second phase of the activity, you might want to provide each member of each group with a piece of newsprint and ask him or her to tear it or draw on it to provide information about the passage he or she has read. This is generally a noisy, messy activity, but it is a valuable way to "open up" the students' ideas about a variety of responses.

7. Again, let the groups present a single response and share that with the class.

8. Over the year, encourage and provide occasional opportunities for students to develop creative responses to their reading.

8.3E RESPONDING TO BOOKS THROUGH MUSIC, ART

Level   Junior high and above.

Objective   To encourage the student to respond to printed material in a medium other than answering questions about it, and to provide the student with the opportunity to experience some delight in his response to reading material.

Description   Rock music and poster art are important parts of the lives of virtually all adolescents. Someone has jokingly suggested that if the content of physics could be put into rock music or placed on posters, every adolescent in America would become expert in the field. There is enough truth in the remark for us to examine the possibilities with some seriousness. The next activities suggest that you use those two popular media as creative ways for students to respond to reading. You could do any of the following:

1. Have class groups take a popular rock tune and change the words to report about a selection they have just read. (They will need to determine the main idea or theme, of course, before they begin.)
2. Have each group perform the number, if possible, with music "backing them up."
3. Have more creative or musical students compose a rock number about some reading they have done and then perform the music for the class.
4. Have students select rock music which they think relates to reading they are doing and bring it to the class or suggest it to their classmates.
5. Compose and practice rock lyrics for reading material that must be memorized.
6. Have students bring their favorite non–pin-up poster and invite them to discuss how the picture or message relates to something the group has read.
7. Encourage the students to make posters about material they are reading.
8. Keep a number of posters displayed around the room and tape a sheet below each that lists reading selections that relate to the themes of the posters.

8.4 READING AND PROBLEM SOLVING

In their continuing attempts to place themselves in the real world, adolescents want to know the real-world value of the books and ideas with which they are presented. For that reason, one of the best techniques schools have for demonstrating the value of a subject is to have the students solve problems through their reading assignments. As a generalized technique or through the specific means of comparison and contrast, predicting and concluding, and other analytic functions, problem solving enables every subject matter teacher to engage students in active learning beyond the printed message.

Those subjects that have labs built into the course should do problem-solving reading almost as a matter of routine. The teacher has to refrain from the trap of personally providing the students with all the information and directions that they need. The teacher should place himself in the role of being a guide and interpreter of the text, not a substitute for the text. In other subjects, such as English, social studies, and mathematics, the teacher has to create circumstances where problem solving makes sense; that is, the teacher stimulates interest and provides a valuable opportunity to read and analyze the reading to solve the problem.

*8.4A PROBLEM SOLVING: SCIENCE

Level   Middle grades and above.

Objective   To provide experiences in the sciences which promote students' critical observation and interpretation of phenomena.

Description Ask the students to read an unusual article or chapter and keep a running list of the incredible statements, potential fallacies, or possible explanations for the strange events. Recently magazines have published many such articles—for example, about the amazing powers of the pyramid-shaped container. A search of the *Guide to Periodical Literature* will reveal many articles at various levels of erudition, among them a simply written article called "The Mystery of Pyramid Powers," *Read Magazine*, Xerox Corporation, Fall, 1977. This article describes, among other things, how vegetables left in pyramid-shaped containers stay fresh much longer than vegetables left in containers of other shapes. After students have made their lists, they can compare them with the other students to gather a full range of questions and speculations. After discussion of these points, the students may try the following:
1. Replicate the experiments cited in the article, keeping a detailed journal of all conditions and observations which may account for the results. Compare journals of several students to see if any explanation arises.
2. Devise other experiments using the supposed powers of the pyramid and keep a journal. Compare results.
3. Ask the librarian for more information on this phenomenon to see what insights this adds.

8.4B PROBLEM SOLVING: LITERATURE

Level   Junior high and above.

Objective   To encourage students to be mindful of an author's clues as they read mysteries or particularly obscure pieces of literature.

Description How often students reach the end of a "whodunit" and are completely amazed at the solution, or read a strange short story and cannot make heads or tails of it. The following ideas may help students be on the lookout for the foreshadowing a skillful author sprinkles along the way to the story's resolution.

1. Begin with short pieces and read them aloud with expression. Warn students in advance that you are selecting the weirdest stories you can find and they are to write a one-sentence explanation at the end. The stories of Ambrose Bierce or the science fiction of Frederic Brown are especially useful for this practice. For shorter versions at easier reading levels the teacher can look to the rewritten versions of many of these authors' works published in *Scholastic Scope* magazine of October 27, 1977, and April 20, 1978. If not available, a teacher can "edit" a long or difficult story by quickly penciling through unneeded descriptive portions and changing some vocabulary before reading aloud. At the end simply ask, "What happened?"

2. Many short mysteries are on the market for this purpose. *Scholastic Scope* magazine has as a regular feature the "Mini-Mystery" which is a five- or six-paragraph detective story in which the hero amazingly finds the "bad guy," but leaves how he deduced the solution for the student to figure out. An added advantage of this feature is that many of the "Mini-Mysteries" are submitted by students. The class may have fun trying to come up with a publishable mystery of its own. In addition, bookstores commonly carry paperbacks which are page after page of similar short riddles or mysteries.

3. Giving away the ending of a story is another idea for allowing students to gain practice in solving literature problems. Again, mysteries are an easy starting place. Ask a student to watch an episode of *Barnaby Jones* or *Hawaii Five-O* which they have seen once already. Since they know who the culprit is, they can concentrate on picking out clues which should have led them to reach the conclusion before the hero announces the solution. If possible, videotape an episode of one of these shows and tell the students the solution before they watch and, as a class, call out significant clues as they watch. The program *Columbo* might be useful here because commonly the solution is shown at the beginning and the plot revolves around the hero's finding relevant clues and arriving at the conclusion the audience already knows. The tape might be stopped at intervals and the students asked to decide what clues the detective should have picked up in that scene.

   For short stories, the solution might be given along with the reading assignment and students asked to jot down clues as they read. Eventually, an *un*solved mystery, such as any of the Agatha Christie novels, can be assigned and the students asked to keep running journals of their suspicions.

8.4C PROBLEM SOLVING: SOCIAL STUDIES, MEDIA-STUDY

Level   Junior high and above.

Objective   To allow students to consider how they are being affected by media consumption by comparing views of "experts" and life with and without the media.

Description   The analysis of any medium is important, but perhaps the best-suited for classroom study is television because of its immediate appeal to students and the amount of time spent with it. Present two views of television: Marie Winn's book *The Plug-In Drug* (or an excellent summary of the book published in *Scholastic Voice* magazine, March 23, 1978); and any of Marshall McLuhan's articles in defense of the electronic media (these may need to be rewritten or summarized for many students).

1. Discuss objectively: "What are the dangers and benefits of television viewing from many perspectives, including health, mental well-being, education, sociology, citizenship, and other areas?" Students can be divided into small groups to cover each aspect.

2. Review the *Guide to Periodical Literature* for several of the many recent articles about families which have given up television for a period of time. Perhaps some students will volunteer to give up television viewing themselves. What was gained? What was lost?

3. Once the various aspects of television have been covered, have students come up with a reasonable "Guidebook for Family Television Viewing" which takes into account the decisions and evaluations about television they have made throughout the study. The guide might include types of programming recommended for each family member, the time allotment per week deemed advisable, plus any hints about room lighting or the like that they pick up in the study.

*8.4D SOLVING MATH–READING PROBLEMS

Level   Middle grades and above.

Objective   To provide practice in predicting answers to mathematics problems with the use of a prediction worksheet.

Description   For some students the total concept of mathematics is very difficult. They seem to encounter even greater difficulties when working with reading problems. They often provide answers that are entirely improbable and sometimes even answers to questions that the problems did not ask. This activity should direct students to predicting an answer even before they begin so that as they apply their mathematics skills to the operation required, they will be aware when they find a solution that is improbable.

For students in greatly accelerated mathematics courses, the worksheet would be used as a self-study *sorting* device to assist with highly complex problems.

1. Prepare copies of the Mathematics Prediction Worksheet in Figure 8–D for the students or put the questions on the chalkboard.

Figure 8–D

MATHEMATICS PREDICTION WORKSHEET

1. Numbers the reading gave me:
   a. _____
   b. _____
   c. _____

2. Questions the reading asked me:
   a. _____
   _____
   b. _____
   _____
   c. _____
   _____

3. What could an answer to those questions be? (GUESS!)
   a. _____
   _____
   b. _____
   _____
   c. _____
   _____

4. Could the number I guessed be *too* high? (Jot down a reason whether you circle *yes* or *no*.)
   a.   Yes   No _____
   _____
   b.   Yes   No _____
   _____
   c.   Yes   No _____
   _____

5. Could the number I guessed be *too* low?
   a.   Yes   No _____
   _____
   b.   Yes   No _____
   _____
   c.   Yes   No _____
   _____

6. Should I guess again?
   Yes _____   No _____
   If the answer is *yes*, reread your problem and go back to 3. and answer the questions again.
   If the answer is *no*, begin to work your problem.

2. As a group, work through the sheet with a problem which the students would find very easy to solve.

3. Continue the group work with the sheet, but increase the difficulty of the problems. You will want to use at least an entire class period with this introductory process.

4. Repeat the use of the worksheet when new *types* of reading problems are introduced to the students so that they have an opportunity for directed practice with thoughtful, systematic predictions.

9 STUDY TECHNIQUES FOR SPECIAL TEXTS

The flexibility of readers is tested as they move from subject to subject, from one selection to another. Each time they read a new article, they are faced with a different purpose, a changed organization, various types of illustrations, and differing degrees of abstraction. Those differences occur from subject to subject as well as within the same course or content. Through the years in school students need help from teachers in learning to recognize those differences and to adjust their mental operations to accommodate changes in the text. Teachers provide help by:

—directing the purpose for study reading;

—calling attention to the author's organization; and

—pointing out techniques for using special textual features, such as diagrams, charts, maps, and formulas.

It is especially important during the secondary school year for students to be shown how to deal with various textual features. The variety and complexity of reading increases during those years and adolescents' minds grow to cope with the abstractions—that is, with the principles or textual organization which can guide intelligent reading. It is during those years, too, that students show an interest in the *process* of learning, in knowing *how* they learn. But, perhaps most significantly, the teacher still controls most of the adolescents' reading, that is, the teacher assigns books and articles to be read for study, for purposes of learning concepts and skills related to the school's curriculum. That makes the setting and the choice of reading different from the students' personal reading.

This chapter describes activities for special bookthinking characteristics of school-related books and magazines. Some of them are more appropriate to specific subjects, for example, map reading or using graphs, but the activities have been constructed for possible transferability into several areas. For example, one of the activities on reading technical directions has broad application, although its particular focus is on reading patterns. As a learning experience, it has the advantage of attracting attention because it asks students to look at a product not many of them will have produced previously. And the transfer value remains high in view of the need for following carefully and systematically the technical directions in science laboratories, vocational courses, home economics courses, mathematics projects, and so on.

Besides those skills which are specialized and often troublesome to adolescent learners, there is the continuing problem of study reading—in every subject—which needs working out by every content teacher.

9.1 STUDY CRITICALLY

To help students revise an unproductive view of studying, teachers need to show them how to study in a critical manner. Crucial to studying critically is setting a purpose for reading and studying so that the mind can be more selective and better organized in sifting and deciding how to use the information and concepts presented in the chapter to be studied. In some instances the teacher may state in advance what the important purposes or topics are; in other instances the students have to decide that for themselves.

Several million times a week, teachers across the country say to their students, "I want you to read the next chapter and then we'll have a test on it." Maybe the statement is: "Read and I'll ask you some questions." But the effect is the same. Students have to decide how to read and study for the test that will follow. How do they carry out that task? Should they memorize the chapter or should they approach it in another way?

Most students seem to approach a study assignment as if their minds were like blotters. They press the pages to their minds as often as it takes to leave vestiges of the print there—in hopes that the questions asked and the vestiges impressed on their memories will somehow coincide. Such an approach not only requires a lot of wasted energy, but it also convinces many students that studying from a book is more trouble than it is worth.

Admittedly, when the students make a personal choice about the purpose for reading, there is a risk involved. But the risk is minor compared to that of acting like an inefficient blotter, hoping an absorption technique is more useful than purposeful organizing of the information read.

*9.1A CRITICAL STUDY TECHNIQUE: PARS

Level   Middle grades and above.

Objective   To use a step-by-step strategy for study–reading.

Description   1. Tell the students that by having a technique or mnemonic device they can guide themselves through the study of a chapter, a book, or a short article. Place the acronym PARS on the board and explain that most of the study–reading techniques follow a pattern that looks like this:

   a. *Preview* the material to get a general sense of its movement and organization—its important headings or concepts.

   b. *Ask questions* before reading to make sure that you are setting a purpose or purposes that satisfy you and your perception of what the teacher will emphasize.

   c. *Read* with those purpose-setting questions in mind.

   d. *Summarize* the reading by checking information gained against the pre-established questions.

Those steps are given various mnemonics, such as SQ3R, which may be useful in guiding students through the steps and in giving them practice in using a technique on all types of study–reading. Experience suggests that the mnemonic be as short as possible; otherwise the students will reject it as too long or too complicated to be of value. For that reason, the mnemonic PARS is quite helpful: *Preview, Ask questions, Read, Summarize.*

2. Explain PARS and give them a brief practice for each step. Convey to them that study–reading involves decision making on their part; it is a reasoning activity and not a power memory exercise. They are in charge—with a mnemonic device to guide the process.

3. Take a brief selection from a content text or use the example on the following page as a handout to the students. Figure 9–A shows a headline and a map that introduce an article in *U.S. News and World Report* (Feb. 27, 1978).

4. Have the students practice the first two steps of the PARS technique.

   P: Just using the headline and the map, what do you think the article will be about? What sorts of information would you expect to find?

   A: Write a couple of questions that you would like to have answered as a result of looking at the headline and the map. For example, "Why is the Kremlin concerned about wheeler-dealers? How could wheeler-dealers develop in the Soviet Union?" and so on.

   R: Collect all the questions and send several good readers to the library to see if the full-length article answers all the questions that were posed. Or, place the article on an overhead projection and have the class read it together, confirming or negating the questions and impressions they formed from their preview of the headline and the map.

   S: Each student should write a one-paragraph summary of the article (or a summary of the discussion of the article as presented by those assigned to read it for the class).

5. Ask the students to apply the PARS mnemonic to a chapter from the text and tell them that you will give them a brief quiz

[1] Reprinted from *U. S. News & World Report*. Copyright 1978 U. S. News & World Report, Inc.

Figure 9–A

A Hotbed Of Capitalism Inside Russia

Kremlin reformers can't keep up with wheeler-dealers from Soviet Georgia, where everything has a price except nationalistic pride.

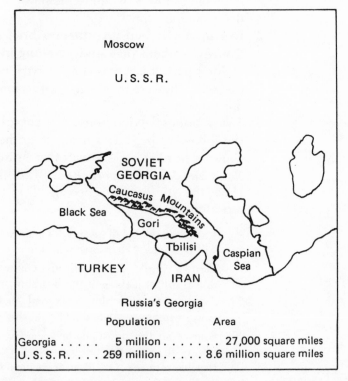

Moscow

U.S.S.R.

SOVIET GEORGIA

Caucasus Mountains

Black Sea

Gori

Tbilisi

TURKEY

IRAN

Caspian Sea

Russia's Georgia

	Population	Area
Georgia	5 million	27,000 square miles
U.S.S.R.	259 million	8.6 million square miles

afterward to see if the approach helps them bring the points together more clearly. In fact, an interesting variation would be to use some of the questions that they posed in the second step (A) as the quiz questions.

9.1B POSING STUDY QUESTIONS

Level   Junior high and above.

Objective   To guide students in forming critical study questions.

Description   Teachers are conscious of asking questions that force students to think. Those critical questions should be asked both before and after selections are read. Though not every selection lends itself to a simple hierarchy for question-asking, the teacher may well use a guide to daily question-asking. Then the teacher can go through a pattern that cuts across various levels of thinking, for example:

Level 1   (Recall):   What three elements were discussed?
Level 2   (Analysis):   Restate the theme in your own words. Compare these social conditions to those during the previous war.
Level 3   (Judgment):   Would you recommend that book to your mother? Why or why not?
Level 4   (Extension):   How would you use these physical laws in everyday living?
                           Can you find music that represents the mood of that story?

1. For study purposes, students should be able to pose questions for themselves that require complex as well as simple answers. If the students know and understand the types of questions the teacher asks, they can at least use a question-asking guide similar to the teacher's.

    On the chalkboard or on a handout, place the following:

    QUESTIONS FOR THINKING

    a. *Recall:*   Who was there? When did he leave?
    b. *Analysis:*   What is the main idea?
    c. *Judgment:*   Is it worthwhile?
                      What value do you see there?
    d. *Extension:*   How would you apply that information in your life?

2. Ask the students to prepare their own ten-question quiz over an assignment in the text or a selection that is given to them. They must have at least one question in each of the four categories—ten in all. Each question should be labeled with its category. Each student should write his or her name and the ten questions on a separate sheet of paper.

3. When the questions are returned the next day, point out that a teacher's questions over the same selection would cover the same kinds of questions that they wrote. In fact, if they can answer the questions that they wrote for themselves, chances are that in many classes they can answer eight out of ten questions on each paper in the class.

4. As an experiment, collect all the question papers and distribute them randomly. On separate sheets of paper the students are to answer the questions that they received in the random distribution.

5. When the questions have been answered, the answers should be returned to the originators of the questions for evaluation. Each originator should grade the answers.
6. Either on the chalkboard or through a student committee, tally the quizzes to see how many papers *did* report satisfactory grades. The results may be quite impressive.
7. When students study, they should be posing critical questions for themselves. If they spread those questions across the categories listed above, they will be asking the same types of questions that a testor would prepare. Even though the questions would naturally vary somewhat, they have a close enough resemblance and focus to provide the information and the basic decisions that the readers need.

9.1C GATHERING INFORMATION THROUGH STUDY QUESTIONS; APPLICATION OF QUESTIONS

Level   Junior high and above.

Objective   To show that the preparation of questions helps gather valuable information.

Description
1. The product of this lesson is to have the students interview a worker about his or her occupation. In preparation, have the students read about an occupation which meets their interests—for example, in a book like *Occupational Guidelines* (Minneapolis: Finney Co., 1977), or *Working* by Studs Terkel (New York: Avon Books, 1972).
2. Based on their reading, ask the students to prepare a list of questions about the occupation. They must have a range of questions, and at least one for each of the categories: Recall, Analysis, Judgment, and Extension (see Activity 9.1B).
3. The answers that the students get from the workers should be returned to class in written form. To aid their memories, they may wish to tape record the interviews. The class discussion should center on the difference in impression that the worker actually gave with the impression that was gained from the book. The questions asked should be the guide to discussing the differences. This discussion could be conducted in small groups or in the whole class.

9.1D PURPOSE DIRECTS STUDY

Level   Junior high and above.

Objective   To set specific purposes for students in order to guide their study of assigned passages in social studies, science, English, health, vocational education.

Description   Too often students just read through assignments and end up with a hodgepodge of vaguely recalled facts. In order to guide the students in purposeful study, the teacher can focus the students' attention on one or two specific questions to be answered by the time they are finished reading. This exercise is divided into four stages which lead students through the process of eventually developing their own skills at setting reading purposes.

Stage 1:   Choose a passage in the content area which hinges on the understanding of a key word. Ask the students to form a definition of this word as the passage is revealed sentence-by-sentence on an overhead projector, or as the teacher reads it aloud. As more of the passage is revealed, the students' definition will change and become more precise as they pick up clues from the reading. Below is a sample of such a passage adapted from the *People's Almanac,* by David Wallechinsky and Irving Wallace, page 1031, "Every Herb Bearing Seed." This book, by the way, is rich in interesting short passages on every conceivable topic.

Ask students beforehand: "What is a lentil?"

Read:

Lentils have a long history of use. Some were found in an Egyptian tomb dating from 2000 B.C. It was for a pottage made of red lentils that Esau sold his birthright to his brother Jacob in the Bible story. Lentils contain as much as 25 percent protein. They are particularly important in the diet of vegetarians. Lentils are made to make the Indian favorite, *dhal.* It is made from lentils which have been boiled until completely soft, and all the water absorbed. It is then left to get cold and hard, so it can be sliced with a knife and eaten.

After practice, the teacher may only have to throw out a key word while making an assignment to give the students "hangers" to put ideas on as they read.

Stage 2:   When the passage is centered around a key idea, the teacher can ask an intriguing question which is answered in the text. The reading, then, is directed to picking up these main notions. The following example is based on a paragraph taken from *Reading Workbook Lessons and Tests* by Samuel F. Zimbat and Wilbert J. Levy (New York: Amsco School Publications, Inc., 1969). However, any interesting textbook passage would work equally well.

Ask students beforehand: "Why does a crocodile want to look like a log?" and "Why does a crocodile need an egg tooth?"

Read:

A crocodile has a favorite method of catching his dinner. He lies quietly in the water with only his nostrils, eyes, and part of his back showing. Thus he deceives his prey into thinking him a floating log. When an unwary bird or animal comes near enough, the crocodile seizes it in his powerful jaws and drags it underwater, and eats it. This doesn't sound like a hard way to get a dinner, does it?

Would you like to know how crocodiles are born? A mother crocodile lays twenty to ninety eggs in the sand. After a time, the heat of the sand hatches the eggs, and the young crocodile breaks the shell by means of a sharp egg tooth that is on the end of its nose. The babies are able to take care of themselves as soon as they are born, and they grow at the rate of about a foot a year.

Stage 3: Once students are familiar with reading to find factual information, the teacher can heighten the skill level by posing an inferential question to guide reading. For example, for the above passage, the teacher might begin, "Ever since the crocodile shattered the nerves of Captain Hook in *Peter Pan*, this beast has had the reputation of being a force in nature to be contended with. As you read this passage, jot down any reasons you find why the crocodile has survived over the years when other species are dying out." The students should come up with answers such as the wily intelligence of the animal or the fact that it is strong and independent from birth.

Stage 4: Eventually the students should be encouraged to pose their own questions to focus their study. For example, the teacher can briefly introduce the topic: "The assignment for tonight is about crocodiles. At the top of your paper, write down something you would like to know about the breeding or feeding habits of this animal. As you read, answer your question." The next day the questions and answers can be discussed. With any luck at all, a few of the questions will *not* have been answered in the assigned passage and students can be asked, "Where *can* you find that answer?" Exploration of other sources can follow.

Stage 5: A more elaborate lesson of the same skill is to have students prepare their own reading quizzes before they read an assignment. The teacher can read aloud the opening few sentences or briefly summarize the topic covered. The students are then asked to write down ten questions they expect to be answered in the passage. Their papers are collected and returned the next day as their personalized quizzes. For this purpose, it is not necessarily important that every one of the students' questions be specifically answered. The unanswered ideas might provide fruitful data for discussion or student speculation. The questions will probably become increasingly realistic as students grow more familiar with the general subject matter and with the organization of their textbook. This idea can be used effectively in science, health, mathematics, and English literature classes as well as in other content areas. Many short stories or novels, for example, begin with provocative one-liners. A classic is the opening to *The*

Bridge of San Luis Rey by Thornton Wilder. All manner of factual and cause–effect inferential questions can be generated and serve as a reading guide for the study of this novel. Gothic novels or mystery stories, including Faulkner's short story, "A Rose for Emily," provide especially intriguing openers.

*9.1E FOCUSING ON KEY WORDS TO BUILD CONCEPTS

Level   Middle grades and above.

Objective   To encourage students to read assigned passages purposefully by using key words.

Description The following three lesson ideas guide students to become aware that not all words are created equal in textbooks. In these exercises, students are asked to make judgments about the relative value of words in getting to the main idea at hand.

1. The following paragraph is taken from the text, *World Geography and You*, by Sol Holt, published by D. Van Nostrand Company, Inc., 1964, page 427. However, almost any well-organized passage will do. This passage has two major concepts: *a.* cows cannot be killed in India because they are sacred, and *b.* the resultant overpopulation of cattle is an economic problem for the country. Each concept is explicitly stated in the opening sentences of the paragraphs, and they appear here in their entirety. The rest of the paragraph is liberally sprinkled with blanks, which can only be filled with understanding of both the main point and the flow of the language. Only key words are eliminated. Either individually or in group discussion the class can decide on appropriate words.

Among Orthodox Hindus all living things are sacred. Nothing that possesses life—whether a human, an animal, an insect, or a worm—must lose it at the hands of a man. A religious Hindu will not _____ a fly or _____ on a bug. This is the Hindu principle of *ahimsa*, or sacredness of life. The _____ of cows by orthodox Hindus is doubly _____ because it is a_____ _____ to _____ a cow or to _____ it. In some Hindu states of India the _____ of cattle is _____ by law.

Because animal _____ is a _____, the cattle population of India has grown tremendously. There are in India today 150 million cattle, or one-fifth of the world's total, and 45 million buffalo, or more than one-half of the world's total. This huge animal population creates a dual problem. On the one hand, the animals must be _____, and on the other hand, the meat of the animals cannot be used for human

_____. No matter how _____ or _____ a cow may be, it is not _____, but it is _____ until it dies a _____ _____. In India there are about 3000 homes for aged _____, supported by religious Hindus, but there are practically no homes for aged

_____.

2. Discuss the fact that all the words for the blanks referred back to the main idea presented in the first sentence or two of each paragraph.
3. The next step is to have students themselves underline lightly in pencil key words in a passage as they read from their text. Perhaps they can be encouraged first to scan quickly through the passage to see where it is going and then go back to find the key words. (This is a version of the PARS technique, 9.1A.) Discuss the value of using key words to verify what the main ideas or themes are. In this way students can clarify concepts and get a better sense of how to extract information.
4. Another variation on this theme is to have students underline the one sentence in each paragraph of textbook reading that presents most completely the main idea of the passage. Work through several paragraphs together in class before asking students to perform this task independently.

9.1F ORGANIZATION OF TEXT; NARRATIVE

Level   Junior high and above.

Objective   To make students aware of the common structure of narrative writing and to help them become skilled in recognizing this form.

Description   While many content area texts have subtitles, graphs, and classic paragraph structure with careful topic sentences to guide the students in ascertaining the organization, the literature text does not give such clues. However, the students must be aware that short stories and novels do, indeed, have structure. This structure must be understood before any deeper, inferential understanding of the literature can take place. The following format provides the students with a chart for identifying the basic components of literature as they read and frees class time for more than mere recitation of who did what to whom with what results.

1. Explain the component parts of all narrative works, and explain how students could fill in the blanks of the basic plot diagram below.

Plot:

Climax

Events of the
Rising Action

Denouement
(Falling
Action)

Setting:
a. time
b. place
c. social conditions

Introduction:
a. people
b. place
c. problem

Characters:
a. physical attributes
b. behavior exhibited
c. motivation of behavior
    (surface motivation for ac-
    tion)
d. conceit: inner, psycholog-
    ical beliefs, hang-ups

Tone:
describe mood, noting keywords

Motifs:
ideas or things that keep re-
curring

2. Demonstrate the use of this common narrative structure with
    videotaped commercials that the students are familiar with. For
    instance, the Folger's coffee advertisement with Mrs. Olsen is a
    perfect example of an advertisement with a narrative structure.

    Plot:

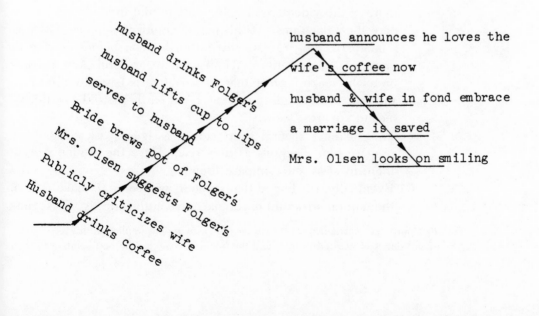

husband drinks Folger's
husband lifts cup to lips
serves to husband
Bride brews pot of Folger's
Mrs. Olsen suggests Folger's
Publicly criticizes wife
Husband drinks coffee

husband announces he loves the
wife's coffee now

husband & wife in fond embrace

a marriage is saved

Mrs. Olsen looks on smiling

a. blushing bride, husband, Mrs. Olsen

b. modern American kitchen

c. husband doesn't like wife's coffee

Tone:
tension, suspense

Motifs:
coffee
reference to color
mountain-grown

Setting:

a. 1970s

b. suburban American neighborhood

c. upper-middle class cast, probably white Anglo-Saxons

Characters:[2]

husband	*bride*	*Mrs. Olsen*
a. tall, handsome, prosperous	a. timid, pretty, eager	a. kindly; older matron
b. drinks coffee; criticizes wife	b. makes poor coffee	b. helps wife
c. hates taste; feels bitter disappointment	c. unlearned in kitchen	c. wise, experienced, compassionate
d. believes it is his right to be satisfied in coffee tastes; attitude of superiority over wife	d. knows duty of good wife; longs to please	d. understands the rigors of young marriage

3. After several commercials are examined as a class, show a few more of the videotapes for students to plot individually. Compare their diagrams. At this point, mundane subject matter is immaterial; the *process* must be made clear before moving to more serious narratives. When students are proficient at commercials, make it clear that *all* narrative is basically the same and that a full-length novel can be as easily plotted as a thirty-second advertisement.

4. For the next several short stories assigned, ask students to prepare plot diagrams as they read. Have the students bring them to class and compare them.

5. Eventually it is hoped that students will come to make note of the natural structure of the narrative automatically. Class time

[2] For other purposes, a class may wish to discuss the assumptions implicit in this scene about attitudes and duties of married couples and the brand of coffee as the best solution to their problems.

then can be spent in application of the themes of the stories, reflective writing assignments, and creative extensions of the literature with only passing mention in class to the stories' rudiments.

6. It should be noted that social studies texts and, to a lesser degree, science texts often use a narrative format for presenting information. Those selections could be analyzed in a similar way. Where narrative is not an organizing device in home economics, vocational studies, and so on, students should be encouraged to find a comparable way to analyze the organization.

9.1G ORGANIZATION OF POETRY

Level   Junior high and above.

Objective   To encourage students to read poetry with a careful eye to the organizational flow of the piece in an effort to better follow the poet's purpose.

Description   Poetry is often a baffling experience for students because of their limited exposure to poetry and their unfortunate preconceived notions that it is close to impossible to comprehend. The following exercises lead students to look for an organizational flow of poetry in the mechanical, grammatical, and the thematic senses. The common device is to engage students actively in the process of creating or recreating the poetry.

1. Cloze tasks for poetry. The cloze procedure is handy for creating student interaction with print. The cloze procedure consists of blanking out either random or selected words in a poem. By doing this the teacher forces the students to take note of the topical and structural considerations of the poem in order to fill in the spaces. The students then must recognize, for example, whether a rhyming word must be filled in or if rhyme is not appropriate to the poem's general format; determine what meaning is implied by the rest of the line which must be maintained by this particular word, or if a change of topic or emphasis is indicated; and select a word which not only denotatively fills the slot, but also captures the connotative flavor or style of the poem.

   It should be noted that any words can be blanked out depending on the teacher's specific purpose: for example, the teacher may choose to work especially on imagery and thus blank out only those expressive nouns, verbs and modifiers which carry images.

   Example: Below is a poem that is useful for this and the following exercises. What makes this poem useful for practicing the organizational skill is that it is simple and predictable in style. Entitled "I Am Hungry," it was written by Eugene Tso.[3]

Complete Text	*Cloze-Task Version*
	(standard every fifth word deletion)
I was hungry and you	I was hungry and _____
landed on the moon.	landed on the moon.
I was hungry and you	_____ was hungry and you
told me to wait.	_____ me to wait.
I was hungry and you	I _____ hungry and you
set up a commission.	set _____ a commission . . .
I was hungry and you	
told me I shouldn't be.	
I was hungry and you	
had missile bills to pay.	
I was hungry and you said	
"Machines do that kind of	
work now."	
I was hungry and you said,	
"The poor are always with	
us."	
I was hungry and you said,	
"Law and order come	
first."	
I was hungry and you said,	
"Blame it on the Com-	
munists."	
I was hungry and you said,	
"So were my ancestors."	
I was hungry and you said,	
"We don't hire after 35."	
I was hungry and you said,	
"God helps those . . ."	
I was hungry and you said,	
"Sorry, come back tomor-	
row."	

2. Similar in effect to the cloze task but a change of pace is the notion of presenting a predictable poem with deliberate mistakes and asking students to locate and correct the mistakes. Using the "I Am Hungry" selection as the lesson, the following version might be presented to the students with instructions to

[3] From *From the Belly of the Shark*, Walter Lowenfels, ed. Copyright © 1973 by Walter Lowenfels. "I Am Hungry" originally appeared in *Akwesasne Notes*, Vol. 3, No. 3, April, 1971. Reprinted by permission of *Akwesasne Notes*.

find the places in the poem where the teacher deliberately
made errors in copying. The following example calls upon students to look for both structural and thematic errors, although a
teacher can plan his or her rewritten version to focus on any one
or more aspects of the passage.

Sample: (the first three verses are left intact in order to allow students to "get into" the poem.)

> I was hungry and I knew
>   it was my own fault.
> I was hungry but you
>   had missile bills to pay.
> I was hungry and you said,
>   "Machines provide jobs for people like you."
> I was hungry and you said,
>   "The poor are always with us."
> I was starving and you said,
>   "Law and order come first."
> I was hungry and you said,
>   "Let me help you out."
>   and so forth in this vein . . .

3. Reported in the literature of reading are several varieties of
   student formula-poetry writing. This idea might be adapted for
   use in studying a poem as well. In the "I Am Hungry" selection,
   the students can demonstrate knowledge of the format and
   theme by responding in kind. For example, after performing
   one of the previous exercises, ask the students, "Who is speaking in this poem? To whom? What is the complaint?" Then
   expand: "Who else in our society has a gripe? Against whom?"
   or, more personally, "What are your gripes? Who or what
   seems to be holding you back?" Then ask students to use "I Am
   Hungry" as a model for creating a poem expressing their ideas.
   For ease the teacher might provide each student with a skeleton
   form of the poem to fill in:

   > _____ was _____ and _____
   >   did _____.
   > _____ was _____ and _____
   >   did _____.

   and so forth for as long as required.

4. A new twist to the often-used haiku format for studying structure and meaning in poetry comes from the paperback, *Haiku
   By Children,* by the Wilhelme International School for Children. This is a delightful collection of haiku written and illustrated by children four to eight years old and is a convincing

comeback to the student who claims he or she just cannot write poetry. This volume, too, has a cogent, one-page explanation of the role of poetry in education and the specific medium of the haiku.

9.2 TECHNICAL DIRECTIONS AND ILLUSTRATIONS

In private life and in much of the reading done in the elementary grades, students deal with general life experiences. They are not accustomed to paying attention to the accuracy and the distinctions that occur in technical directions and illustrations. It does not confuse them in the least to have someone say, "Turn on the water faucet." But it is quite another thing for someone to say to the student, "Replace the ball valve in that faucet; it is worn out." For the person who is uninitiated in the refinements of faucet plumbing, a whole set of technical directions and diagrams must precede fulfilling the direction, "Replace the ball valve." Reading technical directions and related illustrations requires a shift in approach to the text and demands a methodical sense of operation for success.

As is true with most things that we adults already know, we assume that everyone else ought to be able to learn it easily simply because it is resting comfortably in *our* minds. Couple that thought with teenagers' natural inclination to rush through every academic lesson at utmost speed, and the situation does not lend itself to a sense of how to deal with technical reading. The teacher's first job, then, is to slow students down—to show them that it takes time to identify, organize, and utilize technical directions. That probably means engaging in a task periodically that requires the students to follow directions for instance, to produce a model, an experiment, a chart, or some other product.

9.2A TECHNICAL DIRECTIONS

Level   Junior high and above.

Objective   To practice step-by-step reading of technical directions.

Description   Reading directions for various types of projects can appear to be a difficult task to a beginner contemplating a new type of project. The print looks "official" and is technical—meaning that there are terms unique and important to the type of project. Successful completion of the project is dependent on understanding the terms and their contextual meaning.

With increasing male participation in home economics classes and female participation in "industrial arts," there is a wider exposure to more potential interests. Stereotypical attitudes are eroding and, for example, more and more boys are participating in areas once "forbidden" them, like cooking and sewing. For that reason, we here use an example from home economics as a model of how a teacher can help students read technical directions. Because making sewing projects can be a popular activity for boys and girls, an examination of manufacturers' printed patterns can provide an excellent example of reading directions.

1. Begin with an informal discussion about sewing. Talk about the money to be saved, the fun of examining the many types of fabric, and the fun of having something totally unique. Then have students generate a list of things that they think will help them complete a garment that looks even better than an inexpensively purchased one. This might include things like choice of fabric, handwork, pressing seams, and so on, depending on the experience of class members.

2. Look at patterns and pattern language. Choose patterns that do not call for zippers, such as wrap skirts and poncho-style shirts. Have two patterns available (avoid Vogue products—they tend to have a few more complexities than would benefit the lesson), preferably for boys' and girls' projects. Pattern companies might provide multiple copies of a discontinued pattern, an overhead or opaque projector might be used, or lesson sheets could be duplicated. There may be an accomplished sewer in the class who could make this presentation with some earlier guidance.

3. Have students keep a vocabulary list during the lesson and see how many terms they learn.

4. Look at the front of the pattern envelope. Talk about ideas the students get from the photograph or drawing. Look at the placement of the number referred to in the catalog, the size, and any directional indications, such as "jiffy," "easy," or "only four main pieces."

5. Next, look at the back of the envelope. At the top, look at the diagram of the pieces showing the indication of exact number and shape. Move down to the yardage chart and have students determine their sizes from the chart provided. (For a middle school class, perhaps provide tape measures and have students spend a few minutes adding their own measurements to their vocabulary lists.) Next, demonstrate how to find the right amount of 45-inch fabric for their size in the selection they would choose to make (long-sleeved, short-sleeved, and so on). Point out that those numbers refer to the width of the fabric. Next, look at the abbreviations for with and without nap (w, wo) and explain that "shading, pile, or one-way design" means cloth such as corduroy or velvet, where all the pieces must be laid out in the same direction.

Move to the bottom section called "Fabrics" and have students examine the various fabrics that the manufacturer suggests will provide the right texture for the desired result. Have students become familiar with each type listed. (Since the intent here may not be an actual sewing lesson, avoid using a pattern calling for stretch knits.)

6. Go to the direction sheet. Study with students the terms and symbols printed on the left column.

7. Have students next look at the cutting layout diagram for their selection. Point out that shaded pieces indicate the fabric is to be placed face down. Hold up and walk around with a piece of fabric, showing its selvages and grain line.

8. Take out a couple of pieces of the pattern. Emphasize the arrows, the lines for cutting, and the broken lines indicating seamlines. Next, emphasize the notches and dots and what the manufacturer wants done with them.

9. Return to the sewing directions on the printed sheet. Have students find the first point where they are told to use a notch or a dot. Have students practice following arrows to the points of reference on the diagram. Have students look at each diagram as it adds one more step. Finally, ask them to look for any special finishing directions at the end.

10. Remind the students that following technical directions, whether in home economics, science, or vocational or mathematics activities, requires system, attention to detail, and a clear image of the meaning of the terms being used.

*9.2B APPLYING RULES

Level Middle grades and above.

Objective To encourage students to interpret accurately the regulations of games and similar situations in a variety of subjects.

Description Participation in and appreciation of recreational activities in sports is a worthy goal of most physical education courses. Rather than asking students to look at a rulebook and answer objective questions about the dimensions of the court or the size of the equipment, it may be more useful to engage them in exercises that require an understanding of the nuances of the game and how to participate fairly in a game.

Several activities are possible:

1. Select a sport of the students' interest and present them with the current official rulebook and a set of problems to solve. For example, a track devotee might be given the latest American Athletic Union handbook and questions such as these:

   a. In a recent Olympic Games, George Woods of the United States was denied a medal because his shot landed on the flag marker of the location of another competitor's put. How has the new rulebook insured that this will never happen again?

b. What does the chief inspector do if a hurdler knocks down several consecutive hurdles in his race?

c. In an attempt at sixteen feet, the vaulter clears the bar, but his pole passes under the bar. What is the field judge to do?

d. In a modern Accu-track photo finish to a sprint race, the meet referee notices that the two competitors arrive at the tape at the same time, one man's shoulder crossing the line as the other man's chest crosses. Who wins?

e. In the triple jump, the athlete is three steps into his attempted jump when the red light flashes. What is the significance of this and how does the field judge rule?

f. What is the significance of "breaking the plane" in the high jump?

2. After practice with teacher-made situations, ask the students to form groups of those interested in a particular sport and make up situations for the group to solve using the current rulebook.

3. As a regular feature, the old *Saturday Evening Post* ran short articles about strange situations that actually occurred in major league baseball. The *Post* described the unusual turn of events, told the ruling made by the umpire, and explained why this interpretation was made. If copies of this magazine are in the school library, they may be used to test the students—Would they have made the same rulings? What evidence can they find for making alternate decisions?

4. Students may be asked to plan and officiate a "games day" for other students, an elementary school, or summer parks program. They can keep a journal of their experiences and the unusual situations that arose and compare how they handled the problems.

5. Similar situations could be created in the sciences and vocational studies, where mixing chemical compounds, supporting structures with certain hardware, and determining angles for balance and structural effect could all be figured out from the rules or guidelines in a text.

*9.2C MATCHING ILLUSTRATIONS WITH TEXT

Level   Middle grades and above.

Objective   Practice matching dialogue with pictures.

Description   Students often overlook the information that can be gained from illustrations in the text. Captions are often printed in smaller type and are isolated from the rest of the page. If reading the main block of print is an extraordinarily difficult task, it is easy to overlook the picture as an information source and avoid the caption as one more difficult reading task. Teachers who ignore the pictures in chapter discussions and tests reinforce this omission.

An exercise using comics can provide a quick reminder to pump the pictures as a wellspring.

1. Take two or three comic strips using situations that students are likely to be familiar with, such as Dagwood having lunch at the diner, Peppermint Patty trying to get through a day of school, or Snoopy and Woodstock interacting. Blot out the print in the caption balloons and give a copy to each student. Have students supply the print in each balloon. Show the results and discuss what the various products have in common.
2. Repeat the process using a longer segment from one of the heroic comic books.
3. Finish the lesson by having students make a project that can be displayed around the room. So that all students will willingly participate, there should be minimal demand for any special artistic talent. This project might be a collage illustrating a specific theme. It might be supplying captions to a series of pictures, or having students make their own "comic strips" using Polaroid pictures of each other.

9.2D RELATING ILLUSTRATIONS TO TEXT

Level   Junior high and above.

Objective   Use illustrations to make predictions about textual information.

Description   Many textbooks used by students are very nicely illustrated. Some students have formed the habit of looking at illustrations only after reading the print. This habit may have roots in story hours where the picture was held up after the page was read aloud. This may have some value in forcing the listener to imagine the picture before seeing it, but it also may tend to indirectly *undervalue* illustrations. Students who are predominantly print-oriented and, particularly, students who are not completely comfortable with print may benefit from becoming aware of the assets found in pictures. A social studies text in history can provide a useful tool for using pictures in content reading.

1. *A Nation Conceived and Dedicated*, from the American Adventures Program. (By Corinne Hoexter and Ira Peck; Vol. 1: 1620–1860; New York: Scholastic Book Services, 1970.) Have students turn to Part Five, "A People Apart," on page 131. Discuss with students the things they already know and the impressions they have about this period.
2. Have students examine only the illustrations up to page 145 and

discuss the impression they think the authors are trying to give of the period.

3. Ask students to think of five questions they think they will be able to have answered by the text and the captions.

4. Go over the questions with the students and generate some common ones.

5. Have students read the material including "Nat Turner's Rebellion" and discuss the available answers to the questions. Then, ask them to consider whether their estimates of the authors' outlook were confirmed.

9.3 READING SYMBOLS AND CHARTS

Although we live in a world where symbols and diagrams are used extensively, students often seem baffled by the symbols, charts, diagrams and graphs they meet in their content books. Since they have not grown up seeing those charts on billboards and on television, they need direction from an expert—the teacher. They need the teacher's help to learn how to *organize* their minds to approach the symbols and to learn how to deal with the *nuances* of a chart in science or a chart in math or a chart in social studies, and so on. It is often necessary for the teacher to review the legend—the specifics of the symbols used—and points of orientation that will guide the students as they read the chart or diagram or map.

It sounds strange, yet happens frequently, to hear an intelligent adult say that he cannot use a road map to find his way from here to there. He expects the map to give him a set of verbal directions that says, "First go to the light, turn right and drive for three miles, then turn left on the highway marked 37 and drive for sixty miles to Grandma's house." And yet a map, like so many other charts and diagrams, *does* communicate, not in the sense that it gives directions, but in the sense that it enables its readers to build their own sets of directions. The readers become the constructors of the message, using the symbols, the information, and their organization as their message-building tools.

9.3A READING SYMBOLS

Level   Junior high and above.

Objective   To process symbols within a text or selection.

Description   An area of difficulty within content reading is provided by a series of unfamiliar symbols used within the textual material. The printed page containing one or more symbols can appear quite forbidding at first glance. A helpful skill in dealing with symbols is to develop an automatic recall of what they stand for.

1. Have students generate a list of commonly recognized symbols. Start them out with a few examples, perhaps including:

   golden arches
   K-Mart sign
   symbol for pure wool
   shell for Shell Oil
   7–11
   Chevrolet
   states' shapes
   GE
   Bell for Bell Telephone
   VW
   RCA
   Warner Brothers
   Universal Studios

2. When the list is completed, have each student select five or six. Then ask each student to write a short selection including those items, in each case using the symbol in place of the word. Spend some time reading the students' stories aloud, distribute duplicated copies, or use an opaque projector.

3. Next, students should generate their own original symbols. These should avoid print or alphabet letters, relying instead on created designs. Each student should then write a brief story, consistently using the created symbols.

4. The stories should be duplicated so that students have access to each others'. They should then attempt to assess the meanings of the various symbols from the context. At this point, each author should make available a decoding sheet so that students can determine their level of success.

5. Discuss the fact that almost all disciplines use nonverbal symbols (literature uses verbal symbols) as an integral form of communication, especially math and science. They should each then write a brief selection, using the symbols of the course subject, and exchanging them as they did above. This exercise could be repeated regularly, using it as a means of helping students repeat the symbols often enough to develop automatic responses to them—as is needed for easy reading of all symbols.

9.3B MAP READING AND FOLLOWING DIRECTIONS: PLANNING A TRIP

Level   Secondary.

Objective   To provide a practical, fun experience for students that causes them to follow maps and technical directions and to make logical decisions.

Description It is now common for driver's education classes to ask students to pick out a place and map a route there, figuring cost and mileage. However, these lessons often do not go far enough to maximize the learning value of the exercise. Following are several ideas which expand this lesson:

1. Rather than rely on the students' often too-limited frame of reference (most students invariably select Florida), *guide* their choices. For example, have students pick states in random drawings and find reasons for going there. With South Dakota as his assignment, one student can search the library, AAA (American Automobile Association) files, or Chambers of Commerce for points of interest in that state. With those points of interest as his goals, he can then find the best roads, means of transport, and lodging to suit his goals. Cost accounts, clothing needs and the like can be deduced with this destination in mind. More creative and ambitious students may even have found local legends, favorite dishes, state songs, and so on to include in their final reports. Of course, it is of interest and value for students to share their discoveries with the class in oral reports, posters, or "travel agency"-type brochures.

2. Increasingly, older students are afforded more independence of movement. A teacher can take advantage of this by proposing trips that actually can be carried out as a result of the planning. The daily newspapers and assorted publishers have made available lists of interesting trips in given areas. For example, the Rural Electric Mutual Corporation Company of Indiana publishes annual maps of all the local festivals in the state of Indiana. Music lovers might want to go to the Bluegrass Festival in Bean Blossom. They can find information about the dates, cost, and location from this source and then plan a trip there. The Media Ventures, Inc., publishes state travel guides such as *Fifty Best Mini-Trips for Michigan* (and for a host of other states as well) in which students can find one- to four-day adventures in their immediate areas. The American Automobile Association is generally very willing to loan or donate information from its extensive resources about travel. A group of students can select a place that interests them and plan a trip. The key here is for the students to actually *make* the trip and *report* to the class. Points to be covered in the report would include how well the plans worked out, what unexpected problems they encountered and how they might have anticipated them, and an accounting of the roads, cost, and lodging. It might be interesting, too, for the students to keep journals of their adventures or to make a photo essay to record the journey.

3. The current interest in outdoor life among many students can be a springboard for another exercise. The book *Roughing It*

Easy is a storehouse of information about camping. A student might be asked to plan a fishing trip and use this book as a guide for planning equipment needs; finding the best kind of fire for various kinds of cooking; unusual outdoor recipes for readily available ingredients; establishing appropriate toilet, refrigeration and sleeping accommodations; and handling emergency situations. The local department of parks and recreation or forestry departments are rich sources of locations and maps for such enterprises. Pre-planning should include careful consideration of who is going, the time of year, cost limits, equipment available, and the terrain of the camp. Again, if possible, the students will greatly benefit from actually making the trip even if it is only an overnight venture close to home.

9.3C FOLLOWING FLOW CHARTS

Level   Junior high and above.

Objective   To understand and use flow charts.

Description   Flow charts appearing in textbooks can appear overwhelming when seen initially. If students have had some experience in making their own, they will have a more basic idea of how the charts work and how to read them.

1. Create a situation where students need to get a message to everyone in the class. An example might be an important semester exam scheduled the day after a basketball tournament game. Or, late in the afternoon it is learned that an emergency teachers' meeting has been called for the next day and the test schedule must be altered. The teacher will only have time to call one person from each class. The teacher has three classes to cover.

2. Ask the students to draw a flow chart to show how the message to reschedule the test must go from the teacher to every member of the three classes (thirty students per class). For example, have the students create a chain formed by the first person calling two others, and each person thereafter calling two other classmates. (See Figure 9–B on the following page.)

   Leave students the option of deciding whether everyone in the class will be responsible for calling at least one other person, or whether the class has six particularly efficient people who should call five, or whatever.

3. Duplicate or use an opaque projector to have students examine the various forms they used. Have them discuss which is the most practical for their particular situation, that is, as they would apply their chart to their own class.

Figure 9–B

SAMPLE MESSAGE FLOW CHART

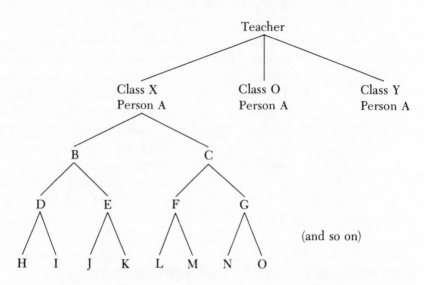

4. Have students discuss some aspect of the school they would like to see changed. Let the discussion begin rather freely, but eventually try to generate a common category, such as smoking, attendance policy, cafeteria rules, and so on. Next, ask students to consider how they might initiate changes in that rule. (It will be important to end up with a category that is student-oriented and one they think quite a few students are concerned about.)

5. Students will need to decide whom to see first, so they should consider who effectively holds the most power in this particular situation. Have students make a list of authority figures in the school system, from most powerful to least powerful. Discuss the versions the students write and try to come to some consensus on the list. On the overhead or chalkboard, show how the addition of boxes and arrows can create a decision-making power flow chart.

6. Next, have students consider the most tactful and/or practical first step in their procedure. Students may have agreed on allowing the chart to show that the school board had the most power but, for example, they would not begin with attending a board meeting if their problem were something as parochial as the student council's having decided that candy would not be sold during the noon hour or that outsiders could not attend the prom. Students should decide which people or offices would be the most appropriate to visit first, and then they should chart out the flow of power as they perceive it.

7. Finally, students should consider who should represent the issue and how they might be selected. (A protest against injustice in the smoking policy might profitably include some representatives with no record of smoking suspensions.) When students determine who could best present their cause (say, a group of five or six people), they should make a chart of whom these people will represent and be responsible to.

8. The process the students went through in charting these sample actions should give them a general sense of how flow charts work. It should also enable them to transfer what they have learned to specific areas of knowledge. They will know how to follow flow charts in their government books, in science processes, and in vocational processes, and will be able to understand historical or relational charts in social studies and in English studies.

9.3D READING CHARTS TO ANSWER QUESTIONS

Level   Junior high and above.

Objective   To use charts to answer questions.

Description   Charts appear on pages of different types of textbooks. They are efficient methods of presenting a body of related pieces of information, but they frequently appear isolated, on the tops or bottoms of pages. Students frequently skip a chart completely, moving on to the next block of print as if the chart were white space. Some of these very students may have been asked to memorize entire charts in the past. They might understandably be inclined to skip over anything written in columns.

Students can gain increasing familiarity with charts by using them to answer specific questions related to information in the text. They provide a ready answer to factual questions. For a practice exercise, choose a selection in which the chart is a carefully planned, motivated supplement.

There are some exercises that students can participate in that will help give them an insight into the advantage of a chart over printed textual material.

1. From a social studies text take a time-line chart and rewrite it into several paragraphs. At random, add one or two sentences of descriptive information about various events. If possible, interrupt the chronological order of the events. Distribute it as a handout and give students a few moments to read through it. Give them an informal quiz over the material. Allow them to use the sheet to answer, and let them write the answers on

scratch paper. Make sure you ask questions only relating to specific events, ignoring the descriptive information you added.

2. Ask students to convert the information you gave them to a more efficient vehicle for answering the previous questions. Show some of their ideas on an opaque projector.

3. Give a second quiz, allowing students to use their own charts to answer. Again ask only for the events that took place and ask the questions out of chronological order.

4. To give students some experience in compiling information from a chart, obtain from a travel agent an airline guide showing flights, times, and so on. If you are unable to find one, make a hypothetical page of your own. Because charts often show columns headed by abbreviations or symbols, go over those appearing in the guide, pointing out that students should do this before beginning to use a chart.

5. From pages that you pass out, ask students to first answer simple questions like whether or not they can fly to Sioux Falls, South Dakota. Add one additional complexity to each round of practice questions until you have students figuring cost- and time-efficient trips between destinations requiring layovers and airline changes.

6. Remind students that they have probably been looking between the two columns to find the point where the lines intersect. Pass out additional practice copies and have students plot the answers with colored pencils.

9.3E READING DIAGRAMS TO SEE FUNCTION

(This lesson might be effectively videotaped so that students could get a close-up view of the machine parts.)

Level   Junior high and above.

Objective To examine the parts of a diagrammed machine in terms of function instead of specific names.

Description Various types of content books have a need to include diagrams within the text. A text in auto shop will, of necessity, be filled with diagrams and various labeled illustrations. The task is made more difficult by the large number of terms that are often needed to label a single diagram. Difficulty with processing all of the terms can be a painful reminder that the job of even the most skillful auto mechanic will sometimes include parts-chasing and inventory and following complex diagrams.

Too often content teachers give an assignment that involves memorizing a diagram, and follow up by giving a test that asks students to fill in the appropriate names on blank lines of a duplicate of the diagram from the text. This may seem like an efficient way to begin a unit, but it can cause a repeat of an old problem for students who have trouble reading all of the words. It can also encourage students to memorize lists of words without regard for the items in the diagram to which they are connected.

Students need practice *a.* in looking at diagrams in *sections* and *b.* in thinking of a function in connection with a specific term. A lesson using a sewing machine provides a workable example of a practice lesson in looking at the function of parts of a machine. This lesson can be taught in the home economics room, or in the classroom with a borrowed sewing machine. Pass out copies of a sewing machine diagram and have a corresponding copy on an overhead projector. (Make sure that the diagram accurately represents the machine to be demonstrated. Try to avoid using an elaborate machine with multiple-stitch options. The diagram can likely be found in a home economics text, or the teacher may already have loose copies available.)

1. Discuss the machine briefly with students, reminding them that its overall function is to sew a double stitch from two angles so that both sides of the work are stitched. This is necessary to make a strong seam that will last over time.

   On the overhead, cover up all but the bobbin and related area. Point to each part of the bobbin mechanism and explain its role in sewing. Thread the bobbin.

2. Next, deal with the head of the machine. Start with the spool holder, and explain each part, following the thread down to the needle. With the needle threaded, sew two pieces of fabric together.

3. Give students an unlabeled copy of the same diagram. Ask them to label each part they recognize by what it does, using as many words as they wish.

4. Have students go back to the labeled diagram and compare it to the one they have just completed. In how many instances do the actual terms seem to be an efficient abbreviation for the functions they have written?

9.3F READING DIAGRAMS AND LABELS

Level   Junior high and above.

Objective   Look at a diagram and compare with the actual object.

Description   For a variety of reasons, diagrams appearing on a printed page create an aura of instant difficulty. The parts tend to look intricate and captions are listed one after another. Students can become increasingly comfortable with diagrams with practice in reading small sections of diagrams and by comparing diagrams to the actual physical objects.

Students in ninth grade are extremely anxious to drive. They are generally not yet old enough to be enrolled in the driver's training class, but are anxious to do car- and driving-related projects. This lesson of changing a tire might be effectively taught in auto shop, but would be almost as effective in the classroom.

1. Show a diagram of a jack reproduced from the owner's manual of a car. (Be sure to have a diagram that depicts the jack to be demonstrated.) Have the students talk about the function of the jack and then examine the real jack after looking at the diagram. Then, set up the jack on a car. (Simulate if doing the exercise in the classroom.)
2. Show a simple diagram of a lug wrench. Have students look at the diagram and then pass the actual lug wrench around.
3. Show a diagram of the lug wrench loosening the bolts on a wheel. Reemphasize the labels of the various parts. Let students turn the bolts after they have been loosened.
4. Finish the process and return to the jack diagram when completed. Finish changing the tire. Again, relabel each part of the jack and let students take turns jacking the car down.

9.3G ANSWERING QUESTIONS FROM DIAGRAMS

Level   Secondary.

Objective   To answer specific questions from reading a diagram.

Description   Diagrams combining both words and line drawing are often encountered as guides for action. Such drawings are successful, however, only when the logic they advance is fully understood. Students can gain greater familiarity with diagrams through guided efforts at an orderly approach to them.

Since many students are interested in car stereo systems, the following exercise dealing with a hypothetical diagram of a car stereo system should be of interest.

1. Have students examine the diagram (Figure 9–C) and then direct them in sorting out the following pieces of information obtained from it:

   a. Where does the sound come from? (left and right speakers)
   b. What are the unit's power requirements? (+12VCD)
   c. What function is served by the FM antenna? (collects FM signals from the air)
   d. What does the symbol ≡ mean? (ground)
   e. Why are there two sets of outputs? (stereo implies two channels for sound reproduction)

f. If one secured a tape playback unit, could it be connected for use with this receiver? Where would one make such a connection? (yes; at the auxiliary input tape)

2. Have students bring in diagrams of things that they are familiar with through other courses or hobbies. Arrange to have them duplicated or made into transparencies, and have the students teach the class to look at the diagrams in some order and to pick specific important information from them.

Figure 9–C

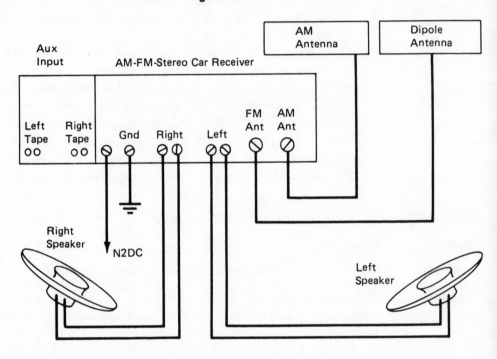

10

TEACHING WRITING WITH READING

Like a speaker and a listener,
a writer and a reader need
to work together. The writer starts a silent dialog with the reader. Thereafter, the writer and
reader are constantly reasoning with themselves and their silent partner.

Over the years teachers have expressed a continuing interest in integrating all aspects of their instruction. That has been true particularly in bringing together the teaching of reading and writing. Since both have written language and organized thought in common, it seems reasonable that they could benefit from being taught together in a deliberate fashion.

Moving from the theoretical position of seeing commonalities in reading and writing to the practical problem of helping twenty-five students learn those commonalities is quite another matter. Too often, it seems, the notion of teaching writing along with reading gets bogged down in a discussion of how to achieve the objectives of both when the number of objectives in either area is already too numerous. One solution is to shift the instructional purpose for integrating reading and writing. The purpose is not to juggle large numbers of skills, trying to keep two sets of similar objectives in the air at the same time. The purpose is more global: to demonstrate the use of writing and reading as similar and complimentary thought-into-language processes. The discusssion in this chapter focuses on several strategies for teaching writing and reading together, but not as a means of developing highly specific skills in either area. For other purposes a teacher may need to work on particular skills, such as might be found in grammar and usage exercises. In this chapter the emphasis will be on the common thought processes used while reading and writing, and the benefit that students will experience from reading with a pen in hand and writing with a book on the table.

FROM PASSIVE TO ACTIVE

Most students perceive reading as a passive activity. One boy, when asked what his mind did while reading, said: "I don't know. I just look at the page and my brain soaks it up." In interviews conducted by the authors, that notion of passivity was repeated often. One major value of making writing a central ingredient in reading assignments would be the alteration of that passive attitude. One way to conceptualize a reader is to imagine that person making notes while reading. Reading to study, for example, is frequently carried out with a highlighter pen in hand. As students find important ideas, they highlight them as a way of returning quickly to those ideas at a later time. Whether or not the student actually returns to the highlighted phrases is probably not as important as the fact that through the use of the highlighter the student works attentively at making decisions about what seems to be important. As a general guideline, therefore, it helps to use writing as a way of prompting the reader to be active, rather than sit and "soak."

10.1 A PROCESS APPROACH: REASONING

BEFORE, DURING, AFTER—Another way to look at the connection between reading and writing is to see that the thought processes in each require the same staging. Reading and writing both require preparation, attention to purpose, and a revision of ideas as a concluding activity.

Every effective teacher knows how important it is to provide adequate preparation for reading tasks. And every effective writing teacher knows how important it is to review and to revise as necessary components of the writing task. It so happens that effective reading and writing both benefit from a similar thinking process, described below.

BEFORE

Prepare adequately. Ask students to call up their experiences and vocabulary related to the topic, and to discuss them as a way of preparing their minds for the task ahead. This preparation activity is akin to a warmup in athletics. It generates the vocabulary and the mental outlines that act as a framework for the upcoming reading or writing task.

DURING

Pay attention to the task. Students need to determine their purpose for reading or for writing and stick to it. By deciding ahead of time what is the purpose and/or the audience for the effort makes the task meaningful and makes it easier to keep to the point.

AFTER

Revise and clarify. After reading or writing, students need an opportunity to sum up ideas or to clarify them. Perhaps they want to reevaluate their own ideas as a result of what they have read. Perhaps they want to clarify the ideas they have put on paper to make sure that the message stated is the one intended.

Whether reading or writing, the three step process mentioned above should remind students that a pencil or a word processor can become an integral part of the working environment. Students can write vocabulary and purpose-setting questions as a preparation for reading in the same way that they might write them for an upcoming composition. During reading and during writing, the student mind is guided by notes and reactions as they arise in the course of fulfilling the purpose of the exercise. And after reading or writing, the student will benefit from writing some kind of summary or reaction, or by reviewing the writing to make changes that will communicate more clearly to the intended audience.

10.1A   ENGAGING IN A DIALOG WITH THE AUTHOR

Level   Middle grades and above.

Objective   To help students interact with the text they are reading.

Description   1. Convey to students the need to react continually to what they are reading. They are to pretend that they are engaging in a dialog with the writer.
2. Their own background will determine what they want to say to the author and how they hear what the author says to them. By using marginal notes in the text or in the book that they are reading they can begin to develop the conversation.
3. Marginal notes can be made on separate sheets of paper instead of on the book page itself.
4. It may be advantageous to convey to students the idea that both the writer and the reader engage in this dialog. In effect, the writer starts by saying, "Here's an idea I am interested in. How about you?" The reader then makes a response: "It has possibilities. Tell me more." And so the two move back and forth in their silent dialog without ever actually meeting each other. Both reader and writer are constantly engaged in questioning the other, predicting the ideas and the language that will occur next, and mentally arranging those ideas to best suit their needs.

10.1B   AN EDITORIAL TO THE AUTHOR

Level   Junior high and above.

Objective   To use an editorial writer's approach to judging the value of a piece of writing.

Description   It is often necessary to help students form the attitudes or the mental set that they need in order to appreciate the role that writing can play in reading. One way to accomplish that end is to ask the students to pretend that they are editorial writers who must give a judgment on the social value of something they are about to read. But instead of sending the editorial to a local newspaper, they are going to send the editorial to the person who wrote the article. In other words they are going to write an editorial about an article and discuss its social, not its literary value, with the author.

An editorial states an opinion and then gives reasons why the writer has that opinion.

Prewrite
Give students directions such as:
Read a newspaper editorial before proceeding. Get a sense of how it proceeds. Go back and scan the reading selection, then write some words or sentences that answer these questions:
1.   What are some facts that you know about the subject?
2.   What are some opinions that you have?
3.   What are some opinions that the author expresses in the article?
4.   Can you explain the reasons that you have for your opinions? Does the author explain his or her reasons?

Write
1.   Reread the sentences you wrote.
2.   Think about your audience, the person who will read your editorial. Your editorial should make your reader want to support your opinion.
3.   Think about how many paragraphs your editorial will have. State your opinion in the first paragraph.
4.   Then use the information you discovered through reading the article to explain why you have the opinion that you do. Use the sentences you wrote to answer the questions above.

Revise
Read your editorial. Did you state clearly your opinion? Did you give reasons that supported your opinion? If not, now is the time to rewrite the parts of your editorial that are unclear.

Mail
Contact the library or the author's publisher to get a mailing address. Send your editorial with a letter explaining the assignment. Ask for a reply.

10.1C   WRITING A SUMMARY

Objective   To learn to write a summary as an aid to thinking while reading.

Description   Writing a summary aids the thinking process that a student needs to use in reasoning through an article or a chapter. The following directions could be printed as guidelines for summarizing an article that they are to read.

Prewrite
When you write a summary, you choose and write the important facts or ideas about a subject in your own words. You can follow these steps to write a summary:
1. Read the material.
2. Think of questions to ask about the information as you read.
3. Using information in the article, write notes as answers to your questions.
4. Read your notes and choose the most important ideas for your summary.
5. Write these facts in a summary of one or two paragraphs.

Write
1. Read your questions and answers. Reread the article.
2. Write a sentence for your summary which describes the main idea in the article. Here is an example:
   Music can have positive effects on a person's health.
3. Write the most important facts from your notes to support your main idea sentence.

Revise
Read your summary. Did you write a clear main idea sentence? Are your secondary sentences based on facts from the article? Have you left out an important fact? If so, rewrite your summary.

10.1D   ADDING THE MISSING PARTS

Level   Middle grades and above.

Objective   To help students understand that their minds are constantly constructing ideas when they read and write.

Description   Help students see that ideas in a composition or in a reading selection are analogous to modular units in some of the toys and games they have played with. A part of the text can be deleted or replaced with a slightly different idea. The whole piece is not destroyed; rather, it is changed or enhanced by the replacement. This idea can be demonstrated by leaving off the ending (or the beginning) of a story and substituting another version. Prepare students for this kind of exercise by reading (or distributing) the following two letters.

Invent an ending

An eighth-grade girl wrote to me about an exercise in one of my books. Her class had read a mystery that took the reader through an episode in which a crime had been committed, then the students were asked to write the ending to the story. Our exchange follows.

Dear Mr. Smith,

We have been reading your mini-mystery about Mrs. Underwood.

Each member of the class developed his own ending, and we shared them and voted on the best one. That was fun, but now we want to know what the real ending is. Please hurry your answer because we are waiting anxiously.

Yours truly,
Kathy

Dear Kathy,

Each of you already has the real ending. The real ending is the one that each of you constructed in your own mind. The Underwood mystery was written as an unfinished story. It was designed to make you both reader and writer, that is, a thinker. You all did a terrific job, especially since you analyzed your endings and voted on the best one in the class. Please send it to me so I will know what the real ending is.

Cordially,
Carl B. Smith

The kind of exercise that asks students to construct a missing element in something they are reading gives them two extremely valuable perspectives: 1) that ideas are communicated in an orderly fashion so that they themselves can project a reasonable continuation of those ideas, and 2) that their minds need to be quite active, whether as readers or as writers.

The teacher needs to make abstractions concrete enough for learners to understand them. The pattern of thought in any article is abstract. By filling in the missing parts of an article, students begin to sense organization and to understand that ideas can be manipulated just like building blocks.

10.1E   THE RHYTHM OF LANGUAGE

Level   Middle grades and above.

Objective   To encourage students to use the flow or rhythm of language as a way of thinking about ideas.

Description   This is a variation on filling in the missing part. It works best using jingles or poetry.

1. Ask students to think of ways in which they get a sense of meaning from the sound or from the rhythm of language instead of simply analyzing ideas. They may want to supply examples from popular songs, leaving out words or phrases that can be easily replaced because the sentiment and rhythm predict it. For example, a song that has the line: "I need you, _____ . I need your love." The blank can be easily filled with a word like "baby" or "honey," because the feeling and the rhythm indicate a term of endearment that has two syllables.

2. Ask the students to replace "hickory, dickory, dock" in the following nursery rhyme with a repetitive phrase of their own — one that fits, of course.

    Hickory, dickory, dock.
    The mouse ran up the clock.
    The clock struck one.
    The mouse ran down.
    Hickory, dickory, dock.

3. See if each student can develop his or her own replacement exercise by using a poem or a popular song. They should leave out a line or a phrase that demands a clear rhythm in order to fit. Preferably the line should be an especially attractive one, which a student can replace with a similarly compelling personal line.

10.2   ESTABLISHING A PURPOSE: PREPARATION

A sense of purpose gives writing the direction and coherence it needs, just as it gives the reader a means for holding ideas together while reading. A sense of audience is closely associated with the notion of purpose. Purpose guides the flow of thoughts but a sense of audience gives the message its flavor and style.

Reminding students of the force of purpose in their writing needs particular attention in the middle and secondary grades. They often become so accustomed to merely writing for their teacher that they tend to lose sight of the variety of purposes and audiences that exist. Occasionally the teacher would serve his or her students well to discuss the many purposes and audiences for which to write. It is often quite beneficial to discuss purpose and audience with a class and to list their suggestions on the chalk board as the ideas come forward. Most important, the class needs to ask themselves what changes in their approach would occur if they shifted from tring to report an event to trying to convince someone of the soundness of an idea or the value of an opinion.

Depending on the sophistication of the students, purpose setting for written communication can be made more interesting by associating different kinds of exposition with different purposes. If the purpose is to provide factual information about a serious accident, it could be reported in the form of a story (narrative), a newspaper report, or a television broadcast — among others.

The audience needs as much consideration as does the purpose for writing. If a serious accident is going to be written about for the high school newspaper, that opens up one kind of vocabulary and background, while an audience of first and second graders indicates a need for greater visualization and for a vocabulary in keeping with their lower-level background.

Not to be overlooked is the motivational value of establishing a purpose and an audience for writing, including writing related to reading. One of the continuing preoccupations teachers have is how to show students the real-world connection between the routine tasks that are performed in the classroom. In that sense, purpose and audience become important motivating factors for the students.

10.2A REPORTING THE FACTS

Level   Middle grades and above.

Objective   To clarify the purpose of delivering factual information in writing, especially through the use of the five W's: *Who, What, Where, When, Why.*

Description   To report factual information is to report those things for which there is objectively verifiable evidence. Thus the emphasis in writing a factual account is on statements for which evidence can be demonstrated. A television newscaster and a newspaper reporter, for example, should present facts about a news event, and should avoid giving their opinions or feelings about what is happening.

Prewrite
1. Imagine you are a newspaper reporter. You are going to write a news story for your local newspaper. First, you must think of an interesting event that happened to you or to someone you know. For example, you may want to report on a soccer game or a class election.
2. Reporters use the five W's to help them write. These are:
   Who? What? Where? When? Why?
   Choose the news event you will write about. Use the five W's to make sure you include all the important facts. Use the five W's to write questions. Write an answer for each question, or use the questions to interview someone.

Write
1. Read your questions and answers.
2. Think about how many paragraphs you will write. Begin each para-

graph with a sentence that tells the main idea. Make sure the other sentences in the paragraph give details that support or explain the main idea.

3. Use the sentences you wrote about the five W's in your preparation. Be sure you write about the facts and not your opinions.
4. Write a headline for your news story. The headline should be so interesting that it will make people want to read the story.

Revise

Read your news story. Did you use only facts and not give opinions? Can you find answers to the five W's in your story? Does each paragraph have a main idea sentence? Did you write an interesting headline? Now is the time to rewrite parts of your news story that may be unclear or incomplete.

10.2B   WRITING A FEATURE STORY

Level   Middle grades and above.

Objective   To show students how to shift from the style and information required for news stories to those necessary for developing a feature article.

Description   What makes a person a hero or heroine? Certainly people who risk their lives fit into that category. Perhaps there are others who help people through difficult periods of their lives, who might also be called heroes and heroines. How would you write about a heroine? Making a decision about the quality of a person requires a personal judgment, a personal opinion. In newspapers and magazines, articles that highlight a special personality, program, or policy are called feature stories. Write a feature story, perhaps based on someone whom you have read about or someone you know.

Prewrite

1. Imagine you are a feature story writer for your local newspaper. A feature story is a story about a subject of special interest to many people. Unlike a news story, it tells more than just the facts about an event. A feature can include more details, background material, and often, the writer's personal feelings about the subject.
2. As a feature writer, whom will you choose as the subject of a story about heroes and heroines? You may want to write a feature about someone you know who has done something for others. People do not have to risk their lives to be heroes and heroines.
3. Before you write, do some reading about your subject. If you choose to write about someone you know, plan to interview that person for your story.
4. The following questions can help organize your writing. As you write the answers, take notes using full sentences.

a. Who is the subject of your feature story?

b. What experience did he or she have? When? Where?

c. Why is the person or what they did of interest to people?

d. How do you feel about what the person did?

Write

1. Read your questions and answers.

2. Plan how you will organize your story. The first part may tell what the subject did. This part of your feature story is like a news story. The facts are told in sequence. Use words like *first, then, next*, and *finally* to help your readers follow the sequence of events.

3. The second part of the feature story may tell about the person's thoughts and feelings, your feelings, and why the subject is of interest to people.

4. Think of an interesting headline for your feature story. A headline should give a hint about the story and attract the attention of the readers.

Revise

Read your feature story. Did you give the facts about what the person did in a clear sequence? Did you tell about the person's thoughts and feelings as well as your own? Will your readers feel as if they know the subject when they have read your feature story? If not, now is the time to rewrite.

10.2C   SELLING THE KITCHEN SINK

Level   Junior high and above.

Objective   To help students alter writing in order to convince an audience.

Description   A television commercial or an advertisement in a newspaper or magazine are all illustrations of the points in this section: each has a clear purpose and sense of audience. Why not use the medium of advertising to sell someone on the idea of reading a book — perhaps your favorite one?

Prewrite

1. Television and radio commercials try to present a product in such a way that people will want to buy it. Commercials often make use of slogans, such as, "Happy Sam keeps you happy with your new car."

    Choose your favorite book. Plan to write an advertisement for that book. If you do a television commercial, you may need pictures and costumes as props. If you write a radio commercial, you may want to use music or other sound effects.

2. To get ready, write down a few facts or events from the book. Write a slogan that will grab the attention of your audience. Your audience

will want to know the title, author, publisher, date of publication, and one or two exciting characters or events in the story.

3. Clarify in your own mind who your audience will be.

Write

1. Read again your facts and slogan.
2. Think about how you will start your commercial. You might start with the slogan.
3. Give facts. You are trying to sell a product. People need to know its name, so use it more than once in the commercial.
4. Commercials have short, snappy sentences. Choose clever verbs, adverbs, and adjectives.
5. Describe how your pictures, costumes or music will fit into the commercial. Someone else should be able to take your script and produce your commercial.

Revise

Read aloud what you have written. Remember that your audience has to see and hear it. Would you want to buy the book? Did you use short, lively sentences? Is your slogan going to grab the attention of your audience? Rewrite any parts that you think could be more interesting or entertaining.

10.3   RESPONDING TO READING

If the reader brings as much to the story as the writer does, then teachers need to find ways of helping students to respond energetically to what they read. After all, meaning is constructed in the mind of the reader. Thus the reader constantly takes ideas from the printed page to try to build something meaningful in his or her own mind.

Although there are numerous ways for a reader to interact with the printed message, the most manageable classroom strategy is to have students write responses to what they are reading. Through writing, everyone can participate at the same time, in his or her own style and pace.

Once the reader has written a response, the written record stands ready for personal review, for group discussion, or for sharing written ideas. A written response allows for thoughtful sharing of ideas, unencumbered by the usual overtones and stresses associated with sharing ideas aloud.

Almost any reading selection in any subject will elicit a written response in which the reader can write down two or three ideas that seem most important or interesting. A sharing of those ideas will exhibit the commonality of reactions as well as the diversity of ideas that are mentioned as important. Seeing both the common elements and the diverse reactions will help students understand the reality of human experiences and human thinking. Given the same literary stimulus, twenty different people with twenty different backgrounds will uncover at least twenty different interpretations.

Some additional strategies for responding to reading include keeping a journal, sharing ideas about reading through letters to peers, writing an interpretive narrative, and using reading as a literary model for personal writing.

10.3A   KEEPING A READING JOURNAL

Level   Middle grades and above.

Objective   To help students think about what they read through regular, personal reactions.

Description   A journal or a diary is a running account of events or thoughts. Those events or thoughts are usually written in the order in which they occurred.

Prewrite
1.   Keep a journal of your thoughts as you read from day to day. It may be a journal of your thoughts on a single book that you read over a period of a month, or it may be a journal of your reactions and thoughts as you read a variety of materials from day to day.
2.   Think about the kinds of reactions you might include in such a journal. You can make your journal more interesting by describing your feelings about the ideas in the reading, rather than merely recording what you think are important facts or events.

Write
1.   Decide each day how many pages you will react to and cover, or what will be the minimum number of paragraphs that you plan to write.
2.   Your journal will be more useful to you if you mark the number of the page in the book that led you to record the thoughts that you are writing.

Revise
Read the entry in your journal. Do the paragraphs tell what happened in the story? Do they tell what your feelings were? You may want to rewrite parts of your journal.

10.3B   SHARING THROUGH LETTERS

Level   Middle grades and above.

Objective   To respond to reading through letter writing.

Description   Friendly letters represent one of the clearest forms of communication. Whether letters are written to other students in the same class or sent across town to students in another school, the sense of personal communication remains clear. A journal may be seen as a private document, whereas a letter opens up the lines of communication between two active minds.

Prewrite
1. Think about the book or the article that you are now reading. Then think about a friend in another room or school, or even in another state. What would you want to tell him or her about this reading selection?
2. List three main ideas that you would want to share with your friend.
3. Prepare several questions that you think your friend would ask about the main ideas which you have listed. Write brief answers to these questions.

Write
1. Read over your main ideas.
2. As you write your letter, write a paragraph about each of your main ideas.
3. Use the questions that you wrote as the subjects for another couple of paragraphs.

Revise
Reread your letter. Does each paragraph give a clear idea? Do you think the letter answers the important questions about the book or the article? Did you ask your friend to write back with reactions and questions? Did you ask your friend to share his or her reading with you? Now is the time to rewrite any portion of your letter that is not clear.

10.3C   AN INTERPRETIVE NARRATIVE

Level   Junior high and above.

Objective   To respond to reading by writing a narrative that interprets the reading selection.

Description   Some people find it easier to present their feelings by describing the emotions of someone else. A short narrative that interprets a reading selection is appropriate for that purpose.
1. Write a first-person narrative (story) that reveals your feelings about the kinds of events in the story that you have just read.
2. Write as if the events are happening to you directly. Use the first person pronouns, such as *I, me, my, mine.*

3.   Think of all the little events or steps that you must tell to help your readers understand your experience and your feelings. You may want to make a chart (see Figure 10-A) to make sure that you identify the steps and the feelings that are important to this narrative.

Figure 10-A

Events	Feelings

4.   When you have written your notes, see if they lead you to some conclusions about your interpretation of the reading. That is what you want to make available to your audience.

Write

1.   Read your notes and conclusion.
2.   Think about the length of your narrative. Perhaps you can write a narrative that has four paragraphs: one to set the stage, two to indicate your feelings, and one to bring the narrative to a close.
3.   Are you ready to add a title to your narrative?
4.   Remember to use first-person pronouns.

Revise

Read your narrative. Did you tell the events in a clear sequence? Did you draw a conclusion based on what happened and upon your feelings about the events? Rewrite any part that is unclear.

10.3D   READING AS A MODEL FOR WRITING

Level   Middle grades and above.

Objective   To use an existing piece of writing as a model for composition.

Description   We get ideas from things around us. Just as each of us has heroes or heroines whom we try to imitate, we also use other people's writing as a model for the writing that we do. Especially when we set out on a new writing venture, it makes perfectly good sense to look at samples of what others have written. They may give us some very good ideas.

Poetry often lends itself to modelling because one aspect of a poem is what we see; that is, the arrangement of the lines, the format of the verses or parts, even the pattern of the rhyme scheme, if one exists.

1. Read the following poem by a fourth grader and note its visual and aural scheme. This student had read a poem that repeated lines for a cumulative effect. She used that poem as a model to produce these verses.

MY FOREST HOUSE*
by
Ruth Simpson

I know a place with a roof of green
And the floor is much the same.

This place I call my forest house.
It's great for playing games.

I love this place more than anything else
With the bluebirds and robins that sing.

This beautiful place, this wonderful place,
Is my forest house in the Spring.

I know a place with a gold-green roof
For the sun is peeking through.

The crickets chirp, the robins sing
As I sit and play in the dew.

I love this place more than anything else,
Where the woodpecker is the drummer.

This beautiful place, this wonderful place,
Is my forest house in the summer.

I know a place with a roof of gold,
And a cool soft floor of green.

This place I call my forest house.
It's the best house ever seen.

I love this place more than anything else
Though I don't live here at all.

This beautiful place, this wonderful place,
Is my forest house in the Fall.

I know a place with no roof at all
And the floor is cold and white.

(continued)

*Reprinted by permission of Ruth Simpson.

This place I call my forest house.
It's always shimmering bright.

I love this place more than anything else
And'couldn't say this any simpler.

This beautiful place, this wonderful place,
Is my forest house in the winter.

2. Find a model for the kind of writing that you want to do. Use
    it to make notes on both the subject and the form that you
    want to use.

Write
1. Read your notes again. Do you have an image in your mind of what
    your composition should look like? Do you have a sense of direction
    for guiding the ideas in the composition?
2. As you write, keep that sense of direction in mind and keep your au-
    dience in mind.

Revise
Even though you want your composition to be original, try matching it
against the features of your model. Does it have a similar look or sense of
movement? When you put yours and your model side by side, are there
things that you would now like to change in your writing to make it more
effective? Now is the time to rewrite.

10.4 REVISING FOR CLARIFICATION

**Students are in the process of learning and therefore are not expected to produce
perfect papers. In that sense, there is always something that a teacher can criticize
or correct. But the goal is to improve, not to be perfect. Student themes, therefore,
place the teacher in the position of praising and providing direction for improvement
at the same time. This matter is further complicated by the need to have the student
become personally responsible for reviewing and revising his or her own paper. If this
is done, powerful lifelong learning habits will be developed.**

A few guidelines, posted or reproduced for students, will reduce frustration
over the question of rewriting. The teacher naturally applies a measure of
common sense to this issue and helps students see the idea of revising and
rewriting as a matter tied to the purpose of writing and to learning how to
grow in clarity of composition.

GUIDELINES FOR REWRITING

1. Proofread every composition — sometimes for specific skills, sometimes for its general sense.
2. A composition submitted to another person must be legible.
3. The purpose for the composition and its audience will determine the extent of its revision.
4. Some compositions may benefit from several revisions before they are ready for public reading.
5. Remember: a public composition carries your signature. Make it clear; make it understandable.

10.4A   A TEACHER NOTATION SYSTEM

Level   Middle grades and above.

Objective   To establish a simple set of notations that a teacher could use to encourage students to carry out personal revisions in their compositions.

Description   Even after the student claims that he or she has proofread and revised a paper, the teacher still may want to review the paper for a variety of purposes. In this section we are assuming that one of the long range goals is to help students become responsible for their own work. One way to aid that process is for the teacher to indicate where improvement is needed but to have the student make the actual changes. A single mark at the top of the paper or in the margin can indicate the need for a change without actually making the change. The mark means that the teacher wants at least one revision in order for the paper to be acceptable for resubmission.

For example, as soon as the teacher notices an error, she or he can place an R (for review) at the top of the paper or in the margin near the error. When the student returns the paper showing that additional work has been done on it, the teacher can then evaluate the paper as she or he thinks is appropriate. A simple notation system can work toward the end of making students conscious of their responsibility. Regarding mechanical errors, the system could use these notations:

> RS = review spelling
> RP = review punctuation
> RG = review grammar
> RH = review handwriting for legibility

Students can use these marginal notations to review their work and make changes. Some teachers find it useful to have students circle the errors that they have located and write the corrections above the circled errors.

In other cases where the purpose of the proofreading was to examine the flow of ideas, or the appropriate use of images and examples, the notations could reflect those concerns:

Flow = logic or coherence of ideas
Language = check vocabulary or phrasing
Images = examine appropriateness of examples or images

Where these more complex issues are the center of attention, the teacher may encourage students to discuss his or her notations among themselves or to discuss these matters with the teacher. The teacher and the students can decide whether or not the paper should show the marks of the revision. When the papers are only between student and teacher, and language growth is the primary concern, the scars of revision may be desirable. Student and teacher may want to see all the marks and notations they have made as visible evidence of the changes that have been occurring. On the other hand, a paper that will be posted on the bulletin board or circulated among students or parents should be rewritten and presented as a clean copy. When the paper is being prepared for public display, the final paper should show respect for the reader and for the image that the writer wants to project to the reader.

The purpose of the paper and its audience are as much a concern in the revision process as they are in planning and writing.

10.4B STUDENT SELF-CORRECTION

Level   Middle grades and above.

Objective   To gradually shift the responsibility for revision and proofreading to the student.

Description
1. Revision by partners or in a team are exercises well-known to teachers of composition. By exchanging and reading each other's papers with a set of guidelines, students learn to look for ways to clarify and improve their papers. They also learn to discuss the clarity of language with one another.
2. At first, independent self-correction should occur only now and then, as for example, in every third or fourth composition. This gives students a chance to see regularly other papers and to see what other readers look for in their reviews. Gradually, through the semester, the burden for revision can be shifted more and more to the individual.
3. In all of these revision exercises, clarification and error reduc-

tion are the goals. As with the team-reviewed papers, so the self-reviewed papers are read by the teacher, who then applies his or her judgment to this particular effort. Does it need more work or is it acceptable, given the purpose for writing? A teacher notation system can be used at this stage for giving the student directions (see a discussion of the notation system above).

4. Keep an improvement chart. It might be an error-reduction chart, and might look similar to the one in Figure 10-B. For example, if a student has identifiable problems with spelling or punctuation, the student might want to aim at reducing the number of those errors from composition to composition. Each composition is listed by date of submission with the type of error that has been searched out. The comments section can be used by the student or by the teacher. Students, for example, may want to remind themselves of generalizations that they need to use in order to reduce certain types of errors. The teacher could also use the comment section as a way of offering encouragement to the student.

5. As the self-correction process becomes more habitual, the teacher will want students to review their compositions for more than one element. Spelling was used in the sample chart merely as an illustration. The same idea could be used to review for organization, for bridging ideas from paragraph to paragraph, and so on. Eventually, at the discretion of the teacher, there can be a proofing of the whole work. The value of a single focus early in the process is that students learn to review for themselves some aspect of their writing that is manageable.

Figure 10-B

Error-Reduction Chart			
Date	Type of Error	Number of Errors	Comments
9/16	spelling	8	Student found six errors
9/20	spelling	6	
9/26	spelling	3	Student found all three

10.4C CLARIFYING COMMUNICATION

Level   Middle grades and above.

Objective   To guide students in clarifying their written messages.

Description   1.   The first and most difficult matter in written communication is making the message clear. We write in order to communicate. The clearer the writing, the better the communication. Since we all fail to write clearly from time to time, we benefit from seeing language samples from our papers that are discussed by other members of the class.

2.   An overhead transparency of an anonymous paragraph can be made by the teacher as a way of discussing clarity (and other elements of written composition). As the group looks at the projected paragraph, the teacher asks: "How can we make this paragraph more clear?"

3.   Any member of the class is then free to write a clarifying word, phrase, or sentence on the chalkboard. The class can then discuss it as an improvement or suggest other ways to improve the comprehensibility of the message. Since clarity of communication is the issue, all sorts of questions about audience, choice of language, perhaps even handwriting, may arise. Since the paragraph is anonymous and clarity is the issue, embarrassment is kept to a minimum, and highly personal and individual learning is encouraged.

4.   This same routine can be used to call attention to specific skills and literary devices — if that suits the purpose of the group.

5.   After observing numerous student samples over a long period of time, most members of the class should see that analytic work applied to their compositions is helpful and a normal part of the process of communicating clearly.

10.4D   THE DRAFT AND REVIEW TECHNIQUE

Level   Middle grades and above.

Objective   To help the student see that the first draft of a composition is only one step toward effective communication

Description   1.   The teacher's role in helping students become more effective in written communication includes developing in them an attitude of personal responsibility for the effectiveness of the communication and giving them guidelines for constructing compositions that are legible, well-organized, and use the conventions of writing as accurately as is feasible.

2.   Students, then, need to see the value in submitting a draft with their own notations, which demonstrate an effort in improving their own papers. This process can be promoted by hav-

ing students write or type double-spaced copy and by having them circle the words or areas that they want to change. The changes can then be made above the circled copy.

3. When the draft with the student's notations is submitted, the teacher does not correct the paper, but rather makes only a few limited comments. If the revising effort seems to be fairly thorough, the teacher may write, "OK." If there are words or phrases that the teacher thinks need additional change, the teacher can circle those areas and return the paper to the student for adjustments. Naturally, the student may discuss these areas with the teacher.

4. Depending on the purpose of the paper, those marked with an "OK" may be acceptable as they are. Those returned with additional circles need more work and are then resubmitted. If the papers are designed for a public display or for a grade, they all should be resubmitted with appropriate adjustments.

5. This technique of drafting and reviewing establishes an attitude about student compositions as interactive communications between student and teacher or between student and an audience. A draft must reflect an attempt to improve the communication. The teacher's response fosters that march toward improvement. In this, as in other suggestions in this section of the book, an attitude is engendered that the student and the teacher *share* the responsibility of developing effective communicators. The burden is not wholly on the teacher with a red pen.

10.4E   WRITING LEGIBLY

Level   Middle grades and above.

Objective   To alert students to their responsibility for legible handwriting.

Description   1. Legibility has to be included as a factor in proofreading. Although upper grade teachers and students do not want to pay attention to mundane matters such as handwriting, legibility is definitely a factor in written communication.

2. We need to make a distinction between neatness and legibility. Some samples of handwriting look neat, but they can not be read easily because all the letters look alike. Another handwriting sample may not look neat but can be read easily because there are clear distinctions among the letters. If m's, n's u's, and w's all look alike, for instance, the resulting script will be difficult to decipher. If i's, e's, l's and t's all look alike, the same is true.

3. By arranging letters in groups that are easily confused, a teacher can alert students to the kinds of factors that cloud their handwriting and make legibility an issue on their papers. After that brief lecture, all a teacher needs to do is to reject papers that are illegible, asking that they be rewritten in legible fashion. Legibility is then encouraged as a matter of etiquette or politeness for future submissions.

APPENDIX A
Activities for Slow Readers

Subjects	Understanding Bookthinking	Motivation	Reader Responsibility
Business Education	1.1A, 1.1B, 1.2A, 1.4A, 1.5A, 1.5B	2.1A, 2.1B, 2.2A, 2.2B, 2.2C, 2.2D, 2.2E, 2.2F 10.4C, 10.4D	3.1A, 3.2A, 3.3A, 3.3B, 3.4A, 3.5A 10.4E
Career Education	1.1A, 1.2A, 1.4A, 1.5A, 1.5B	2.1A, 2.1B, 2.2A, 2.2B, 2.2C, 2.2D, 2.2F 10.4C, 10.4D	3.1A, 3.2A, 3.3A, 3.3B, 3.4A, 3.5A 10.4E
English	1.1A, 1.1B, 1.2A, 1.4A, 1.5A, 1.5B	2.1A, 2.1B, 2.2A, 2.2B, 2.2C, 2.2D, 2.2E, 2.2F 10.4C, 10.4D	3.1A, 3.2A, 3.3A, 3.3B, 3.4A, 3.5A 10.4E
Fine Arts	1.1A, 1.1B, 1.2A, 1.4A, 1.5A, 1.5B	2.1A, 2.2A, 2.2B, 2.2C, 2.2D, 2.2E, 2.2F, 10.4C, 10.4D	3.1A, 3.2A, 3.3A, 3.3B, 3.4A, 3.5A 10.4E
Foreign Language	1.1A, 1.2A, 1.4A, 1.5A, 1.5B	2.1A, 2.2A, 2.2B, 2.2C, 2.2F	3.1A, 3.2A, 3.3A, 3.3B, 3.4A 10.4E
Health/ Physical Education	1.1A, 1.1B, 1.2A, 1.4A, 1.5A, 1.5B	2.1A, 2.2A, 2.2B, 2.2C, 2.2D, 2.2F 10.4C, 10.4D	3.1A, 3.2A, 3.3A, 3.3B, 3.4A, 3.5A 10.4E
Home Economics	1.1A, 1.1B, 1.2A, 1.4A, 1.5A, 1.5B	2.1A, 2.1B, 2.2A, 2.2B, 2.2C, 2.2D, 2.2E, 2.2F 10.4C, 10.4D	3.1A, 3.2A, 3.3A, 3.3B, 3.4A, 3.5A 10.4E
Mathematics	1.1A, 1.1B, 1.2A, 1.4A, 1.5A, 1.5B	2.1A, 2.1B, 2.2A, 2.2B, 2.2C, 2.2F	3.1A, 3.2A, 3.3B, 3.4A 10.4E
Science	1.1A, 1.1B, 1.2A, 1.4A, 1.5A, 1.5B	2.1A, 2.2A, 2.2B, 2.2C, 2.2D, 2.2E, 2.2F 10.4C, 10.4D	3.1A, 3.2A, 3.3B, 3.4A, 3.5A 10.4E
Social Studies	1.1A, 1.1B, 1.2A, 1.4A, 1.5A, 1.5B	2.1A, 2.1B, 2.2A, 2.2B, 2.2C, 2.2D, 2.2E, 2.2F 10.4C, 10.4D	3.1A, 3.2A, 3.3B, 3.4A, 3.5A 10.4E
Vocational Education	1.1A, 1.1B, 1.2A, 1.4A, 1.5A, 1.5B	2.1A, 2.1B, 2.2A, 2.2B, 2.2C, 2.2D, 2.2E, 2.2F 10.4C, 10.4D	3.1A, 3.2A, 3.3B, 3.4A, 3.5A 10.4E

(continued)

Activities for Slow Readers

Subjects	Vocabulary	Recall	Analysis
Business Education	4.1A, 4.1B, 4.1C, 4.2A, 4.2B, 4.2D, 4.2E, 4.3A, 4.3B, 4.3C, 4.3D, 4.3E	5.1A, 5.1B, 5.1C, 5.1D, 5.1E, 5.2A, 5.2B, 5.2C, 5.2D, 5.3D, 5.3E, 5.4B	6.1B, 6.2A, 6.2B, 6.2C, 6.2D, 6.3A 10.1, 10.1D
Career Education	4.1A, 4.1B, 4.1C, 4.2A, 4.2B, 4.2D, 4.2E, 4.3A, 4.3B, 4.3C, 4.3D, 4.3E	5.1A, 5.1B 5.1C, 5.1D, 5.1E, 5.2A, 5.2B, 5.2C, 5.2D, 5.3D, 5.3E, 5.4B	6.2A, 6.2B, 6.2C, 6.2D, 6.3A 10.1, 10.1D
English	4.1A, 4.1B, 4.1C, 4.2A, 4.2B, 4.2C, 4.2D, 4.2E, 4.3A, 4.3B, 4.3C, 4.3D, 4.3E	5.1A, 5.1B, 5.1C, 5.1D, 5.1E, 5.2A, 5.2B, 5.2C, 5.2D, 5.2E, 5.3B, 5.3D, 5.3E, 5.4B	6.1B, 6.2A, 6.2B, 6.2C, 6.2D, 6.3A 10.1, 10.1D
Fine Arts	4.1A, 4.1B, 4.1C, 4.2A, 4.2B, 4.2D, 4.2E, 4.3A, 4.3B, 4.3C, 4.3D, 4.3E	5.1A, 5.1B, 5.1C, 5.1D, 5.1E, 5.2A, 5.2B, 5.2C, 5.2D, 5.3D, 5.3E, 5.4B	6.2A, 6.2B, 6.2C, 6.2D, 6.3A 10.1, 10.1D
Foreign Language	4.1A, 4.1B, 4.1C, 4.2A, 4.2B, 4.2D, 4.2E, 4.3A, 4.3B, 4.3C, 4.3D, 4.3E	5.1A, 5.1B, 5.1C, 5.1D, 5.1E, 5.2A, 5.2B, 5.2C, 5.2D, 5.3D, 5.3E, 5.4B	6.2B, 6.2D, 6.3A 10.1, 10.1D
Health/ Physical Education	4.1A, 4.1B, 4.1C, 4.2A, 4.2B, 4.2D, 4.2E, 4.3A, 4.3B, 4.3C, 4.3D, 4.3E	5.1A, 5.1B, 5.1C, 5.1D, 5.1E, 5.2A, 5.2B, 5.2C, 5.3D, 5.3E, 5.4B	6.2A, 6.2B, 6.2C, 6.2D, 6.3A 10.1, 10.1D
Home Economics	4.1A, 4.1B, 4.1C, 4.2A, 4.2B, 4.2D, 4.2E, 4.3A, 4.3B, 4.3C, 4.3D, 4.3E	5.1A, 5.1B, 5.1C, 5.1D, 5.1E, 5.2A, 5.2B, 5.2C, 5.2D, 5.2E, 5.3D, 5.3E, 5.4B	6.1B, 6.2A, 6.2B, 6.2C, 6.2D, 6.3A 10.1, 10.1D
Mathematics	4.1A, 4.1B, 4.1C, 4.2A, 4.2B, 4.2D, 4.2E, 4.3A, 4.3B, 4.3C, 4.3D, 4.3E	5.1A, 5.1B, 5.1C, 5.1D, 5.1E, 5.2A, 5.2B, 5.2C, 5.2D, 5.2E, 5.3D, 5.3E, 5.4B	6.2A, 6.2B, 6.2C, 6.3A 10.1
Science	4.1A, 4.1B, 4.1C, 4.2A, 4.2B, 4.2D, 4.2E, 4.3A, 4.3B, 4.3C, 4.3D, 4.3E	5.1A, 5.1B, 5.1C, 5.1D, 5.1E, 5.2A, 5.2B, 5.2C, 5.2D, 5.2E, 5.3B, 5.3D, 5.3E, 5.4B	6.1B, 6.2A, 6.2B, 6.2C, 6.2D, 6.3A 10.1, 10.1D
Social Studies	4.1A, 4.1B, 4.1C, 4.2A, 4.2B, 4.2C, 4.2D, 4.2E, 4.3A, 4.3B, 4.3C, 4.3D, 4.3E	5.1A, 5.1B, 5.1C, 5.1D, 5.1E, 5.2A, 5.2B, 5.2C, 5.2D, 5.3B, 5.3D, 5.3E, 5.4B	6.1B, 6.2A, 6.2B, 6.2C, 6.2D, 6.3A 10.1, 10.1D
Vocational Education	4.1A, 4.1B, 4.1C, 4.2A, 4.2B, 4.2D, 4.2E, 4.3A, 4.3B, 4.3C, 4.3D, 4.3E	5.1A, 5.1B, 5.1C, 5.1D, 5.1E, 5.2A, 5.2B, 5.2C, 5.2D, 5.2E, 5.3D, 5.3E, 5.4B	6.2A, 6.2B, 6.2C, 6.2D, 6.3A 10.1, 10.1D

Activities for Slow Readers

Subjects	Critical Thinking	Applied Reading	Special Skills
Business Education	7.1A, 7.4B 10.1A, 10.1B, 10.3A, 10.3B	8.2A, 8.3A, 8.3B	9.1B, 9.1C, 9.1D 9.2A, 9.2B, 9.2C, 9.2D, 10.1C, 10.1E, 10.2A
Career Education	7.4B 10.1A, 10.1B, 10.3A, 10.3B	8.2A, 8.3A, 8.3B	9.1B, 9.1C, 9.1D, 9.2A, 9.2B, 9.2C, 9.2D, 10.1C, 10.1E, 10.2A
English	7.2A, 7.2B, 7.4B 10.1A, 10.1B, 10.3A, 10.3B	8.1A, 8.1B, 8.1D, 8.1E, 8.2A, 8.2B, 8.3A, 8.3B, 8.3C, 8.4D 10.3D	9.1B, 9.1D, 9.2C, 9.2D, 9.3B 10.1C, 10.1E, 10.2A, 10.2B
Fine Arts	7.4B 10.1A, 10.1B, 10.3A, 10.3B	8.2A, 8.3A, 8.3B, 8.4D	9.1B, 9.1C, 9.1D 9.2A, 9.2C, 9.2D 10.1C, 10.2A
Foreign Language	7.4B 10.1A, 10.3B	8.3A, 8.3B, 8.4D	9.1B, 9.1D, 9.2C, 9.2D 10.1C
Health/ Physical Education	7.1A, 7.4B 10.1A, 10.1B, 10.3A, 10.3B	8.2A, 8.3A, 8.3B, 8.3C	9.1B, 9.1C, 9.1D 9.2A, 9.2B, 9.2C, 9.2D, 9.3B, 9.3E, 9.3F, 10.1C, 10.2A
Home Economics	7.1A, 7.4B 10.1A, 10.1B, 10.3A, 10.3B	8.2A, 8.3A, 8.3B, 8.3C	9.1B, 9.1C, 9.1D, 9.2A, 9.2B, 9.2C, 9.2D, 9.3B, 10.1C, 10.1E, 10.2A
Mathematics	7.4B 10.1A	8.1C, 8.2A	9.1D, 9.2C, 9.2D 10.1C, 10.2A
Science	7.4B 10.1A, 10.1B, 10.3A, 10.3B	8.2A, 8.3A, 8.3B, 8.4D	9.1B, 9.1C, 9.1D, 9.2C, 9.2D, 9.3B, 9.3E 10.1C, 10.2A
Social Studies	7.1A, 7.2A, 7.2B, 7.4B 10.1A, 10.1B, 10.3A, 10.3B	8.1A, 8.1B, 8.1D, 8.1E, 8.2A, 8.2B, 8.3A, 8.3B, 8.3C, 8.4D	9.1B, 9.1C, 9.1D, 9.2B, 9.2C, 9.2D, 9.3B 10.1C, 10.1E, 10.2A, 10.2B
Vocational Education	7.1A, 7.4B 10.1A, 10.1B, 10.3A, 10.3B	8.2A	9.1B, 9.1C, 9.1D, 9.2A, 9.2B, 9.2C, 9.2D, 9.3B, 9.3E, 9.3F, 10.1C, 10.2A

APPENDIX B
Check Your Teaching Against These Questions

Questions	Yes	No
1. Do I know how to approach reading in my content subject?	☐	☐
2. Do I know how to motivate students to read content books?	☐	☐
3. Do I know what aspects of adolescent development to use to promote reading in the content texts?	☐	☐
4. Do I know ways to prepare students for the vocabulary in my content text?	☐	☐
5. Do I know how I can help improve the student's recall of information?	☐	☐
6. Do I know ways to improve the student's analytic techniques?	☐	☐
7. Do I know what I can do to prod critical thinking?	☐	☐
8. Do I know ways to help the student use information creatively?	☐	☐
9. Do I know how to help students with problems that are unique to my content text?	☐	☐
10. Do I know how to integrate writing with reading as an aid to learning?	☐	☐

INDEX

Accountability, as reading motivation, 24
Activities for slow readers, 245–247
Advertisements, 25
  and reading motivation, 30–31
Acronyms, for recall, 104–105
Affixes, and vocabulary building, 80–82
Alphabetical system, of mnemonic devices, 109
Analysis activities for slow readers, 246
Applications, and motivation, 33
Applied reading activities for slow readers, 247
Analyzing
  and author's purpose, 177–122
  and line of reasoning, 129–143
  and main idea, 122–128
Argumentation, for drawing conclusions, 179
Argument to the man, 139
Art, 186–187
Association, 102–110
  and acronyms, 104–105
  for events/situations, 106–107
  and images, 103, 107
  and important people, 105–106
  and mnemonic devices, 103, 108–110
Association game, 70
Ausubel, David P., 110
Authenticity of sources, 139
Authors
  editorial to, 226–227
  engaging in a dialog with, 225
  interaction with, 11, 18
Author's purpose, 117–119
  and propaganda devices, 121–122
  and slanted writing, 120

Bandwagon technique, 121–122
Begging the question, 139–140
Bibliographic data, and note taking, 116
Biorhythms, 182–184
Bookthinking, 6–8
  activities for slow readers, 245
Books
  and topic selection, 47–48
  See also Textbooks
Business education activities for slow readers, 245–247

Career education activities for slow readers, 245–247
Categorizing, 97–102
  with concrete objects, 101–102
  feedback on, 100
Cause and effect
  and line of reasoning, 132–134
  as propaganda device, 121
Charts, 216–219
Civil Tongue, A (Newman), 137
Classifying, and motivation, 38–40
Cloze procedure, 14, 67–68, 205–206
Communication clarification in writing, 242–243
Comparative reading, and motivation, 30–31
Comparison and contrast
  in line of reasoning, 131–132
  and media study, 137
  and social studies, 134–135
Comprehension
  and reading speed, 60
  See also Literal comprehension
Concluding, 174–179

Concluding (*continued*)
  and argumentation, 179
  and divergent thinking, 177–178
  and supportable conclusions, 178–179
Concluding signals, 177
Concrete objects, and categorizing,
    101–102
Consonant blend, 87
Consonant digraph, 86–87
Consonants, and word identification,
    86–87
Content book, importance of, 8–10
Content reading, vs. story reading, 18
Content teacher
  decisions by, 2–3
  See also Teacher
Context clues, 84
Creativity, 181, 185–187
Critical thinking activities for slow read-
    ers, 247
Crossword puzzles, 76, 77

Dale, Edgar, 81
Decision making, and course planning,
    2–3
Definitions and meanings, and vocabulary
    building, 75–76, 83–86
Detail
  locating of, 94–97
  and main idea, 125–126
  in oral directions, 90–91
*Developmental Reading in Middle and
    Secondary Schools* (Hafner), 184
Diagrams, 9–10, 219–222
Divergent thinking, in conclusions, 177
Draft and review in writing, 243–244

Emotions, 180–185
  finding satisfaction for, 184–185
  identification of, 181–182
  and reader distress, 34
  reporting of, 182–184
English activities for slow readers, 245–247
Error-Reduction Chart, 241
Evidence, predicting from, 172–173

False analogy, 140
Feature story, writing a, 231–232
Fine Arts activities for slow readers,
    245–247

Fistful of words, 44, 49, 51
Flexibility, and reading speed, 58–60
Fog Index, 67
Foreign language activities for slow read-
    ers, 245–247

Generalities, 121
Governmental agencies, and career infor-
    mation, 27

Hafner, Lawrence, 184
Handwriting, legible, 243
Hasty generalization, 140
Hayakawa, S. I., 118
Health/Physical Education activities for
    slow readers, 245–247
Hidden Persuaders, The (Packard), 118
Holt, Sol, 201–202
Home Economics activities for slow read-
    ers, 245–247
Hook systems, 108
How To Make Flibbers (Lopshire), 92

"I Am Hungry" (Tso), 206–207
Ideas, interaction with, 11–14
Ignoring the question, 140
Illustrations, 211–213
  and vocabulary building, 83
Images, and recall, 103, 107
Index, use of, 8
Inference questions, 164–165
Information Sequence Categories, 99
Interest
  range of, 51
  and topic selection, 49–51
  and vocabulary growth, 73–74, 76–77
Interest reading, and motivation, 43–44
Interpretive narrative, 235
Interrogative categories, 99

Job-related reading, as motivation, 24–26
Journal of reading, 234–235

Key words, 201–202

Laboratory reports, 160
Language, rhythm of, 228
Language arts, and comparison/contrast,
    135–137
Language Function Categories, 99

Language in Thought and Action (Haya-kawa), 118
Learning theory, and recall, 110
Legibility in writing, 243
Letter writing, 234–235
Licenses, and motivation, 31–33
Limited alternative, 140
Line of reasoning
   and comparison/contrast, 131–132, 134–138
   and cause and effect, 132–134
   and logical flaws, 138–143
   and order of ideas, 129
   and number sequence, 130
   and time sequence, 130–131
Link systems, 108
List, in vocabulary building, 65
Literal comprehension, 89–97
   and detail, 94–97
   and oral directions, 90–91
   and written directions, 91–94
Literature, and problem solving, 188–189
Logic, 138–143
Lopshire, Robert, 92

Main ideas, 122
   identification of, 40–42, 123
   locating, 123–125
   outlining for, 128
   supportive details for, 125–126
Map reading, 214–216
Mathematics,
   activities for slow readers, 245–247
   and problem solving, 190–192
Maturation
   and reading choice, 45–46
   and topic selection, 52
Media study
   and line of reasoning, 137–138
   and problem solving, 190
Memorization, and vocabulary building, 78
Mnemonic devices, for recall, 103, 108–110
Motivation
   activities for slow readers, 245–247
   guidelines for, 21–22
   with reality, 22–23
      and advertisements, 30–31
      and applications, 33

      and career-entry requirements, 26–29
      and job-related reading, 24–26
      and licenses, 31–33
      and thought purpose, 23–24
   in recall, 88–89
   using success, 33–44
      and interest reading, 43–44
      and main ideas, 40–43
      and organizing information, 38–40
      and summarizing, 37–38
      using test directions, 35–37
Multiple meaning vocabulary, 70–72
Music, 186–187
My Forest House (Simpson), 237–238

Name calling, 121
Narrative, and text organization, 202–205
Newman, Edwin, 136–137
Newspapers
   and reading selectivity, 46–47
   and vocabulary building, 75–76
Note taking, as organizing technique, 115–116
Number sequence, and line of reasoning, 130
Numerical systems, of mnemonic devices, 109

Object system, of mnemonic devices, 109–110
Oral directions, 90–91
Organizing, 110–116
   by note taking, 115–116
   by outlining, 113–115
   by purpose setting, 111–112
   by summarizing, 112–113
O'Rourke, Joseph, 81
Outlining
   for main ideas, 128
   as organizing techniques, 115–116

Packard, Vance, 118
Paragraphs, and main ideas, 40–41
PARS, 194–196
Personal interest, and topic selection, 52–55
"Piece of Steak, A", 171
Pleasure reading, 180
Poetry
   My Forest House (Simpson), 237–238

Poetry (*continued*)
   reading, 237–238
   and Study Techniques, 205–208
Predicting, 167–174
   and charting, 169–171
   by comparing facts, 171–172
   of endings, 173–174
   from evidence, 172–173
   overview of, 167–169
Prefixes, 80–82
Propaganda, devices for, 121
Problem solving, 187–192
   and literature, 188–189
   and mathematics, 190–192
   and media study, 190
   and science, 188
   and social studies, 190
Purpose, in study techniques, 198
Purposes selection, 55–58
Purpose setting, and recall, 111–112
Puzzles, 76–77, 79–80, 83–84
Pyramid principle, 19–20

Readability level, 14
   and slow readers, 16
   and study guides, 16–17
   and vocabulary, 15, 67
Reader Responsibility activities for slow
     readers, 245
Reading
   applied, for slow readers, 247
   and concluding, 174–179
   and creativity, 181, 185–187
   developing flexibility in, 58–62
   and feeling, 180–185
   interaction in, 11–14
   as model for writing, 236–238
   and motivation, 21–44
   passive vs. active, 224
   and predicting, 167–174
   and problem solving, 187–192
   purposes for, 55–58
   responding to, 233–238
   and thinking, 12–13
   and topic choice, 46–51
   writing taught with, 223–244; *see also*
     Writing
   See also specific names and subjects;
     Motivation

Reading guide, and literal comprehension,
   97
Reading journal, keeping a, 234–235
Reality, as motivation, 22–33
Recall
   activities for slow readers, 246
   and categorizing, 97
   and literal comprehension, 89–97
   and motivation, 88–89
   and organizing, 110–116

Reporting facts, 230–231
Review in writing, 242–243
Revising writing for clarification, 238–244
   clarifying communication, 241–242
   draft and review technique, 242–243
   student self-correction, 240–241
   teacher notation system, 239–240
Roots, and vocabulary building, 80–82

Science
   activities for slow readers, 245–247
   and problem solving, 188
Scholastic Scope, 138, 189
Self-correction system in writing, 240–241
Skimming, and reading speed, 60–62
Slanted writing, 120
Slow readers, activities for, 245–247
Social studies
   activities for slow readers, 245–247
   and comparison/contrast, 134–135
   and problem solving, 190
Special skills activities for slow readers,
   247
Special test
   study techniques for, 193–222
   See also Study techniques
Speed
   increasing, 58–60
   and skimming, 60–62
Stereotyping, 142
*Strictly Speaking: or, Will America Be the
   Death of English?* (Newman), 137
Story reading, 18
Study guides, use of, 16–17
Study questions, 196–198
Study techniques
   for critical studying, 194–196
   and key words, 201–202

and PARS, 194–196
for poetry, 205–208
and slow readers, 16, 17
and study questions, 196–198
and text organization, 202–205
Subject-specific meanings, and vocabulary
    building, 70–72, 77–86
Success
    and motivation, 33–44
    See also Motivation
Suffixes, 80–82
Summaries, 37–38, 112–113
    writing, 227
Super Athletes (Willoughby), 138
Supporting statements, outlining for, 128
Syllabication, and word identification, 87
Symbols, 213–214

Teaching, self-questionnaire on, 248
*Teaching Reading in Secondary School
    Contents Subjects* (Smith, Smith and
    Mikulecky), 3
Technical directions, 208–211
Technical information, 9–10
Technical writing, 159–160
Techniques of Teaching Vocabulary (Dale
    and O'Rourke), 81
Test directions, and reading motivation,
    35–37
Testimonial, as propaganda device, 121
Test preparation, and topic selection,
    50–51
Test taking, 100–101
Textbooks
    critical features of, 4–6
    and instructional decisions, 2–3
    interactive attitude with, 11–14
    readability, of, 14–17
    utility of, 10
Thinking, and reading, 12–13
Thought purpose, and motivation, 23–24
Thumbtack theories, 108
Time
    assignment of, 6
    in vocabulary reassessment, 64–65
Time sequence, and line of reasoning,
    130–131
Topic selection, 46–49
    and book selection, 47–48

by interest, 49–51
and personal interest, 52–55
student-determined, 48–49
Transfer, as propaganda device, 122
Tso, Eugene, 206

Utility, attitude of, 10–11

Vocabulary
    activities for slow readers, 246
    assessment techniques for, 64–68
    building of, 68, 86–87
    and concluding, 176–177
    guidelines for, 64
    and readability level, 15
    in test directions, 36
Vocational Education activities for slow
    readers, 245–247
Vowels, and word identification, 87

Willoughby, David P., 138
Word identification, and vocabulary
    building, 86–87
World Geography and You (Holt),
    201–202
Writing
    adding missing parts in, 228
    clarifying communication in, 241–242
    draft and review technique in, 242–243
    editorial to the author, 226
    engaging in a dialog with the author,
        225
    establishing a purpose in, 229–233
    a feature story, 231–232
    interpretive narrative, 235–236
    keeping a reading journal, 234–235
    legibility in, 243–244
    and line of reasoning, 132–134
    preparation, 229–233
    process approach to, 224–229
    reading as model for, 236–238
    reasoning in, 224–229
    reporting the facts, 230–231
    responding to reading, 233–238
    revising for clarification, 239–244
    rhythm of language, 228
    selling the product, 232–233
    sharing through letters, 234–235
    student self-correction, 240–241

Writing (*continued*)
    a summary, 227
    teacher notation system for revisions,
        239–240
    and topic sentences, 43
    W's five, 230–231

Written directions, 91–94
W's, five (*Who, What, Where, When,
    Why*), in writing, 230–231

Zigzag skim techniques, 61–62